Effective Communication on the Job

Effective Communication on the Job

THIRD EDITION

edited by
William K. Fallon

A Division of American Management Associations

Library of Congress Cataloging in Publication Data
Main entry under title:

Effective communication on the job.

   Includes index.
   1. Communication in personnel management. I. Fallon,
William K.
HF5549.5.C6E35 1981   651.7   80-69701
ISBN 0-8144-5698-7

First Printing

Preface

You are what you communicate. Of course you are. The way you dress and wear your hair may say something about you, but the way you communicate, both verbally and nonverbally, says much more. You have heard that we should see ourselves as others see us. Carrying this further, we should also *hear* ourselves as others hear us and *read* our own notes, memos, letters and reports as others read them.

Good communication skills are surely among the most important ingredients of business success. Even if you aren't a salesperson, you have a selling job to do throughout your entire career. You have a product to sell—and that product is you! Whatever your job is, you must get messages across to people, whether they are your subordinates, your peers, or your bosses.

That's what *Effective Communication on the Job* is all about—getting messages across. In this new third edition, some 36 authors give you expert advice on the many aspects of this vital topic. Their writings have been selected and sequenced to reflect a problem-solving approach. The first chapter is an introduction that explores the entire process of communication and its many ramifications. After this, the material is divided into five separate parts. The first part is comprised of two chapters that discuss the bridges that must be crossed and the barriers overcome. The second part consists of seven chapters on how to improve your communications skills in general. The third part contains seven chapters that discuss various facets of downward, upward, and peer communication, from the performance review to huddling and the rumor mill.

The fourth part of the book contains eight selections on the everyday applications, such as nonverbal communication, interviewing, holding meetings and even *arguing*. In the final part, the reader actually gets a complete course in business writing. Twelve chapters cover the subject from the general to the very particular, beginning with the inherent problems and following through with specific instructions on how to write letters, memos, and reports. The section concludes with two very practical chapters—one on how to measure the readability of your writing and another on how to write job descriptions.

The two earlier editions of this book were highly successful and we hope that this new version will meet with the same kind of acceptance. The book follows the same general structure of the previous edition, but only three of the chapters are holdovers. They were included because of their excellence in content and exposition as well as their ability to withstand the test of time.

Many thanks to those at AMACOM, particularly Florence Stone and Bob Finley, who gave advice and assistance in culling the literature for the very best material available. Thanks also to Eileen Altman and Tobi Levenberg for their aid down the homestretch. And a special note of appreciation to Elena Bose, who played a key role in making it all happen. Finally, I want you to know that I've had a lot of fun selecting the pieces in this book. I hope that you will have just as much fun reading them.

William K. Fallon

Contents

Introduction:
The Give and Take
of Communication

Marion M. Wood

Management is frequently admonished to communicate with its employees: Find out what they are thinking and how they feel about their jobs and the company; let them know what's going on; let them help with decision making. But employees aren't waiting to be addressed anymore. They are taking the initiative. When they want something, they protest and ultimately strike or sue if they don't bring about the change they want.

This is a turnabout for management. Authoritarianism, or one-way communication, rarely works anymore in getting people to become somebody, do something, or believe something. Management recognizes the importance of promoting lasting and good relations with and among its employees—and enlightened managers, at least, are becoming more aware of the need to stop talking occasionally and listen.

Thus a new era of two-way communication has evolved in the industrial world. After the rise of unions opened up communication channels for labor, others throughout the workforce gained new bargaining relationships with management. Executives, young and old, found a brighter world of options through the help of executive search agencies. And, most recently, minority employees and women have been given new freedom from traditional restraints by the federal government's requirements for affirmative action programs designed to promote equal employment opportunity.

The resultant heterogeneity of the new workforce has created new interpersonal relationships and unique interpersonal communication problems. Men and women are having to work and talk together as peers in areas they have never shared before. Men are working for women supervisors and managers, women are working for women and men are joining clerical pools. Male WASPs are training men and women of minority ethnic groups for work they themselves once dominated. Whites are working for black executives.

Interpersonal Communication—Cement of the Organization

Mediators are trained to work out communication problems arising between management and labor; marriage and family counselors are trained to work out communication problems in their areas of expertise. But managers without special training must cope with difficult communication problems daily. Managers must perform their functions—and hold organizations together—through interpersonal communication.

A person usually spends 70 percent of waking moments in interpersonal communication, but the higher he or she goes in management, the higher this percentage becomes. Communication time breaks down this way: 9 percent is spent writing, 16 percent reading, 30 percent talking, and 45 percent listening. If a manager is a poor communicator—especially a poor listener—hours of people's time and dollars of company profits are wasted.

The problem is, interpersonal communication really cannot be *taught*; at least, not the way calculus, accounting, or corporate finance is taught. Communication is a very personal experience, a very *inter*personal experience, in which at least two persons are actively involved. People *participate* in communication; they don't *do* it alone.

Managers can be taught to write more effectively and to give a better oral presentation. But they have to teach themselves to listen actively. Training in communication is largely training in how to polish tangible outputs of oral and written communication. One has to have something to say and someone to say it to, however, before he or she can write or talk.

Needed: Knowledge of the Other Person

Clearly, *good* writing and *good* talking are products of the human mind. A *good* communicator knows how to put thoughts together so that they are expressed with some meaning for someone else. A major tenet of communication, therefore, is that the initiator of a communication knows something about the person or persons he wants to express his meaning to and then takes that knowledge into account in expressing himself. This is vital because the meanings we attach to various words, concepts, and experiences can form the greatest barrier to effective communication. We use words and symbols to express our meanings, but these very words and symbols hold many meanings for other word-and-symbol users. Meaning is not a property of words: it's a property of the human mind.

However, no matter how much we know about the other person—our audience—before communicating, we must still have far more information in order to make that experience worthwhile for everyone involved. We often get this information at the time when we are interacting.

Sensitivity and Flexibility

Essentially, then, someone can know all about sentence structure, gestures, and grooming before entering a communication situation, and he can know quite a bit about the people he will be talking with—but the success of the communication depends on what happens during the interaction. At least one communicator—and, preferably, all who are participating—must have a sensitive awareness of what is appropriate behavior for that particular situation and the flexibility to adapt his responses to events as they occur. Knowing what is "appropriate" entails a combination of experience, intuition, and luck. You cannot be taught sensitive awareness. You have to discover it for yourself and seek to widen your awareness to be ready to cope with new human relationships, surrender old expectations, and face up to inevitable surprise.

Active Listening

This sensitive awareness is, in fact, active listening. Like writing, speaking, and reading, listening is part of the integrative complexity of the human mind. It has to be understood as a multisensory process. We use all senses to transmit, and we use all senses in perceiving a message. Listening is commonly mistaken as a function solely of the ears. But the listener must have all senses alert to the multiple clues of meaning. To listen actively is to listen "with a third ear." But listening is not a matter that readily lends itself to measurement; this is why so little emphasis has been put on listening in management training.

Nevertheless, learning to listen is vital in learning to communicate. And it is not always easy—especially in groups or meetings where you can feel anonymous or lost in the crowd. In such situations, it is easy to leave the burden of communicating to the speaker. But the fact that the speaker has a microphone and notes and the audience has comfortable seats doesn't mean that it is time for the speaker to work and the audience to relax. On the contrary, it is tougher to listen when you are one of many listeners. A speaker can't communicate alone. He or she needs audience participation.

Communicating in a large group is very different from a one-to-one situation in which we can help each other by asking questions, clarifying, rewording, and working out inevitable kinks that are causing static. In a group situation, each member of the audience can communicate with his face, eyes, body, and numerous other clues. Through such feedback, you can show the speaker when you don't understand, when you do, when you're bored, when you're interested, when you're tired, and when you're alert and want to move along faster. A good speaker watches constantly for feedback information; he is sensitively aware of this feedback and of what's going on "out there."

Problems of Listening

Listening is never an easy task. In fact, researchers have determined that we listen at about 25 percent efficiency. The basic problem is that most people talk at about 125 words per minute, whereas they listen and understand at three or four times that rate. This means that the listener can do one of three things: actively assist the sender in the effective transmission of his message; use the time fruitfully on some other thinking project (if he's not interested in hearing what's being said); or simply let his thoughts wander aimlessly.

Problems of Speaking

It's a toss-up whose task is more difficult: the listener's or the speaker's. The odds are against the speaker since he or she will be blamed if the communication flops—no matter how well prepared, organized, and presented the talk is. Without helpful feedback from the audience, the speaker is powerless; there can be no meaningful interaction. A sleeping or bored audience is no more than a sounding board. Perhaps the only thing worse is when the audience appears to be listening and understanding when, in fact, it is not. Buoyed by a seemingly positive response, the speaker moves onward enthusiastically, only to find he's the victim of a hoax when the questions start.

Consider, too, that the speaker with an audience of more than one is actually addressing each one in the audience on a one-to-one basis—without the obvious benefits of one-to-one communication. In other words, the speaker is addressing X number of people—individually, simultaneously. Each one is listening as a person, not as a group.

Clearly, the larger the audience, the more complex and difficult it is to have effective communication. Each individual is perceiving the speaker and the message in a unique way. The speaker receives conflicting feedback: While part of the audience is flashing, "You're great," others are signaling, "Will you ever stop?" If the speaker works to gain the attention of the bored or increase the understanding of the confused, he risks losing the attention and interest of those who are already with him and waiting impatiently to move ahead.

Too often, speakers fumble with useless notes, read nervously from books, stare vacantly out the window (or at one segment of the audience only) when talking, "ah-er" an audience up the wall, fail to vary the tone or speed of their voices, and never change expression or move from the podium. In short, they are not *relating to* the audience. They are talking at, not communicating with, the audience. They appear totally unaware that no one is listening and that no communication is occurring. Nothing is going on between them and the person or persons they're addressing.

A Dynamic Process

In face-to-face communication, and to a lesser extent in other situations, one doesn't serve solely as a talker or a listener—but as both. Communication is a dynamic process. The so-called "sender" also listens actively to feedback; the so-called "recipient" also transmits feedback. Everyone involved in the situation is moving toward "communication equilibrium," or the point where the persons interacting are genuinely exchanging meaning.

Verbal and Nonverbal

One mind can communicate with another both verbally and nonverbally; *verbally* denotes "with words," either orally or in writing, and *nonverbally* denotes "without words." Great emphasis is placed on vocabulary and syntax, and we often think of words as the essence of human communication. But they are not. Only 10 percent or less of our meaning is transmitted by words in face-to-face communication and another 30 to 40 percent by the way the words are used. All the rest—more than half of our meaning—is transmitted nonverbally. Our eyes, our body, our clothes—all that we are and do—express our meaning.

To concentrate on words, then, as speaker or listener, as reader or writer, is clearly not the most effective way to communicate. Meaning is in our minds, not in the words that we speak or write. Good speakers punctuate words with an infinite variety of nonverbal clues.

But attending too closely to clues other than words can be just as fatal for a listener. It may lead to evaluating the speaker not on his ideas but on the way in which he is (or is not) presenting them. To listen actively is to listen with one's whole self; to listen with all one's senses in order to hear the other person's mind.

Training for active listening is perhaps the most useful preparation for carrying out management functions. On an average, managers spend 1,200–1,500 hours a year meeting and talking to people—out of the 1,800–2,400 hours of a normal work year. If effective listening is not taking place during these hours, much valuable time and information are lost or wasted.

Today's workforce poses new communication problems for management, but so will tomorrow's. To communicate effectively with all the unique audiences we will encounter throughout our lives, we have to be continually alert to the meanings and feelings of the other participators. This is possible only by listening for clues, by listening for feedback, and by developing our sensitivity and awareness to what is going on in the total situation and in the minds of others.

Part One

BRIDGES AND BARRIERS

1

Why Don't They Understand?

Philip Lesly

Almost everyone goes through each day thinking he or she is courting others—soliciting their support, seeking their good will, currying
their favor, seeking their love, or at least neutralizing their hostility.
But a major portion of the time we not only fail; we actually repel
those we court or reinforce the antagonism of our opponents.

Why does so much of what we think is communication turn out
to be discommunication?

There are libraries of books, films, tape cassettes, lectures,
workshops, seminars, and videotapes on how to communicate. Yet
almost no available resources analyze why all of us discommunicate—and what can be done about it.

I

In the comparably abundant field of sex, materials are almost
equally divided between how to do it well and how to cure what's

From *How We Discommunicate*, by Philip Lesly. © 1979 AMACOM, a division of
American Management Associations.

wrong. The balance is rather close between Dr. Alex Comfort and Drs. Masters and Johnson. The difference is that in sex, most people know when they have problems and are eager to seek solutions, while in communication, people are unaware of their goofs or feel sure it's the other person's fault when dialogue breaks down.

The analogy is worth carrying further. When a man can't achieve an erection or a woman can't reach orgasm, it's evident that something has failed in the interchange between two people. Traditionally, the afflicted person blamed the partner for lack of technique or allure or understanding. There was a breakdown in communication, the person's ego was threatened, and the blame was directed outward. But the flood of sex education of the past generation has forced most people to recognize that although it takes two to fail at sex, it's usually necessary for each partner to look inward.

The flood of materials on communication has not reached that stage of acceptance. When a parent finds a youngster failing to follow the parent's precepts, the parent blames the youngster. In reverse, if Pop doesn't dig what all of today's kids are doing, it's because the old man doesn't get the message. When management, after spending perhaps $100 million a year to communicate its concepts of what an economic system should be, finds that masses of employees are still critical of business, executives gather at isolated spas to discuss why the workers can't be reached.

The explosion of communication to which everyone is subjected has multiplied the trouble areas in the same way television has multiplied our exposures to the world and frayed our nerve endings. When people went through life with little or gradual exposure to events or changes, they adjusted readily. With exposures to information and messages coming at people now in barrages, the task of trying to reach them with one bit of information or a specific message is far more difficult; and scarcely anyone even understands the new problem, let alone knows how to deal with it.

As a result, the world is full of boobytraps ready to explode—pressure charges of disruption—and we are walking into them like an untutored clodhopper rather than with the refined skills the new conditions require.

Each of us sees the effects of discommunication all around us. Parents and children discommunicate so much we have coined a term for it—the generation gap. Husbands and wives display their discommunication in the offices of marriage counselors and divorce lawyers. Employers measure their discommunication in turnover, absenteeism, and strikes. Doctors diagnose it in epidemics of pill popping, dissipation, government controls, and malpractice suits.

Presidential candidates say simply, "Trust me," and find their biggest problem is the public's distrust. Nations communicate their principles and purposes, and their neighbors increase their armaments. Radicals go through contortions to spread their conviction that all society must transform itself, and see the multitudes grasp more firmly to their privileges and comforts. Terrorists plant bombs or grab hostages to "send them a message," and find that the public demands rejection of the terrorists' causes.

Within groups the malady is just as virulent. Labor leaders struggle to hold onto the support of their rank and file. Most professional and trade organizations find their memberships splintering faster than their influence can be imposed on those they are employed to sway. Almost the first sign of maturity in any group—women's liberation, black activism, taxpayer revolt, financial conservatism, libertarianism—is a growing dissonance among the supporters that is attributed to a breakdown in communication. And the fading out of the highly touted new way of life of the 1960s—the commune—resulted from the failure of communication among the communers.

II

One of the worst examples of discommunication is what we have done with the term "communication." It is used in more ways and to mean more things than "love"—and with even more upsetting consequences.

It's used to describe many mechanics and mechanisms; advertisements by American Telephone & Telegraph, IBM, and Xerox deal with their equipment as communications and their use as the answer to any communication problem. Advertisements for communications specialists under Positions Available specify expertness with telephones, teletypewriters, computers, even satellites. Books on communications techniques describe blackboards, slide projectors, flip charts, and motion picture projectors.

It's easy to imagine a compatible marriage between two people who are both "in communications"—she a switchboard operator and he a service man for copying machines.

In military affairs and world politics, when reference is made to a nation's communications it usually denotes transportation facilities: highways, rivers and canals, railroads, airplanes and landing fields, and motor vehicles. Historians in all eras treat these physical means of exchanges between people as the communications networks that helped determine events.

Means of communication are what is meant when we speak of communication media—newspapers, magazines, journals, books, radio, television, and motion pictures. These are funnels for communication, not its substance. The need for all of these to obtain materials to disseminate is one of the primary causes of discommunication, as we shall see.

Another source of difficulty is treating the relationship between participants in communication as if they were communications themselves. In fact, "relating to each other" has become a fuzzy synonym for communicating. That creates the impression that whatever a man and woman do with each other—or a parent and child, an employer and employee, one racial group and another—is per se communication. One sex manual defines lovemaking that results in simultaneous climax as good communication. It is necessary for two parties or groups to relate to each other to have communication, but to define association as communicating is like saying getting wet is the same as swimming.

The fuzziness is compounded by focusing on particular forms of communication. That is comparable to writing a book about polo and titling it "The World of Sports." The different forms that have been treated in this way, as communications in themselves, include art, music, body language, aggressiveness, submissiveness, tactile exchanges, seductiveness, sermons, speeches, and gestures—in addition to the many ways statements are directed at audiences.

And then we have the growing number of mystiques about communications that purport to explain how two parties come to understand each other—including the secrets of charisma, rapport, extrasensory perception, transactional analysis, biofeedback, and cybernetics—not to mention messages from God, departed ancestors, and various spirits.

A person may employ all of these—mechanisms, media, relationships, elements of the whole, and mystiques—and still not be able to achieve effective communication. For communicating involves almost every aspect of everyone's waking life; and the complexities involve billions of possible ideas, bits of information, contacts, and interrelationships.

Obviously it is necessary to cut through this mass of concepts and materials to grasp what the individual needs to know. To understand why we discommunicate and how to avoid doing it, *we must deal with what meets the purposes of most people most of the time.*

In doing that we run into trouble immediately. Billions of dollars have been spent exploring space and the bottom of the sea; but what can truly be called research about communication—the universal process that makes us all human, that makes the world go, that can become so disrupted it brings catastrophe—has involved far less investment than one mission to Mars. Most of what is labeled research in this field is useless discommunication at its worst—posturings to gain academic stature or efforts to prove that television is a better place for advertisers' dollars than magazines, or vice versa.

As a result, we are dependent on intelligence applied to observation for most of what we know. But that is not to depreciate the value of what we come up with. Pythagoras, about 530 B.C., surmised that the earth was round only on the basis of intelligence applied to observation. Democritus, about 420 B.C., with no tools to aid him described the Milky Way as a multitude of small stars. And Jesus, Mohammed, and other religious leaders deduced what were the susceptible currents in people's attitudes and learned to move them, without the benefit of opinion polls or chi-square diagrams.

III

Failure to correctly evaluate the importance of communication is not confined to those who assign research projects. In fact, it permeates our whole society's outlook. This is one of the most complex and demanding human disciplines, yet it is treated as casually as playing catch or spinning a top.

Everyone automatically learns to speak, so we all assume we know how to communicate. As a result, almost everyone goes through life carrying out one of the most vital functions as uninformed, untrained amateurs. Most people spend far more time learning to hit a ball or dance or swim than they do learning how to avoid getting their lives fouled up through discommunication.

People insist on knowing about tangible things they must cope with—their cars, tennis rackets, cameras, ovens—but go blindly into the arena of attitudes and ideas without ever checking their equipment. The skydiver who neglects to examine his parachute pays for his error quickly, but the person who just assumes his communications will be all right may go through a long life without realizing why things seldom go smoothly.

This function that everyone copes with throughout life and that is vital to the functioning of all society is one of the most neglected subjects in the training of the child, getting almost no conscious attention in the home or in play groups and being miserably taught in the schools.

Yet it is probable that once people realize how much trained skill in communication (and especially adeptness in avoiding discommunication) can do for the individual, it will be studied almost as avidly as the latest line on sex.

In about 400 B.C., Plato wrote in *The Republic:*

> What is there greater than the word which persuades the judges in the courts, or the Senators in the Council, or the citizens in the assembly, or at any other political meeting? If you have the power of uttering this word, you will have the physician your slave, the trainer your slave, and the money maker . . . will be found to gather treasures, not for himself, but for you who are able to speak and to persuade the multitude.

More than 2,300 years later, Winston Churchill, Mahatma Gandhi, Franklin Roosevelt, and Adolf Hitler "persuaded the multitude" with their ability to reach into the psyches of people; and Barry Goldwater in 1964, George McGovern in 1968, and Gerald Ford in 1976 demonstrated how discommunication—the foot-in-mouth disease—can lose great stakes.

It is an anomaly of our time that great numbers of young people are inspired to strive for Olympic medals, selection as astronauts, medical degrees, and membership on professional sports teams, but scarcely any are moved by the great opportunities for achievement, power, money, and recognition that await the master communicator. True, many flock to journalism schools, but what they seek amounts to technicians' roles—investigative reporting, producing TV news shows or dramas, putting together a newspaper each day. When they acknowledge that they have the urge to change the world with their communications, they mean they want to deflate established institutions or destroy persons in power. And their courses give scant recognition to the sensitivity to human attitudes that is needed to mold opinions, or the great discipline and effort needed to avoid the many traps of discommunication.

The contradictions inherent in this amateur-oriented casual approach are all around us.

Everyone who plays a musical instrument, even poorly, is aware of the need for precision. Doctors know that every prescription must be compounded with precise balances of ingredients, that every cut of the scalpel must be studied with infinite care; if they slip, their patients are ready to take them to court to punish their inexactitude. Executives wouldn't think of being casual about the data input for their computers, and their insistence on error-free information and zero-defect operation is a mark of professionalism. Physicists know that errors of millionths of a millimeter or a second of time will result in disorder. Athletes know that every game is "a game of inches." Millions of drivers, often casually trained, know that one wrong push on a pedal or twist of a wheel can be fatal, and so make advance recognition of consequences instinctive.

Yet all these take for granted the imprecision of communication. In fact, a speaker who selects his words and phrases carefully is often considered pompous and pedantic. As we shall see, such strong feelings rise against the elitism of careful expression that they lead to many of the worst instances of discommunication, such as the quite content-less utterings of the "Uh, you know, I feel like . . . you get what I'm driving at?" variety.

At the opposite pole lie attempts to so elevate and enhance ordinary thoughts and actions that they are often embellished into oblivion. When, for example, someone writes, "If we commission a computer check on the cost-benefit ratios of this proposal, hopefully the readout will provide confirmation or rejection of the feasibility and advisability of the proposed undertaking," when he could say, "Let's get the computer to check what the chances are this will pay off," he is probably making himself sound more acceptable to his colleagues, who feel that simple and direct language has no advantage.

The consequences of muddled discommunication comprise a catalogue of most of the problems we face. Yet either the malady is ignored, or the equivalents of witch doctors are called in to treat them.

If a computer—the darling of modern master managers—spewed out checks instead of bills, the manager would get to the root of the error quickly. But when efforts to communicate get results opposite to what's expected, they blame the recipients of their messages and tinker with surface traits.

Modern people view the computer with awe for its ability to keep millions of bits of information organized. Though the computer has mechanical means of storing and issuing its data, its complexity readily justifies the extensive training devoted to its mastery. But the bits that go into the total mix of communication—the words that can be combined into infinite combinations, the nuances, the inflections, the gestures, the volume, the lights and the shadows—add up to many billions. How foolish to treat that amalgam as something to pick up casually and use for a lifetime without conscious care! Communication poses greater demands than any other element of human existence; and to attain optimum mastery of it, we must seek the most skillful and expert help.

2

Communication Barriers: Individual Quirks and Corporate Personalities

Joseph A. Rice
John B. Colby

Why do some people fail to communicate? Perhaps, for some, the problem is a simple lack of writing skills. For others it may be an unwillingness to try or a fear of being pinned down. Some can't communicate because they don't understand the particular meanings their companies attach to special words.

It is a costly error to treat all employees alike in terms of their communication problems. But this error is a fairly typical one. Let's look at some cases.

Mike Baker was an engineer who liked to talk about literature. He vehemently objected to the stereotype of engineers as "illiterate." Mike worked for a giant corporation that had come upon hard times when the aerospace business went into the doldrums. He was devoted to the company, and he was aggressive, industrious, and

From *Supervisory Management*, April 1976.

19

bright. Mike was a natural choice to direct a team to revive the company's faltering fortunes.

Mike and his team developed an innovative and pragmatic method for ascertaining when machinery would fail. It was a highly sophisticated incipient-failure detection technique. They tested it at a refinery and it worked. But instead of moving toward marketing the concept, Mike decided to do further testing. Six months later the team solved another problem for another refinery. Again they went back to their lab. With the situation in the parent company getting worse by the day, Mike and his team barricaded themselves behind mounds of data. To the question, "Why don't we put it on the market?" Mike responded, week after week, "We need to do more testing."

Some engineers are comfortable only inside the lab. They refuse to end a job, to say "Enough!" and communicate with those responsible for turning their findings into cash. Though the walls of their company are crumbling around them, they keep on testing. And the phenomenon is not limited to the engineering field. Perfectionists who find it difficult to complete a task are found in every sphere of the working world and at every level.

Bill Scott worked for a research center affiliated with one of the major oil companies. His speciality was finding ways to improve oil well production. His friends kidded him and said his favorite sport was to don rubber boots and slosh around in slush pits. But Bill knew more ways to coax oil out of a formation than just about anybody. His crowning achievement was a vastly improved well-stimulation process. Within six months, everybody in the industry had heard about it, and Bill's peers regarded him as a genius. The trouble with Bill was that he couldn't—or wouldn't—do anything but his own research. When the patent for Bill's invention was written up, somebody else had to collect the data and do the writing. Somebody else had to work with the company's attorneys. Somebody else had to write the speeches Bill gave—reluctantly—to oil industry conferences. Somebody else had to worry about press releases, articles in the industry journals, and the final report that went to affiliates. Bill Scott had drawn a narrow self-image of himself. "I'm an inventor," he said. "Communicating that stuff is not my job."

Because Bill discovered a process worth a billion dollars, he got away with not communicating. But that kind of situation is highly undesirable. And not many employees can get away with it anyway; Wayne Davis didn't.

A COSTLY SILENCE

Wayne invented small things. He consistently improved existing machinery and techniques, but he never made a dramatic breakthrough. He invented and improved and poli;hed and tested as a sideline to his main job, which was offshore drilling. Whenever he invented a time-saving device or implemented some other improvement, Wayne simply told his boss. He never got proper recognition or credit for his many contributions over a 12-year period. Eventually Wayne's immediate supervisor received a nice promotion and Wayne was eased out of the company. At his age, 41, it was difficult to relocate. He finally found a job selling marine engines.

Only after long reflection did Wayne realize that his failure to communicate had undercut his own position. When Wayne sat down and figured out what his improvements and minor inventions had been worth to the company that had dismissed him, he was stunned. The amount was many times the salary he had earned during those years.

Constant communication—written and oral—about what they are doing is vital for employees in every field. It need not be viewed as corporate gamemanship or an exercise in egotism. If all of Wayne's contributions had been known, the company would not have wanted to let him go. Honest communication should focus on facts—not on stepping on or blaming others or on exaggerations intended to bring unearned praise or rewards. The fact that others have misused communication doesn't make it an invalid or dishonest device.

SUCCESS KILLED CHARLIE

Charlie Morris was a key man in a manufacturing organization that had grown from six people to 75 in less than a year. Because Charlie had a background in law as well as engineering, he was involved in nearly every phase of developing contracts, working with subcontractors, and supervising employees.

Charlie was a human dynamo, a man of unbounded energy. He didn't understand why others could not keep up with his pace—and he didn't much care. He seemed to go out of his way to step on toes. When the organization was new and small, people made allowances for Charlie. As it grew, however, the newer employees were shocked at the bluntness of his manner, the caustic tones of his memos and directives.

Success killed Charlie. As the company developed more and more new contracts problems inevitably arose. When that happened, Charlie could be counted on for clear thinking—expressed in imperative memos that literally shouted commands. "I'm not a public relations man," Charlie would say. "I'm here to get action out of these bastards. By God, I'm gonna do it!"

Charlie's attitude almost lost the company a multimillion-dollar contract. He did not realize that everyone who works with customers or subcontractors *is* a public relations person. PR, like other forms of communication, is not the exclusive duty of the public relations department. That department simply does more PR work than others. Treating customers and the public with tact and dignity is an assumed duty of every job. The best public relations technique is candor served up graciously.

Ben Harding came out of World War II with one goal in mind—to become a millionaire. By the time he was 43, he had built a small company into a large one and had sold it for nearly three million dollars. Seeking new worlds to conquer, he took over the presidency of a giant corporation. And though the giant corporation has continued to grow, Ben has lost one key person after another to competitors.

What is Ben doing wrong? Nothing in his experience prepared him for holding a viable meeting or discussion with subordinates. In the Air Corps, his job was to listen attentively during briefings: Everything was spelled out. Later, in building his first company, it had been a matter of making the decisions and asking other people to implement them. Never in Ben's experience had there been much occasion for listening to alternative proposals, discussing possibilities, allowing people to involve themselves in the decision-making process.

If Ben's success had depended on his ability to conduct an effective meeting, he would never have become a millionaire. Ben schedules meetings late in the afternoon, thereby inviting disinterest. He makes thinly veiled criticisms of individuals under the guise of speaking for the general welfare. He controls meetings so stringently that people are afraid to interrupt.

A big part of communication is listening. No one is so successful or so knowledgeable that he can't learn from someone else. You can stick to an agenda and avoid getting off on tangents without giving up the benefits of thoughtful two-way communication.

At the other extreme from the executive who allows for no feedback is the employee who is so timid about accepting responsibility that he avoids any suggestion that might place a decision-making responsibility on his shoulders. Travis Bruce was one of these. When his boss—the plant manager—asked him to "check into what needed repair and correction around the plant," Travis looked around and made a list of 19 items. The items were not organized by priority and Travis did not bother to estimate costs. He didn't think about or consider Occupational Safety and Health guidelines, employee complaints, or plant inspectors' reports. He simply made a head count of holes in the roof and rust on the machinery.

The plant manager probably had heard about most or all of the 19 problems. He expected Travis to apply judgment to data, to establish priorities, to make sensible recommendations. But Travis didn't want to say anything that his boss might disagree with—so he refused to commit himself on any subject. People with this kind of communication problem need to be given step-by-step instructions to help them learn how to make decisions.

JARGON NE'ER WINS THE DAY

When a banker writes a customer that "we will exercise our option to accelerate the collateral," he is using bankers' jargon. In effect, he is hiding his meaning from the layman. Objectionable as that practice may be, Walter Hart has extended it even further. Walter is a petroleum engineer who talks in terms of viscosity indexes and centipoises so exclusively that only another petroleum engineer can understand him. His colleagues with backgrounds in electrical engineering or even chemical engineering have been reduced to laymen.

The speaker, or writer, who follows the term "viscosity index" with the words "it spreads about like mayonnaise" has made peers of laymen for a moment. In defining a technical term, he has increased his hearers' knowledge and done it in a way palatable to them.

In each of these cases, a different communication problem was evident. And although each of the problems is common, no two communication problems are ever exactly alike because no two people are exactly alike. Communication is as distinctive and individual as fingerprints. In the largest of corporations, in the most bureaucratic of environments, communication is still a highly individual matter. To fail to see this is to complicate the problem.

CORPORATE PERSONALITIES

Yet many managers fail to recognize how personalized communication is and must be. Perhaps this is because a manager's awareness is far more controlled by his environment than most realize. Just as individuals have personal traits that affect their communicative ability, so do corporations. Predictably, a manager will evaluate problems and people in terms of his corporate environment. Let's look at some cases.

The Watercress Wicket

In the Watercress Corporation, a heavily engineering-oriented company, it is virtually impossible for an engineer at a given level in one department to communicate with a peer in another department. To reach the person down the hall, he must go up several levels and work his way back down. This we call "going over the wicket." It results in considerable paperwork and delay.

At Watercress, everything is rigid and codified and incredibly inflexible. Watercress is an immobilized giant, waiting for some David with a slingshot to come along. The Watercress engineer, as viewed by the Watercress manager, is as successful as his ability to work within the wicket. Not to work within the wicket is to be identified as having communication problems.

The Bullrush Pyramid

Bullrush is another giant engineering-oriented corporation. It has wickets, like Watercress, but it is more famous for its pyramids. At Bullrush certain words are not heard below the 40th floor. Other words are used between 40 and 35, still others between 35 and 30, and so on down the pyramid. The word *policies*, for example, finds its way into print at floor 40 and up. A person on the 39th floor would substitute *guidelines* for it.

The Bullrush engineer responsible for writing reports, making oral presentations, or getting projects approved must learn the words appropriate to his level and eschew all others. If he doesn't, a manager is likely to identify him as one with a communication problem.

The Maginot Line

The Maginot Corporation has wickets and pyramids, like Watercress and Bullrush, but it is most notable for the defensive writing patterns of its employees. At Maginot, every memo is equivocal, every report is hedged, every recommendation is hidden, every communicator is entrenched. Managers seeking to avoid blame encourage obfuscation.

The employee who approaches communication with misconceptions, apprehension, and reluctance limits his promotability. The corporation whose managers devote their energy to wickets, pyramids, and entrenchments limits the communicative ability of its employees. In an era of crunch, crisis, consumer hostility, and corporate realignments, an individual or a corporation must be able to communicate—to peers and to laymen, rapidly, persuasively, without defensiveness, and with clarity.

WHAT IS THE PROBLEM?

An axiom of scientific work is that if you can state the problem correctly, you have gone a long way toward solving it. This may be true of communications problems, too. Two answers frequently seem to occur to managers who feel that their employees have communication problems. One answer is to assign noncommunicators to a writing school. The other is to "improve vertical communications"—usually by increasing the number of downward-directed memos.

But will a writing school solve the problem of a person who insists on interminable testing? Or one who ignores feedback? Or collects data by the ton? Will these noncommunicators be helped by learning to "organize their material"? By learning to construct paragraphs? By improving their spelling and sentence structure?

The interminable tester may be a person who fears to move from the known (a successful project) to the unknown (a new, poorly defined assignment). His fears may be allayed if his next assignment is clearly explained to him—particularly if he is asked to help define the project. If this is done, then he in effect is drawing his own map of unexplored territory. Fears diminish as knowledge increases.

Corporation wickets, pyramids, and Maginot lines are indeed difficult to deal with. It is not that there is active, determined resistance. It is more like immense inertia. Or like trying to battle through a room full of loose cotton. But these problems can be dealt with. First, the employee must try to state the real problem. If, for example, he finds himself in a wicket corporation, he then knows one immediate answer: Play the game and go over the wicket. This eliminates the self-inflicted pain of trying to go by a more direct route.

A creative employee may also try the carbon-copy solution. In this plan, the original of the message goes over the wicket, which takes time. But the carbon goes straight to the person who needs to act on the message. When the original gets to him, he can report that the needed action has already been taken. Used selectively, this makes everyone look good. In time, of course, the carbon-copy approach will be detected. But if the course of action has led to better performance or profits, it might lead to needed changes in procedures.

The pyramidal and Maginot-like corporations may suffer from internal fears. Managers tend to use jargon and "academese" when they are dealing with numerous unknowns, or because they feel it is more important to avoid saying something wrong than it is to say something right. The answer to dealing with such situations is simply to start communicating clearly and boldly. If, when you try this, your boss calls you in to discuss your "communication problem," you'll have the perfect opportunity to discuss the real problem.

Communication problems, because they are individualized, cannot be solved by applying a one-size-fits-all solution. But this does not mean the problem can't be solved. The key to any solution is to analyze the problem and the unique aspects of the situation and supply the needed remedies.

Part Two

PRESCRIPTION FOR SELF-IMPROVEMENT

3

How to Plan
Your Communications

David Emery

The fundamental objective of most face-to-face communications on the job is to *sell an idea*. The do-this-or-else-and-never-mind-why type of order is a thing of the past in enlightened organizations: It went out with the realization that people are different from machines. People need to *understand* a communication in order to give their best support to it. They need to *accept* an idea before they will do more than simply go through the motions.

That's why communications must be sold, and this applies to more than direct orders. When a report on some operation is required, the person reporting must appreciate why the information is needed and the possible uses it will serve. When a supervisor wants his people to grasp recent changes in company policy, he rarely succeeds if he simply passes the information on. Most important of all, when it comes to the problem of changing people's attitudes, off-the-cuff communications have an excellent chance of falling flat or, worse still, of arousing resistance in the listeners.

To help management avoid such difficulties, the following five-step approach has been developed. Its objective is to provide a brief checklist guide for *planning* more effective communications. The list can also serve as a tool for *reviewing* the strong and weak points of past communications.

These five essentials of communication have been phrased in the language of salesmen for two reasons: (1) to serve as a constant reminder that communications must be sold; and (2) to put the ideas in familiar language so that they will be easier to remember and to apply.

At the beginning, a word of caution may perhaps be necessary. In no sense is a high-pressure approach to communication being recommended here. In fact, one of the main purposes of this check-list is to eliminate bulldozer-type communications. The term "sell," as used here, means *communicating in the way that produces first understanding and then acceptance.* Here, then, is your guide.

1. KNOW YOUR PRODUCT

As a communicator, the first thing you have to be clear about is what you are actually trying to communicate. To do this, it will help to pin down:

Your immediate objective. Is it to get action, change attitudes, acquire information, or what?

Your long-range objectives. Is your immediate objective compatible with them? Is your message so formulated that the listener will see how it ties in with his long-range objectives?

Pertinent background situations. What has made this communication necessary? Are there any related events that should be considered?

2. KNOW YOUR CUSTOMER

The more you know about the person or group you are communicating with, the better are your chances of getting your message across. To make sure you're taking full advantage of the information you already have, check over in your own mind:

The best party to reach. Does the individual or group you now have in mind possess sufficient authority and responsibility to handle your communication? If you're dealing with one man, is he the one most likely to understand what you need? Have you considered whether it would be better to speak to a single person or to the group as a whole?

The other party's background and experience. Has he been in similar situations before; if so, how did he react? Does he have any strong, fixed attitudes toward this subject?

His personal values. Do you know what this individual or group is trying most to achieve? What bearing could these goals have on understanding and cooperating with your communication?

The present state of his affairs. Has anything happened in the immediate past that may have affected his present mood so as to make him favorably or unfavorably disposed toward your idea?

What the listener probably expects and hopes for from you. If there's any doubt, be sure to clarify in your own mind exactly what authority and responsibility the listener bears in relation to you. In view of this and your previous communications, what is he likely to expect from you, and what is he likely to depend upon you to provide? Are you offering the bare minimum, the fulfillment of his hopes, or far more than he expects? How is this likely to affect his motivation?

3. KNOW YOURSELF

This pointer doesn't often appear in sales manuals, but maybe it should. It is a key factor in communication because *who you are* and *what you want* are bound to be top questions in the *listener's* mind as he judges your message. For this reason it's a good idea to re-examine:

Your fundamental goals. In other words, what you as an individual really want out of your job in the way of satisfaction over good work and increased authority and responsibility. These goals—while they may be quite different from the objectives of a specific communication—will influence the way you deliver the message and the way others react to it. An important question to put to yourself in this connection is, "Does this particular communication serve my fundamental goals?"

What you stand to gain or lose from this communication. "What's in it for him?" is a common question in the listener's mind. If you can answer it satisfactorily for yourself *and* the listener, the chances of gaining acceptance for the rest of your communication are greatly increased. Some successful managers say it's a good idea to *begin* each communication with a frank statement about what you personally have to gain from it: "Tom, it would be a feather in my cap and a credit to all of us if we could speed up the handling of those *XYZ* orders. That's why I'd like your suggestions on. . . ."

Your communication habits. Do you sometimes over- or understate your case? Do you tend to talk too much, cut in on others, or assume too much knowledge on *their* part?

4. PLAN YOUR APPROACH

Every salesman knows how important the details of his customer approach are in helping to create a favorable response. But managers—under the pressure of top-heavy schedules and inadequately trained personnel—sometimes overlook the points listed below. Then they wonder why the other party reacted in such an unexpected manner. Even when you are under considerable pressure, it pays to ponder:

Timing. When is the other party most likely to be a good listener? When will he be alert—or relaxed? When is he likely to be facing the very problem you want to discuss?

Location. Salesmen are sensitive to the importance of the setting of a discussion because they know how it affects a man's mood and his readiness to listen. When is *your* customer most likely to listen and understand? Would it be better to see him alone or with others? Should the meeting take place in your office or in his; on the open floor, at lunch, or where?

Style. Naturally, you're not going to try anything artificial in the way you communicate. There are, however, little things about the way you kick off a communication that can make a difference in the listener's attitude toward what you have to say. For example, is he more likely to react favorably to the positive approach ("I think we may have the answer to the *XYZ* problem") or to the negative ("I think we're headed for trouble on that *XYZ* problem")?

Clarity. Another point for you to consider in planning your approach is what—if any—illustrative devices you can use to clarify and emphasize key points in your message. Would pictures or a diagram help? If your man is the type who thinks better in concrete terms, do you have a specific example of the problem in mind? Would it help to have scratch pads or a blackboard handy so that both of you can sketch your ideas as they come up?

5. AIM AT LASTING SATISFACTION

It always leaves a bad taste when, as soon as you've signed on the dotted line, the salesman begins to take you for granted. But this type of behavior hurts even more when it comes from someone you more or less permanently depend upon, such as your superior. To make sure that *your* subordinates are not inadvertently subjected to on-again-off-again communication:

Follow through promptly with whatever action your communication suggested you would take. "Always follow through" is one of the oldest supervisory recommendations in the book, and it's still one of the most frequently overlooked. Usually, the pressure of new orders or unforeseen difficulties is to blame. However, there is one way of minimizing the risk of failing to follow through: When you're *planning* a communication, be careful not to make any promise of future action if there's doubt in your own mind as to whether you'll be able to carry it out.

Check every communication for its possible long-range effects. No matter how well you communicate for *today*, you have failed if your message sets up a roadblock for *tomorrow's* communications.

Try to foresee how your communication may affect others' communications. Many a mix-up has been precipitated because a manager in Department *A* spoke before considering how what he had to say would jibe with the policy of Department *B*. Such embarrassments can largely be avoided by pre-checking important communications with your associates as well as with higher management.

A lot to watch? Yes, it is, and of course you won't be able to run an exhaustive check of the points listed above on every communication. But, as you become familiar with them, you will more or less automatically come to know which parts of this guide are most important for the different kinds of communications you issue in the course of your work.

Meanwhile, until this list has become a built-in part of your communications-planning apparatus, *and long after it has*, there's one point that will go far toward keeping you out of trouble: *Listen when you communicate.*

4

Face-to-Face Communication: Breaking Down the Barriers

Robert Schachat
Joel Anastasi

Learning face-to-face communication skills may seem about as necessary as taking a course in breathing since both activities appear so natural to most of us. But anyone who seriously aspires to a successful career in management is asking for trouble if his or her communication skills are poor.

Considerable evidence suggests, and our experience confirms, that the poor communication skills of managers and supervisors are major contributors to low morale, high absenteeism and turnover, worker unrest, shoddy productivity, even sabotage. And any manager or supervisor saddled with these kinds of problems is likely to have an unhappy, if not short, career. Today's supervisors must be "people developers." They must know the individuals they supervise: their concerns, feelings, attitudes. Strong face-to-face communication skills can help you as a supervisor achieve this understanding. Most of us can vastly improve our communication

From *Supervisory Management*, April 1978.

skills by dropping some common bad habits and by following some simple tips. Before discussing these, however, we should define what we mean by face-to-face communication. Obviously, it is a process by which people send and receive verbal and nonverbal messages. On a deeper level, it is a very important process by which people, through verbal and nonverbal exchanges, have a chance to uncover and discover themselves and others.

When we communicate effectively, we begin to break through the differences and insecurities that make us fearful and suspicious of one another. We can work out our conflicts and develop genuine relationships—relationships in which we can accept and enjoy ourselves and others with a minimum of demands, manipulations, and controls.

Since face-to-face communication has always been a part of our normal daily lives, why don't most of us communicate more effectively?

The fact is most of us never learned how to communicate well. As children, we were told to behave, to control our feelings, and not to talk back to authority figures. Slowly we began to shut up inside ourselves our feelings and, out of a fear of punishment, to control our natural desire to say how we felt. In addition, in competing for affection and recognition with other children, we tended to set up barriers between ourselves and them and to treat our young peers like business competitors.

As we've grown up, these feelings and attitudes have stayed with us. They are also reinforced in adulthood. Don't we work for impersonal organizations where sharing feelings and personal concerns is frowned upon, and where competition for recognition, position, and money is encouraged?

The only way to break out of our old communication patterns is to become aware of the obstacles to good communication that exist and to develop the communication skills that will enable us to tear these obstacles down. Let's look at some of the most common barriers to effective face-to-face communication, identify how these barriers affect us in our professional and personal lives, and consider some ways of breaking through.

BARRIER #1: FEAR

Most of us are afraid to talk about who we are and how we feel. We don't measure up to our idealized versions of ourselves; and in a culture that condemns failure and demands success, we're afraid of letting others see our inadequacies. We hold our feelings in or, worse, assume what we consider "the proper image"—that is, one that will cause others to accept us, care for us, and find us worthwhile and competent. That's worse than holding in feelings, for assumed roles and images strain communication between people, unnecessarily increasing self-doubt and insecurity.

Can you think of people in your personal life or at work with whom you're afraid to express your true feelings—maybe a boss, a co-worker, or a friend? Think how this fear interferes with your happiness or your ability to get things done. Or, turning the question around, can you name some people who may be afraid to express their feelings to you? Think how this fear might affect their happiness, sense of well-being, and, especially in the case of subordinates, ability to work productively.

Tip: Turn fear into trust. The first step is to tell someone about your own difficulty in being open and to explore the reasons why. We need to create situations where we and the people with whom we associate are free to say what we want to say, for only then can we be creative and productive. Is it worth opening yourself up? As a supervisor, you can serve as a model of openness and reinforce openness in others.

BARRIER #2: NOT LISTENING

Listening is hard work. Countless thoughts shoot through our minds, distracting us and blocking our understanding of one another. Effective listening requires that you concentrate, that you clarify the speaker's message, and that you deal with the feelings the message is arousing. In short, it demands that you actively listen.

Tip: Actively listen. To do this, restate for the speaker the content and feelings (when applicable) you heard expressed in his or her message. For example:

Speaker A: "Joe should not have been a supervisor here."

Speaker B: "You think Joe is a poor supervisor?"

Speaker A: "No, he's a good supervisor. It's just that he belongs in sales, not production."

Or, another case in point:

Speaker A: "That's the last straw! Can't you supervise? Why do

I always get the dirty work? It's like summer camp for the rest of the guys here!"

Speaker B: "You feel picked on because of the extra assignment."

Speaker A: "Yes! Do you know this is the third extra work assignment I've had this week?"

Speaker B: "How about our taking a look at our work assignment plan?"

In the first example, Speaker B actively listened to A, and A was able to clarify the message for B. In the second case, B used active listening to show understanding and acceptance of A's feelings, allowing A's anger to dissipate. The two could then go on to a problem-solving discussion unhampered by antagonism.

Active listening can help communication in several significant ways:

1. It slows down the communication process, offering more time to think, feel, and reflect.
2. It helps clarify the communication.
3. It raises the speaker's self-esteem by demonstrating an interest in what the speaker is saying.
4. It can help defuse the speaker's anger or emotional state by letting him or her know that you fear, accept (but not necessarily approve), and understand.
5. It helps the speaker clarify his or her own thinking by giving some feedback on what feelings and attitudes you are hearing.

BARRIER #3: DEFENSIVE BEHAVIOR

We become defensive when we feel we are being threatened or attacked. At such times we tend to stop listening to the speaker's message and to start considering how we may be seen more favorably, win, dominate, impress, escape punishment, and the like. Our defensiveness creates, in turn, defensiveness in the initial speaker, and the dialog, if unchecked, becomes increasingly destructive.

Tip: To avoid behaving defensively, we must keep from getting hooked by other people's labels, fingerpointing, demands, and efforts at manipulation. To do that, we must be aware of that behavior in others. Second, we must let others know we are receiving negative messages, and we are uncomfortable with them. As you'll find, letting people know that you feel uncomfortable about what they are saying or doing is your best defense against control and manipulation.

You can avoid arousing defensiveness in *others* by following these guidelines:

1. Avoid interpreting other people's behavior. It can cause them to become defensive, regardless of how insightful the judgment may be. Check out your assumptions first before you draw conclusions about someone's behavior. You may find that your interpretation is off target, and you may get to know the person a little better.

2. Avoid giving advice. Telling someone what is good for him or her and what action to take can make that individual feel inferior and increase the person's defensiveness. On the other hand, asking the individual what he or she thinks will help open the person up to advice.

3. Avoid giving commands. Your attempts to control someone or to change that person's behavior make the individual think you believe he or she is inadequate. The result: resistance.

4. Avoid evaluations, judgments, or fingerpointing. Such communications are likely to make a person angry and unresponsive. Also, they are more often intended to inflict pain than to foster communication.

5. Avoid being detached and aloof. People need to feel valued as persons rather than as objects of study or production. We need to feel warmth, concern, and empathy to be open and nondefensive.

BARRIER #4: DEALING WITH FEELINGS

One of the biggest problems in face-to-face communications is dealing with our own and other's feelings. Feelings are an indicator of our comfort level with ourselves, with others, and with our ideas. And not dealing with them can be a source of considerable conflict among people. It can undermine the best of relationships and prevent the development of new ones.

The more in touch you are with your feelings about someone or something, the clearer you will be about what action you should or should not take.

Tip: The skillful expression of your feelings can create an open, supportive climate. When confronted with strong feelings (like those you experience when you are in conflict with someone), take time to examine them. Also, give words to those feelings in order to communicate them to yourself and the other person. When you feel anger, pain, fear, love, or joy about some specific event, place, or person, say so. For example: "I'm annoyed at your being late again." Sometimes similes will help you express your feelings ("I feel like a small fish in a big pond").

Statements like "You're irresponsible," or "You're stupid," do not show your feelings. Rather, they are expressions of hostility that conceal your real feelings of anger, pain, and/or frustration; they create more distance and trigger the other person's defensiveness. Good communication depends on your expressing your feelings about someone's behavior, not about his or her personality. Defense-reducing responses that focus on behavior might be, "I'm angry with you for missing that appointment," "I'm disappointed in you for going back on your promise," or "Your statement about my productivity really bothered me, and it's been upsetting me all day."

The free expression of feelings is important for physical, psychological, and interpersonal reasons. When anger is denied, for example, it turns inward and usually emerges as depression, hostility, or some other undesirable emotion. Respect and accept your feelings. They are, after all, the real you. If you can accept your feelings, you can accept yourself. If you can accept yourself, you can accept others.

Here's some advice on how to deal with another's feelings. The best way is by actively listening to them. Listen to the feelings and show you understand and empathize by expressing what you perceive them to be and why. Consider this dialog:

Speaker A: "This is a terrible rating. . . . How could you do this to me? You aren't capable of evaluating my performance."

Speaker B: "You're angry because I didn't give you a higher rating."

Speaker A: "Yes, I've worked hard and late night after night."

Speaker B: "You feel you've been evaluated unfairly?"

Supervisor B's response indicates that he or she really listened to the employee's feelings. The speaker did not react defensively. Thus the chances are much greater for an effective problem-solving session during which the supervisor and the employee can jointly decide on what behaviors will lead to a better rating in the future.

BARRIER #5: POOR FEEDBACK

Our behavior sends messages to those around us. When someone shares with us their reactions to our messages, they are giving us feedback. Sharing feedback can help us understand each other's behavior, feelings, and motivations.

Fingerpointing and judgmental statements are not feedback. They are devices for getting even and hurting others, and they have no place in face-to-face communication. Their use has attached a stigma to feedback, causing many people to refrain from exposing themselves to constructive, helpful feedback.

Tip: Keep feedback constructive. To do that, follow these guidelines:

1. Offer feedback in a caring, supportive way. Let the receiver know you are interested in improving your relationship.

2. Give feedback in private (or among other supportive people) when there are clear indications that the listener is ready to receive it. If he or she is not ready, the message either won't be heard or will be misinterpreted.

3. Describe the receiver's behavior. Report exactly what took place, withholding your ideas as to why things happened or what was meant by them. Let the receiver of the feedback describe what the behavior means or let him or her invite you to explore its meaning together.

4. Give the feedback close to the event so the details can be reasonably well remembered.

5. The feedback should refer to something that can be changed in the individual.

6. Respect the right of the receiver to do what he or she wishes with your feedback. Don't demand a change. The receiver may see things differently from you. Be willing to look into yourself to examine why you are unable to accept that particular behavior.

BARRIER #6: HELPING BY TELLING

Helping is commonly perceived as telling or showing someone how to do something or as giving advice. A far more effective "helping" technique is to assist others to help themselves. That means listening to them, asking questions, and assisting them in identifying and selecting possible solutions, thereby encouraging independence and self-reliance.

Tip: Be an interviewer. The capability to define the problem and identify its solution is usually within the person who needs the help. By asking questions and actively listening, you can help someone accurately state the problem and find the answer.

Helping others help themselves is an important part of being a good supervisor. It fosters self-esteem and confidence, leading to greater self-reliance and, ultimately, higher productivity.

To repeat, face-to-face communication is a skill that must be learned and practiced. We live in a world that doesn't ordinarily support or reinforce this skill, so we must work especially hard to acquire and develop it.

Fortunately, many organizations recognize that poor communication is a frequent cause of people-problems. These organizations are responding by creating their own interpersonal communication programs, bringing in programs from the outside, or sending employees to public communication workshops. If the trend continues, effective face-to-face communication may one day be more common than it is now.

Although there are barriers to good communication, they can be overcome using the tips outlined in this article. We hope that you will join us in using these tools and in helping others use them, too, so that you and your relationships at home and at work can be more productive and joyful.

5

Communication Skills Are Critical

Alan J. Weiss

In an organization, improving your ability to influence others is essential to advancement. And perhaps the most important ingredient of building influence is being able to communicate effectively. So when you want to change someone else's behavior, you must communicate to the person clearly:

- The behavior you desire.
- The reasons why his or her present behavior is unacceptable.
- Immediate feedback on changes in his or her behavior.
- Reinforcing feedback to maintain the person's changed behavior for as long as you desire this new behavior.

Communicating in this way supplies the initial and ongoing motivation needed in any supervisor-subordinate relationship. Communicating is critical to effective supervision since how effective one's verbal skills are determines a supervisor's influence, ability, and even power.

Most people are not terribly effective at influencing others pre-

From *Supervisory Management*, June 1978.

cisely because their verbal and interpersonal skills are not well honed. And this isn't surprising. Every day we read newspaper reports of high school seniors being able to read at only a sixth-grade level and of advertising copy being intentionally aimed at grade school reading-comprehension levels. Similarly, it is no coincidence that a barrage of books bemoaning the decline of the English language has recently hit the bookstores.

But this ineffectiveness in communication surely can't exist in the business world, you say? Let's look at an example.

THROWING THE PITCH

The first thing sales trainees are taught in business—regardless of whether they are to sell typewriters or insurance, goods or services—is "the pitch." And a major reason for this training is that the pitch has been designed, tested, and refined to produce the most effective communication for influencing others—namely, the prospective buyers. After all, getting someone to spend money requires formidable influence.

And let's go back to the home office for a moment. Are new managers ever formally trained in the skills that will enable them to produce the most forceful possible case when they are seeking to influence others? They are not. While some are exposed on a rather uncoordinated basis to experiences such as "effective letter writing," "telephone techniques," or "effective listening," very few ever experience a systematic, disciplined approach to developing communications skills *with the specific objective* of influencing others both inside and outside the organization.

Now, granted, the regimented, cut-and-dry sales pitch might be inappropriate training for the average manager or supervisor, but surely there is some reasonable equivalent that would help a manager be more effective in his or her job. This is especially true since a manager needs a range of communicative techniques in order to carry out even the most basic job responsibilities. At one extreme would be nonverbal communication (of which perhaps extrasensory perception would be the ultimate example), and at the other would be bodily harm (in other words, as a noted political scientist once observed, warfare is nothing more than the least subtle form of persuasion).

It is beyond our purview to study every communication process

in depth, but we can discuss some basic techniques that are necessary in business situations and communicative modes normally used
to influence others. In Figure 5-1, nonverbal communication does
not include physical threats or violence against another person.
While threats and violence can be a most effective way to exert
influence, we will not consider it to be a frequent mode of operation
in business—unless the business is loansharking.

At this point, let's also establish a basic communication flow
process. (See Figure 5-2.) Within this basic process, spoken communication can suffer on two main dimensions. One is "interference";
this stands for environmental interference as well as the misunderstandings that come from using incorrect language. Spoken communication can also suffer because the vantage points of the speaker
and the listener can affect what they mean, what they say, what
they hear, and what they get, making distortion of the message almost inevitable. Let's examine each of these elements.

INTERFERENCE AND THE BUSINESS LUNCH

Environmental interference is literally anything external to the communication that detracts from one party's ability to hear clearly what
the other party is saying. A simple example of this occurs every time
we try to conduct a meeting in a room with a noisy air conditioner,
when there is loud drilling in the street outside, or with a pipe
smoker who incessantly fiddles with his pipe and bangs it on an
ashtray.

Another example is trying to conduct business over lunch. Contrary to popular belief, a restaurant is probably one of the worst
places for a manager to try to exert influence. This is heresy, you
say? Perhaps, but consider this: In almost any restaurant, the environmental detractions from communication are legion. These include people talking, people walking by, ordering the meal, the act

Figure 5-1. Communication modes frequently used to exert influence.

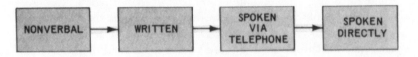

(Increasing ability to influence shown by arrows)

Figure 5-2. A model of basic communication flow.

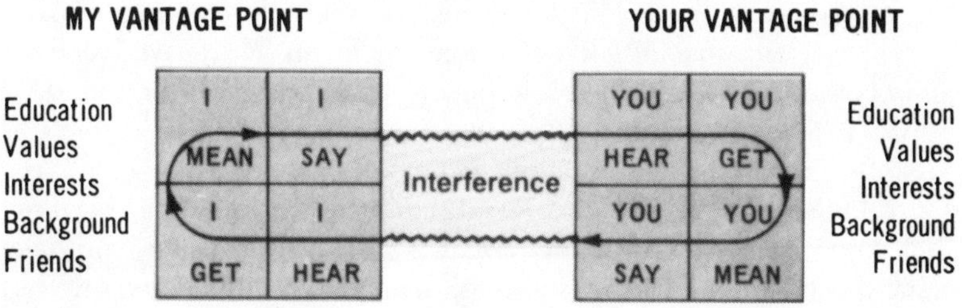

of eating, visiting the rest room, or even *not* visiting the rest room out of fear that precious time will be lost. In fact, business lunches take so long, not because they are so much fun, but because it takes so long in this type of environment to communicate complex issues accurately. Unfortunately, many a business lunch participant finds that the issues being discussed over dessert are just about the same as those that greeted the appetizer. Buying a person a meal can, of course, be effective for establishing a certain image, repaying a debt, or creating a debt in the mind of the other person, but business lunches are seldom useful occasions for trying to influence a person.

The moral, then, is that when you are seeking to influence others, select an opportunity and locale relatively free of environmental disturbances. Remember that even the most carefully prepared persuasive appeal is no match for a telephone that rings and must be answered every ten minutes.

THE NEED FOR PRECISE LANGUAGE

The second component of the colored line of interference is much more difficult to avoid: incorrect language. While this might include questions of improper grammar and syntax, these are not the main issues here. No, more important to the ability to influence others is the appropriateness of the words themselves. Using words precisely is essential if we are to achieve a condition wherein "you hear" exactly what "I say."

For example, consider the age-old game of "telephone": One person whispers a message to another person, who then whispers it to another, and so on. Of course, by the time the message reaches

the tenth person in the game, it turns out to be considerably different in form and content from the original. Why does this happen?
The confusion of the original message is primarily due to:

Inexact speech. "We'll need some help on your part," doesn't
answer the question of, "How much help?" Or, "What kind of
help?" In every communication, we should try to be as explicit as
possible, anticipating uncertainty *before* we say something.

Technical or "in" jargon. People are reticent to reveal that they
don't know what you're talking about if such an admission will make
them "outsiders." They might go along for the moment, but
whether or not they actually change their behavior is problematical.
Always be simple and direct in communications, and try to avoid
faddish terminology.

Loaded language. No matter how great your persuasive powers
or how impressive your style, certain "red flag" words and phrases
can render you powerless. Religious, political, and sexual references
are examples of these. Using these terms can only besmirch you in
the eyes of others, so avoid them at all costs. Similarly, criticizing
third parties can be a serious indiscretion; they may be acquaint-
ances or even friends of the person you are trying to influence.
Never assume you really "know" anyone well enough to confide in
him or her, unless the person is a longstanding and trusted friend.
In general, consciously stay away from emotionally loaded language
and, more specifically, avoid using those particular terms unique to
your experience or situation that are sure to be misunderstood.

SPEAKER/HEARER DISTORTIONS

Communication can also suffer as a result of the way the speaker
and the hearer process information. (The four aspects of this process
are represented by the four quadrants at either end of the diagram
in Figure 5-2.) Speakers and hearers both contribute to the distortion of the message because of:

Highly different vantage points. When I *say* "a little money" I
might *mean* $200 to $300. But when you *hear* "a little money" you
might *get* the idea that I am only thinking of $20 or so. Thus our
frames of reference are light years apart, causing a much different
interpretation of the same phrase. In fact, the more qualitative the
language used (for example, when using such words as "reasonable,"

"comfortable," and "quality"), the more likely it is that our separate vantage points will cause a communications breakdown. Of course, not all concepts are quantifiable. In such cases, be sure to test the internal interpretation of the person you are talking with. "Let me see if I understand. By 'a little money,' do you mean $20? Or do you mean more?" "You just said 'quality is important,' but I'd like to know how important? And precisely how do you define 'quality'?"

Not listening. This is probably the single most devastating factor in communications breakdowns. *Not listening* is quite different from environmental interference or *not being able* to listen. Of the many reasons that people don't listen, three are most prominent:

1. They have a hidden agenda. In other words, many times when we are trying to communicate with another person, the other is not thinking about the conversation at hand but about a more pressing priority. (One example of this would be a conversation with a subordinate at the end of the day, at a time when the subordinate is wondering if he's going to be able to get to the automobile repair shop before it closes to pick up his car.) If you sense this preoccupation in the other person, test your perception by asking for precise feedback on the topic. "I would go ahead with this course of action, but I think there are still too many uncertainties. What's your opinion?" If the other's response shows that you are correct and that he or she has a more important priority in mind, arrange to discuss the matter at a different time; you're wasting your time to attempt it now. Similarly, if you're the one with the hidden agenda, don't bother trying to influence anyone else; such a task is obviously not your highest priority at the moment either.

2. They have anticipated what you are going to say. One common misconception among people with corporate ambitions is that the most persuasive managers are those who can respond to and rebut objections most quickly. So often these people are not really listening to the points being raised in a conversation but are instead silently mapping out their strategy for refuting the argument. Unfortunately, this is gross miscalculation for someone trying to get ahead in the political organization.

The deliberate pause, the carefully framed response carries much greater impact in a conversation than does the sharp rejoinder. Moreover, carefully weighing your words and considering your response tend to impress the other person by showing that his argument deserves real attention. Finally, there are so many times when another's response cannot be anticipated correctly that you would do well never to try. In short, it is accuracy, not speed, that carries influence in a conversation.

3. They are offended. (This is a carryover from the "loaded language" mentioned previously.) A person's interpretive process literally gets turned off by a remark that seriously offends his or her sensibilities. The point of mentioning this phenomenon here is that not only should you avoid offending the other person, but also you should guard against letting someone "blow your fuse" with a chance or intended remark. After all, you are the person trying to influence the conversation; you cannot allow yourself to be incapacitated so easily or your mission is doomed.

NONVERBAL BEHAVIOR

Its current notoriety to the contrary, nonverbal behavior—such as shrugs, arched eyebrows, and frowns—in and of itself is not a very powerful tool in trying to exert influence. You can probably encourage certain behaviors and discourage others with such silent actions, but many nonverbal signs carry the risk of being misinterpreted. (This is more of a danger today than ever before, what with the publication of so many books dedicated to helping us interpret each other's shrugs and moans. These books generally espouse a pseudo-psychoanalytic approach to understanding behavior and, as such, should be avoided.)

Similarly, if you attempt to exert influence with a technique that is predicated upon whether the other person has folded his arms or raised his eyebrows, you will soon find yourself in deep trouble. The problem is that without specific words and statements to base your comments on, you are taking unnecessary risks that can very well backfire. "Your folding your arms shows you've rejected my idea." "No, I'm considering it very carefully, but please don't try to read my mind!"

Despite this ban on trying to interpret others' nonverbal behavior, you can utilize nonverbal behavior yourself in *augmenting* your spoken message. When combined in a subtle fashion, these two techniques provide an impact that is hard to beat. To make the most of your own nonverbal behavior:

Look the other party directly in the eye when you speak and when you listen. This is an uncomfortable activity for some people, but it is a highly effective means of listening effectively, avoiding environmental interference, and exerting influence overall.

Don't loom. Give the other person breathing room. It doesn't take a book on body language to know that when you get too close to another person, your very proximity takes on a threatening implication. In the political organization, the emphasis is on persuading, not pressuring.

Don't conduct. Effective use of hands and arms can underscore key points, but overdoing it will detract from your message, threaten the other person, and make you look pompous at the same time.

Keep your posture erect and attentive, whether you're seated or standing. If you're trying to show how important it is for someone to change their behavior, you won't convey this with a slouch. Like using eye contact, when your body is alert you reinforce your spoken message and impress the other person with the seriousness of your argument.

THE WRITTEN WORD

Trying to influence others is an activity that is not confined to person-to-person encounters. Often it involves communicating via business letters, memoranda, project proposals, or project reports or studies. Unfortunately, many managers and supervisors who are able to communicate perfectly well in person become hopelessly ineffective when they try to put their thoughts on paper.

But communicating via the written word is important in influencing others. Often it is the only practical method of communication available. And sometimes spoken communications and agreements must be documented "for the record" by a written statement or contract. So written communications are important, and to succeed in the political organization, managers or supervisors must learn to express themselves on paper.

There are, of course, basic guidelines that must be followed in writing. The most rudimentary of these—writing legibly and understandably, using correct and consistent grammatical rules, being correct in the spelling of words—we will assume are well known and need not be repeated. Let's concentrate instead on some guidelines that might not be so obvious or so well known. When you write for the purpose of influencing others, it is imperative that you:

Separate the behavior desired from the objectives to be met. It is useful to provide several different alternative behaviors that the individual can use rather than forcing him or her to make a go/no go decision. The objective to be met—in other words, the motivation for the behavior change—should come first in your message and be the most prominent aspect of the message. Once the objective has been "sold," you can discuss the various behaviors you are seeking. For example, good sales letters usually begin with the question, "How would you like to increase your income?" not, "How would you like to use our product?"

Organize the data so that the reader's key concerns are answered quickly. Otherwise, the reader will become preoccupied and won't digest many of the facts you present. Basically, you should very quickly try to answer the reader's unspoken question: "What's in it for me?"

Provide your own devil's advocate. Any plan or suggested action is fraught with some risk. Concede that fact, show what the perils are, and then demonstrate how you propose to deal with them. This not only shows how thoroughly you have considered the action you are requesting, but it will also save much time that is usually spent answering such questions as, "Have you considered. . . ?" and, "What if. . . ?"

Use hard facts. Unlike the spoken word, in writing you cannot retreat behind disclaimers like, "I didn't really say *that.*" If you're not sure of your facts, check them out. If you can't check them, then admit that they're only assumptions. If you label an assumption as a fact and you're found to be wrong, your credibility will be destroyed—and so will your influence.

Success in the political organization goes not always to the swiftest nor to the strongest, but it often goes to the most eloquent. Influence is dependent on the twin powers of persuasion and salesmanship, and both of these are aspects of good communication.

GLIBNESS IS OUT

Lest the wrong impression be created, let me emphasize that effective communication as we have described it is not mere glibness, which is slick talk or words without content. In exerting influence, the content of what you say or write—what objectives should be met and what behaviors should be used—is all-important, especially since others are most likely trying to exert influence against your proposals. Communication without a vital case is as futile as a valid case without effective communication. The one complements the other.

Finally, by understanding how adept communication can help you to wield greater influence, you become much more cognizant of when "empty" communication is taking place. And you'll recognize more readily when someone is truly trying to communicate something to you and when they're merely trying to dazzle you with verbal footwork.

6

Chances Are You're Not Communicating

Wayne Sanders

Communication is commonly defined as the sending of information from one person to another. My definition, however, is more precise: Communication is the sending *and* the *understanding* of information from one person to another.

The successful supervisor knows that effective communication with superiors, peers, and subordinates is of the utmost importance in performing his or her job. Yet many supervisors also believe that the mere act of speaking constitutes communication. Nothing could be further from the truth. Studies show that 75 percent of the time spent in giving directions and information to others is wasted because what is being said is not being understood. And ineffective communication on the management level can result in organizational chaos. If you, as a supervisor, want to become more professional in your communication techniques, you must accept the fact that your current methods probably should be improved.

For example, most people simply tell another person what they want and expect that person to understand. That is a mistake. How

From *Supervisory Management,* October 1979.

often have you heard one of your subordinates ask another, "What are we supposed to do?" after you've spent ten minutes giving them both what you thought were clear instructions. Don't blame them. You're the one who may not have been communicating.

SOME COMMON MISCONCEPTIONS

One of the most common methods a supervisor will use to see if subordinates have understood what he or she has said is to ask "Are there any questions?" The supervisor should ask instead, "What did you hear me tell you to do?" This kind of feedback is important in the communication process. It's not enough to ask the individual if he or she understood what was said, for this would put subtle pressure on that person to say that he or she did, whether or not it was true.

Many supervisors are reluctant to ask a subordinate to repeat instructions because they feel it gives the individual the impression that they think he or she is not capable of carrying them out. However, it's better to do this than to let your employee make a major error. You can take the pressure off your subordinate by saying, "It's important that we do this correctly, and at times it seems I'm not communicating well. Could you just repeat what you heard me tell you to do?"

The cause of a communication problem in most cases will be lack of concentration. How often should you ask an employee for feedback before he or she realizes that it is important for him or her to concentrate on what you're saying? I've discovered that it doesn't take long. In fact, when it is expected that he or she understand, an employee will insist on better methods of communication from the supervisor. For your part, either you seek and insist on total understanding on both sides, or you fail in what you are setting out to do.

The communication problem may also be attributable to the ambiguity of what is being said. Most educators agree that short, simple sentences are the best vehicle for getting messages across. However, this type of sentence structure doesn't guarantee the elimination of misunderstanding.

A short, simple sentence—for example, "I never said he stole money"—can have many different meanings. Let's take each word in the sentence and emphasize it and see what the sentence means in each case.

◇ *"I* never said he stole money." Meaning possibly someone else said it, not I.

◇ "I *never* said he stole money." Now I'm denying I ever said it.

◇ "I never *said* he stole money." I may have *thought* he did, though.

◇ "I never said *he* stole money." Someone did, but not him.

◇ "I never said he *stole* money." He borrowed it, embezzled it, got it as a gift.

◇ "I never said he stole *money*." Maybe not money, but a car, savings bond, and so on.

The sentence itself is straightfoward enough at first glance, but the interpretations drawn from it are numerous. The same can happen during discussions with your subordinates. To reduce misunderstanding and increase the chances of getting your message across, consider using some form of nonverbal communication as well. Supervisors should use gestures, eye contact, and other types of body language when communicating. Visual signs and aides, such as charts, diagrams, and so on, are also helpful, increasing the retention of subject matter by 30 percent.

SOME HELPFUL TIPS

I stated earlier that communication is the sending and understanding of information from one person to another. With this definition in mind, I suggest that you adopt the following ideas. I believe that they can make the difference between success or failure when you communicate.

Speaking
◇ Take time to think about what you want to say.
◇ Speak as if you were writing. Have an introduction, body, and summary to your presentation.
◇ Look at the person to whom you are speaking and be as clear as possible. Remember the meaning lies not only in the words used but in the manner in which they are presented.
◇ Facial expressions, body language, and tone of voice convey a message to your audience. Use them as much as possible.

Listening

◇ Concentrate on what is being said.

◇ Recognize your prejudices (against the speaker, the message, and so on) and make an effort to overcome them. Try to understand the message even if the speaker doesn't come across the way you would have liked.

◇ Ask questions if something is unclear, but do not interrupt until the individual has finished making his or her point.

◇ Make sure you understand what the speaker wants you to know. If you do not, ask him or her to repeat the key points.

Effective communication is the key to success in all areas of business, and the odds are with the person who can both speak and be understood and listen and understand.

7

Tools for Spotting and Correcting Communication Problems

Edward L. Levine

Effective communication—no organization or manager can function well without it. In terms of one-to-one, face-to-face communication, effective communication is measured by the quality of the communication process itself and the consequences of the communication encounter for work productivity and job satisfaction.

Of these two measurements, the last would seem to be the easiest to determine. By then, though, it might be too late; any damage that might result from faulty communication would already have occurred. Fortunately, you don't need to wait that long. There are three tools that you can use to identify whether the communication process is going smoothly or poorly. These will also give you immediate information as to why the process is effective or not so that you can take action to improve the situation. And when you are able to enhance the quality of the communication process, you will dramatically increase the chances of positive consequences following the communication exchange.

From *Supervisory Management,* June 1980.

FACTORS AFFECTING INTERACTIVE CHEMISTRY

You can probably recall any number of times when you got together with your supervisor or subordinate to discuss important matters, but the discussion never really got off the ground. You had the sense that the two of you were not really communicating. I use the term "interactive chemistry" to describe the degree to which information and energy are exchanged and *accepted* by each party in a one-to-one communication encounter. When your discussion does not get off the ground, the chemical reaction is poor or lacking.

Successful interactive chemistry is related to a number of factors, including communicator credibility, the similarity between the two people, the message's quality or content, and the history of the relationship. These are factors that lie *under the surface*. Two other factors—whether the parties are listening to each other and the form and quality of the interaction process—are *observables* or *symptoms* of the interactive chemistry. As such, they may be watched as the communication encounter takes place, and action may be taken to enhance the chemical reaction.

The communication process can be improved by working on the symptoms themselves or by working on the subsurface factors. For now, I will concentrate on the symptoms, but it should be apparent that both symptoms and subsurface factors are not completely independent of each other. In other words, as we work to improve the form and quality of the interaction and the listening process, improvements will be made in the subsurface factors as well.

Let's consider an example. You and your subordinate have gotten together to talk about the subordinate's career development. During the course of the meeting, your subordinate senses you are not really listening to his or her statement of career needs. Rather, you are merely repeating company policies about career development from the company manual. The communication encounter is marred by embarrassing silences on your part because you have failed to listen, apprehend, and keep track of what your subordinate has been saying. Your face shows a bored expression, and you are yawning a good deal. You are looking at some papers on your desk, not at your communication partner. You offer few concrete suggestions on ways for the subordinate to attain career goals. You interrupt the subordinate several times and cut the meeting short by pointing out that you have another meeting to attend.

Your subordinate's reaction is predictable. A bored or annoyed expression creeps into his or her face. There is much staring at the clock on the wall. Your subordinate's contributions to the discussion wane, so you do most of the little talking that occurs. As the meeting proceeds, your subordinate thinks, "Gee, my own supervisor doesn't know much about career development in this company. Maybe that's true of other things that I must get assistance on to succeed here. Everybody knows that stuff in the company manual was obsolete months ago. Well, of course! Managers are different from us underlings; they've got it made. What do they care about us? I'm going to remember this for a long time to come."

You can readily see that your *credibility* has suffered. Your subordinate has drawn clear *lines of distinction* or *difference* between the two of you, and the quality of the messages exchanged is poor. One glaring incident has been added to the evolving *history of the relationship* between you and your subordinate. All these, of course, are subsurface factors.

Along with my main point about the relationship between the process and the subsurface factors in interaction chemistry, the example I just gave of poor communication also contains the aspects of the communication process that will concern us here. These are the nonverbal signs that have occurred during the meeting, the frequency and direction (manager to subordinate, or subordinate to manager) of the messages, and the form the messages take. The social sciences have developed over the years a number of techniques that enable us to take a reading of these three aspects in an objective, systematic way. There are three, in particular, worth noting. Before we explore these techniques, though, I must emphasize the need for proper preparation and practice. You cannot put these techniques to use immediately merely by reading about them. You need to try them out first, and get feedback where it is feasible. Perhaps you might enroll in a training course that uses role playing and subsequent feedback discussions to try these tools out.

COMMUNICATION TOOL #1
Reading the Nonverbal Messages of Others and Controlling Your Own

Can we read the nonverbal messages of others reliably? Yes, but only within rather narrow limits. Can we control our own nonverbal messages? Yes, but only if we work at it. In order to see more clearly what can and cannot be done with nonverbal messages, let's consider them in more detail.

There are two categories of nonverbal communication. One is *body language*. The other I call *speech-surplus*. *Body language* includes facial expressions; eye contact; body position or posture; body orientation; the space between our body and that of our communication partner; whether we touch our partner or not; and hand, arm, and body gestures.

Facial expressions may communicate a number of emotions or messages in such a way that others can recognize them with some degree of reliability, at least others who come from the same cultural background as we do. However, the number of facial expressions is much more limited than the number of emotions that we may experience. For example, the same facial expression may be used to express impatience and disgust or to express interest and puzzlement. You can probably look in the mirror and produce facial expressions that correspond to these and other emotions.

Eye contact is the extent to which we gaze directly at the face and eyes of our communication partner. Eye contact that is somewhat frequent and of some duration will generally convey the impression of interest and trustworthiness. On the other hand, overly frequent eye contact that lasts just a short period of time—in other words, when the eyes are darting to and from the face and eyes of our communication partner—may suggest anxiety and deception.

Body position or posture may indicate degree of interest in the subject of conversation and even indicate our feelings of status or power in comparison to our communication partner. At the extreme, if we turn our face from, and our back toward a person, we are communicating that the individual has little power, and his or her words are of no interest. An overly erect posture may suggest tension or low status. An expansive, slouching, foot-on-the-desk posture may suggest relaxation or high status.

The degree of liking one has for another may be conveyed by our body orientation. Communicators tend to lean toward those they like and away from those they dislike.

The amount of space we maintain between ourselves and others may suggest how much we like them. Moreover, we probably ought to move closer when we deliver good news, or further away when we deliver bad news, in order to maintain a positive relationship between ourselves and our communication partner.

Touching the other person on the arm or shoulder may be an effective way to indicate warmth and acceptance, if the context makes it appropriate. It may also help to persuade our communication partner to accept our message.

Hand, body, and arm gestures may complement facial expressions in communicating our emotions. They may also be used to illustrate a point we are trying to make. Gestures used to illustrate a point may consist of drawing a kind of picture in the air, stabbing with a finger, or tapping on the desk to highlight a word or phrase. Tremors, nail biting, picking or squeezing at one's body or face, drumming the fingers, and other such gestures are often associated with tension. Covering the eyes or ears with the hands may suggest fatigue or deception.

In contrast to body language, *speech surplus* refers to the tone of voice used, how loud or soft we talk, how quickly words are delivered, and the number and duration of silent pauses between our statements. A monotone may indicate fatigue or boredom. Speaking too loudly or too rapidly may suggest anxiety or deception. Too many silences may indicate unwillingness to discuss a matter or confusion. (Silence will come up again later in the discussion.)

You probably noticed the wishy-washy nature of the statements I have made about nonverbal communication—statements characterized by *"may* indicate" or *"may* suggest." This is because the state of our knowledge about nonverbal communication is far from complete. Moreover, the context of communication and the cultural background of the partners to the communication will affect the meaning attached to the nonverbal messages we send and receive. For example, in a particular encounter we may interpret lack of eye contact as indicative of anxiety or deception; but if our partner is a Mexican-American, it may be a sign of respect. For these reasons, our capacity to interpret the nonverbal messages of others and to control the nonverbal messages we send is quite limited.

How can we make practical use of nonverbal communication in light of the many kinds of nonverbal cues that exist and the difficulty of attaching fixed meanings to them? We should look at nonverbal cues only in the most basic ways. As suggested by Mehrabian, one of the foremost researchers in this area, we should consider nonverbal cues along three lines. First, nonverbal cues may bear on the *degree of liking* one person has toward another. Secondly, they may bear on the degree of *dominance or status* one person possesses compared to another. Third, the degree of *responsiveness* and *attentiveness* can be contained in nonverbal cues.

The most important advice I can give concerning the reading of others' nonverbal messages is to be alert to these three dimensions, and be wary of *overinterpreting* or drawing definite conclusions about nonverbal messages *without discussing them verbally*. This will help you pin down more exactly what they mean. Also, it will alert your communication partner to some unintended inferences you are drawing about the communication process.

It is especially critical to translate nonverbal cues into verbal messages when these nonverbal cues do not match the verbal messages being exchanged. Lying, or the masking of true opinions and emotions, may often be spotted in this way. For example, suppose your subordinate tells you that things are going really well but keeps his or her eyes on the floor. If this occurs, you should tell what you are seeing in the nonverbal behavior and probe for additional information.

Also, there may be instances when a nonverbal message strongly indicates dislike for you or what you are saying, or an overly submissive attitude or disinterest (you think). These are signs that must not be ignored. If they are discussed and handled properly, they can serve to enhance the interactive chemistry and cement a relationship. If left undiscussed, they may serve to sour a relationship and create substantial barriers to effective communication.

The key to being able to discuss these issues is the creation of a permissive, nonthreatening climate so that the subordinate feels comfortable in sharing his or her feelings, beliefs, and opinions. Without full communication in these areas, nonverbal cues may never be fully understood, and continuing deterioration in communication effectiveness will take place.

To control the nonverbal messages you send and enhance communication, I would recommend the following:

1. Be attentive to eye contact. You should gaze at the face and eyes of your communication partner frequently and with some amount of duration. However, don't stare too long at your partner. This may create a feeling of competitiveness and discomfort.

2. Have your facial expression and posture reflect interest and acceptance, if not liking. This may be accomplished by arching the eyebrows, smiling, maintaining a fairly erect posture, and nodding as the other person speaks. Your facial expressions and posture may be practiced in the mirror.

3. Maintain a reasonable social distance—approximately four to six feet from your partner.

4. Lean forward and use gestures that are not too exaggerated to emphasize an important point. For example, tap lightly on your

desk to "spice up" the conversation; don't smash it with your hand or fist.

5. Speak at a reasonable pace, not too slow to bore your communication partner and not too fast to be misunderstood. Modulate your voice in tone and amplitude: a monotone is obviously boring. Speech courses or toastmaster's groups can be helpful in achieving these objectives. Prior preparation for a meeting will likewise assist here.

6. Since lying or masking true opinions or feelings often come through nonverbally, they should be avoided. We are generally not very good at lying nonverbally.

COMMUNICATION TOOL #2
Flowcharting the Messages

The use of a flowchart is based on the notion that an effective one-to-one communication process is marked by a lot of talking on the part of *both* people. A high rate of activity and mutuality of communication generally lead to high productivity and high job satisfaction. The flowchart is a simple, systematic way to determine whether a high rate of activity and mutuality of interaction are present.

The procedure for flowcharting is simple. But it can be made slightly more complex, if more information is desired. Figure 7-1 illustrates the procedure. The form allows you to tally (on the left side), merely by drawing a line, every time you direct a verbal message (suggestions, opinions, questions, and so forth) to your

Figure 7-1. Flowchart form.

Date of Meeting _7-18-79_   Name of Subordinate _Sam Smith_

No. of Interruptions	No. of Silences
111\1	11
Me to You	You to Me

Length of Meeting: _15 minutes_
Comments:_____

subordinate. A tally is made for each separate message you utter. You may likewise tally (on the right side) the frequency of communications directed from your partner to you.

The tally pattern shown in Figure 7-1 reveals an extremely one-sided communication process. This will often suggest that a communication problem exists, one you may not even be aware of. You are dominating the conversation! For some situations this may be all right. For example, when you are training a subordinate in a new work method, this may be a typical flow pattern. However, in most other situations, more participation by your subordinate would usually be expected and desired.

The number of silent periods that last for more than five seconds may be tallied in the upper right portion of the form. One tally mark is registered for each five-to-ten second silent period. Figure 7-1 reveals that there were only two silent periods lasting ten seconds or less. Along with the large number of messages exchanged over the 15-minute period, this suggests a high rate of activity.

The number of times you interrupted or were interrupted by your subordinate may be entered in the upper left portion of the form. Interruptions are times when you started to speak or were in the middle of a statement but were cut off by statements of your partner, and vice versa. If the number of interruptions is high, this will often indicate a communication problem. From the form, it appears that your subordinate tried to speak on a number of occasions but was cut off by you. This is based on the fact that your subordinate only spoke twice, but there are five interruptions.

You should make the tallies on a form like this as the communication process is taking place. Once you have practiced a bit, you should be able to make these marks without detracting from the communication process at all.

Finally, the form in Figure 7-1 contains a section for you to write in comments for your own use. You can record your impressions or explanations of the process as you experienced it and use the comments for improving the process as you prepare for future meetings.

Perhaps the most worthwhile way to complicate this process is by keeping tallies for specific time segments of a meeting. Suppose you have prepared in advance for a fact-finding meeting with your subordinate. You have anticipated that you will spend the first five minutes in discussing the issues with your subordinate, then you will launch into a series of questions to gather facts and opinions.

Finally you will conclude by thanking your subordinate and giving instructions for future action. You could make up a form like that shown in Figure 1 of each one of the meeting segments as you have planned. You might expect that the first and last segment will show more interactions from you to your subordinate than the second segment. Ideally, none of the meeting segments should show as one-sided a pattern as the form in Figure 7-1.

You can probably think of additional ways to modify the form to meet your needs. However, you should not make the procedure so complicated that its completion will, in and of itself, detract from the communication process.

COMMUNICATION TOOL #3
Charting the Form and Quality of the Communication

Knowing the rate and mutuality of interaction may give you a start in overcoming communication problems; but you may need even more information to diagnose and remedy communication problems. The tool I am about to describe will provide such information. The information should provide you with insight into the *form and quality of the communications* shared by you and your subordinate. However, the method requires a good deal of practice. It also requires a great deal of objectivity about your own communications, so it should only be used when other methods have not led to the solution of communication problems.

The tool is adapted from the work of the eminent social psychologist R. F. Bales, and is based on the idea that one-to-one communication in a work setting deals with two major issues—*task accomplishment* and *social-emotional issues*. Task accomplishment refers to those aspects of the communication process aimed at producing *outputs* from the meeting (solutions to problems, a new list of objectives to shoot for, new knowledge about work procedures, and so on). Further, task accomplishment involves the exchange of suggestions or decisions, opinions or evaluations, and information of a factual nature. People in one-to-one communication may either give or ask for any one of these three categories of communication (suggestions, opinions, or information). As a result that portion of the communication process devoted to task accomplishment may be divided into six categories, each of which is listed below with a few examples to help in its definition.

1. *Gives suggestion/decision.* "Let's proceed with the new product." "How about trying out Jim on the territory." "We'll go with your idea about increasing morale."

2. *Gives opinion/evaluation.* "I think that there are other alternatives to consider." "That is an idea whose time has come." "In my judgment, it can't work."

3. *Gives information.* "It is 3:15 PM." "Our work needs to be completed by the end of the day."

4. *Asks for suggestion/decision.* "What do we do now?" "What shall our decision be?" "How can we hit our target for this month?"

5. *Asks for opinion/evaluation.* "What do you think of Jane's idea?" "What do you feel is the economic state of our test market site?" "What is this report on company communication problems really saying?"

6. *Asks for information.* "What time is it?" "When do we need to get this work out?"

The social-emotional aspect involves the "cement" that keeps you and your subordinate working together harmoniously and energetically. The portion of the communication process dealing with social-emotional issues may be categorized as either positive (binding) or negative (nonbinding, splintering). Positive social-emotional communications include indications of solidarity—(for example, the use of the pronoun "we" to refer to you and your subordinate and praise for the two of you, such as, "We really work well together")— occasional joking, sighing, side comments, personal stories to release pent-up tension, and agreement or acceptance of ideas, suggestions, and information. Negative social-emotional communications include exhibitions of aggression or hostility (for example, interrupting the other person or saying, "That's a dumb idea"); showing tension (evident from the use of "uh" and "er uh," the drumming of fingers, pulling at one's ear or gripping of a chair hard); disagreeing in a hostile way with suggestions, opinions, and information; and excessive release of tension to the extent that work tasks are not able to be handled (for example, 40 minutes of jokes and tall tales in a 45-minute meeting).

To chart the form and quality of communication you can set up a form like that shown in Figure 7-2.

As a one-to-one meeting proceeds, you would make tallies in the proper category, one tally for each type of message exchanged. You would place the tallies under the space for your communication or that of your subordinate depending on who initiated the message.

Figure 7-2. Charting the form and quality of communication.

Date of Meeting _____ Name of Subordinate_____

No. of Silences

Subordinate Interactions

Positive Soc. Emo.	GIVES			ASKS			Negative Soc. Emo.
	Suggestions	Opinions	Information	Suggestions	Opinions	Information	

My Interactions

Positive Soc. Emo.	GIVES			ASKS			Negative Soc. Emo.
	Suggestions	Opinions	Information	Suggestions	Opinions	Information	

Length of Meeting_____

Comments: _____

Sometimes you may code a single message in two or more categories. An example might be when you ask, "How about both of us
taking a long lunch break today so we can discuss this problem away
from the office?" This could be coded by making a single tally in the
categories Gives Suggestions, Asks Opinion (if you are really seeking
an evaluation of this suggestion), and Positive Social-Emotional. One
valuable lesson to be learned from this example, in addition to how
to tally, is the idea that many of the messages we exchange *contain
both tasks and social-emotional components mixed together.* At any
rate, you can readily see that the tallying is more complicated than

the tallying for the flowchart. So prior preparation and practice are musts.

With the addition of a place to tally the number of silences (five to ten seconds long) in the upper right-hand corner of the form, it should be clear that this tool pretty much duplicates the information in the flowchart. The total number of communications initiated by you as compared to those initiated by your subordinate may be determined by adding all the categories. Also, a space is provided for your comments.

How do we interpret the information provided by this tool? As with the flowchart, we could look at activity rates and mutuality in the process. Also, we could look at the differences between the number of "Gives" messages and the number of "Asks" messages. Also, we could look at the number of "Positive" versus "Negative Social-Emotional" messages. Generally, a productive one-to-one meeting will be characterized by a lot of "Gives," particularly "Gives Suggestions," few "Asks," a relatively equal number of communications initiated by you and your subordinate, a high rate of activity (few silent periods, many communications), and a relatively frequent occurrence of positive social-emotional communications.

When you have diagnosed a problem, if one exists, you can then take corrective action. For example, if there are a high number of "Asks" relative to "Gives," this may mean that you and your subordinate have not prepared adequately for the meeting. Or it could indicate that you need to call in an expert. Another problem that might arise is that there are too few positive social-emotional messages exchanged relative to task-based messages. This may mean that you are not delivering sufficient praise and indications of solidarity to cement the relationship between you and your subordinate.

PUTTING IT ALL TOGETHER

We have discussed three communication tools to help you spot communication problems. The three tools—reading the nonverbal messages of others and controlling your own, flowcharting the messages, and charting the form and quality of the communication—deal with the observables or symptoms of the interactive chemistry taking place between you and your subordinate. Perhaps I can anticipate a reaction from you sharp-eyed readers. You are probably saying, "But wait! The symptoms include whether the parties are listening to each other, as well as the communication process itself. The tools seem to deal only with the process." My response is that if you make use of the tools, you will *have to listen* more actively and attentively than you ever have before. And you will be able to spot and correct listening problems on the part of your partner.

Because they require a great deal of concentration, there is always the danger that the tools I have described here may detract from the effectiveness of one-to-one communication. This may happen if you are not fully prepared and well versed in their use. Or you may overly complicate the suggested procedures if you seek to record too much information during a meeting. Finally you may begin to lose sight of the real objectives of a one-to-one meeting because you have begun to concentrate so much on the process. For example, you may be focusing on communication flow and nonverbal signs when the purpose of the meeting is to plan work objectives. For these reasons, the tools discussed here are to be used only when you are having a specific problem, or when you think your overall communication effectiveness could stand substantial improvement.

Two more points before I end the discussion. One is that these tools are useful not only for one-to-one communication but for group meetings as well. Secondly, you may be faced with a communication problem that these tools cannot help you solve. In this situation the use of a third party in your office, or an expert from outside the organization, may be the answer.

Communication effectiveness is a key element in productivity and job satisfaction. No matter what strategy or tools you choose to overcome communication problems, they must be solved to allow for maximum achievement of your work goals.

8

How Do You Rate as a Listener?

Jean W. Vining
Augusta C. Yrie

"I'm sorry that I didn't return your call. My secretary misunderstood your message."

"May I speak to Mr. Smith? I'm returning his call. What? There's no Mr. Smith there. Is this 123-2322? It is. Then I must have received the wrong message."

Do these conversations sound familiar? Perhaps they sound all too familiar, reflecting similar situations that frequently occur in your own department. Have you ever wondered why so many messages are incorrectly reported? Perhaps the personnel in your organization do not know how to listen effectively or do not recognize how important listening is if a message is to be transmitted correctly and appropriate follow-up action taken.

You, as supervisor, are well aware of the need for effective listening skills. Instructions on doing a job that are not clearly understood can lead to costly mistakes. And an incorrectly reported telephone message from a client or customer can mean the loss of

From *Supervisory Management*, January 1980.

that individual's business. But employees are not the only individuals with poor listening skills. On occasion, you, too, may be guilty of ineffective listening. That can be even more costly to your organization.

Ineffective listening skills are certainly not unique to your organization, this generation, or even to this century. They've been around at least from the time of Socrates who complained that the youths he tutored were generally poor listeners. Only recently, however, has the importance of receiving and transmitting verbal ideas clearly, concisely, and coherently been emphasized. Much of the research in the past in communication focused on written messages.

WHY PEOPLE LISTEN

Individuals listen for a number of reasons, including to receive a message; as a basis upon which to make a decision; to obtain needed information; and to enhance their ability to instruct, supervise, guide, manage, or counsel others. Any of these reasons for listening may be used repeatedly each day by an executive and his or her subordinates. In each instance, listening errors can occur. The message perceived by the listener and the resulting transmitted message may be entirely different from the sender's intended message.

Receiving and comprehending abilities vary with an individual's surroundings at the time that the message is received. They may also be influenced by previous listening experiences and by noises present at the time that the message is transmitted. Still another factor relates to the words used in the message. People are able to hear more accurately and to convey a message more correctly when familiar vocabulary is used. For your part, that means that a conscious effort should be made to use terminology that is easily understood by all personnel in your organization. To assist new employees in becoming operationally familiar with the terminology of their jobs, you might consider providing a list of terms relevant to the particular situation, department, or industry.

IMPROVING LISTENING

As with many skills, practice in listening tends to improve one's ability to listen effectively. As a supervisor, you'll find that as your listening skills grow, your managerial effectiveness will increase because your decisions will be based on a clear understanding of the facts. Also, you will be perceived by your subordinates and your co-workers as a manager who listens before acting. Because of your new image as a listener, your decisions may be implemented more smoothly and more quickly by both your subordinates and fellow workers.

You can actively work to improve your own listening competency and that of your staff by practicing the following techniques and advocating that your people try them, too:

- Learn to let the speaker express his or her thoughts without interruption.
- Learn to listen between the lines because what the speaker actually says may not completely represent his or her intended meaning.
- Concentrate on developing retention ability. Do not take too many notes—make your memory work for you.
- Do not "tune out" the speaker if you find the subject or speaker to be boring.
- Do not become hostile or emotional just because the speaker's ideas differ from your own.
- Learn to ignore distractions.

You can identify your listening weaknesses and rate your listening effectiveness by using the quiz shown in Figure 8-1. It will help you to pinpoint specific areas that need improvement and evaluate your overall listening competency.

How did you rate as a listener? If you scored 32 or more points, you are an excellent listener—a positive receiver of ideas through listening. A score of 27 to 31 makes you a better-than-average listener. A score of 22 to 26 points suggests that you need to consciously practice listening. It is a signal that there are weaknesses that need to be eliminated. If you scored 21 points or less, many of the messages that you receive are probably garbled and are not likely to be transmitted effectively. By consciously working to eliminate the "never" and "rarely" responses, you should significantly improve day-to-day operations and your relations with subordinates, co-workers, and superiors.

Besides taking the listening quiz yourself, you should encourage your subordinates to take it. Encourage them to rate themselves and to refer to the quiz as they work to change their listening behavior.

Figure 8-1. How do you measure up as a listener?

Directions: Read the questions listed below and rate yourself on each of the listening characteristics using the following scale:

Always	= 4 points
Almost always	= 3 points
Rarely	= 2 points
Never	= 1 point

Listening Characteristics   *Responses*

1. Do I allow the speaker to express his or her complete thoughts without interrupting?   4 3 2 1

2. Do I listen between the lines, especially when conversing with individuals who frequently use hidden meanings?   4 3 2 1

3. Do I actively try to develop retention ability to remember important facts?   4 3 2 1

4. Do I write down the most important details of a message?   4 3 2 1

5. In recording a message, do I concentrate on writing the major facts and key phrases?   4 3 2 1

6. Do I read essential details back to the speaker before the conversation ends to insure correct understanding?   4 3 2 1

7. Do I refrain from turning off the speaker because the message is dull or boring, or because I do not personally know or like the speaker?   4 3 2 1

8. Do I avoid becoming hostile or excited when a speaker's views differ from my own?   4 3 2 1

9. Do I ignore distractions when listening?   4 3 2 1

10. Do I express a genuine interest in the other individual's conversation?   4 3 2 1

The listening evaluation quiz can help both you and your employees assess the department's listening competency and identify specific areas that need improvement. Consider how much would your business and managerial abilities improve if everyone in your organization listened effectively each day. When was the last time you really listened to those around you? Why not start listening today?

9

The Way We Word

Paul R. Timm

"Communication breakdown" has just about taken the place of original sin as an explanation for the ills of the world—and perhaps with good cause. As our world becomes more complex and as we spend more time in organized activities, the need for interpersonal understanding has never been greater. And just as important, the cost of failure has never been higher.

The Latin root word for communicate is *communicare*, which means "to make common." So the degree to which a message sender and receiver have a *common understanding* of a message is the measure of how effective the communication process has been. And although we take this whole process pretty much for granted, the way our language works is not well understood by most people.

SOURCE OF MISCOMMUNICATION

First, it may seem ironic that language—the very basis of what many view as real communication—poses one of the most pervasive

From *Supervisory Management*, May 1978.

sources of misunderstanding in our communicative processes, but it does.

Let me explain: We have all developed our own ways of using words and symbols to describe what we mean to others. How we process and arrange words is our personal language structure. Our sensory experiences—that is, our perceptions of the physical world to which we attach words and symbols—can be likened to data cards for a computer. And in these terms, our language structure is analogous to a system program, which tells the computer what to do with the new data. So communication failures often arise between people either because of differences in how they relate words to experiences or because of the way they process the words they speak or hear.

There are two ways to improve verbal communication skills: Either increase a person's vocabulary so that more precise "data cards" can be produced, or improve the match between language structures and objective reality. Increasing someone's vocabulary will usually be a far less fruitful approach than working on structures, because only in those situations where there is a seriously inadequate vocabulary—such as when a person is learning a new language—would an emphasis on improved vocabulary be significantly valuable. Clarifying language structures by examining our logic and showing discrepancies between the way we "process" words and the way the real world behaves is a far more valuable approach.

Let's look at several assumptions about word use that may be causing some of the more common problems in the ways we process language.

FACT VS. ASSUMPTION

Many problems of miscommunication arise when the way we structure our language does not distinguish between fact and assumption. And to presume that people in general—including ourselves—know an absolute fact when they see one is a dangerous presumption.

In truth, the vast majority of information we receive is inference or opinion, not fact. Something we personally observe or experience can be regarded as a fact—at least for us. But just about anything else should be considered inference or opinion. The times that we run into misunderstanding and disagreement with others are when we state inferences or opinions as though they were facts. The problem is that the language we normally use does not automatically make the distinction clear. So we must make an extra effort to do so.

For example, under normal circumstances, we can state direct observations—"I saw Tom leave the plant at five o'clock"—as facts. But if we take the fact about Tom leaving the plant and try to elaborate on it, what we say becomes an inference. For example, when we say, "I saw Tom leaving the plant *to go home,*" we are now adding a new dimension to the message that may or may not be true, in fact. That Tom left the plant can be verified by observation, but that he went home is merely inferential on our part.

An inference is a conclusion based upon incomplete information, and much of what we talk about is based on inference. By necessity, we communicate inferences all the time. But problems arise when our listeners are unclear as to whether we are inferring or speaking of fact. Our language often tends to muddy this distinction, so inferences have a way of coming out sounding awfully factual.

Again, let me restate: There is nothing inherently wrong with drawing inferences. Inferences are necessary for people to make day-to-day sense out of the world. We seldom have the luxury of having *all* available data at our disposal before we draw conclusions. The important thing is that we recognize inferences as such and that we word them in ways that will help us and our listeners avoid confusing them with facts. Failure to do so can often lead to confusion and argument.

For example, if you like the sales manager's dress, and you say, "Hey, I like that dress," fine. That's a fact. You are clearly expressing a factual, as-it-relates-to-me statement. You like the dress and there's little room for misunderstanding. If, however, you say, "That's a nice dress you're wearing," you're stating an opinion that sounds like a fact, and there's more room for interpreting what you really mean. Do you like the fact that the sales manager is wearing a dress instead of her customary pantsuit, which you think is too masculine? Do you like the fact that you can now get a better look at the sales manager's legs? Are you being sarcastic and not really complimentary? There's more room for interpretation in an opinion. (Of course, nonverbal dimensions such as tone of voice and facial expression can clarify the point you are trying to make.)

Nobody can argue about what you "like." If you say, "I didn't like that movie," that's your right and other people will respect it. But if you say, "That was a rotten movie," then others may be put on the defensive, especially if they liked the movie.

HOW TO RESPOND?

When an opinion is not identified as such, the receiver of the message has to make a decision on how to respond—whether to be "nice" and agree with you or be true to his or her feelings and say that it was not a "rotten" movie. If contrary opinions are offered, the risk of starting an argument is increased.

Another example: If I state the opinion that, "Frank is stupid," it may appear on the surface that stupidity is an inherent characteristic of Frank. But what, in fact, I am saying is that:

◊ My personal experience has supplied me with a meaning for the word "stupid."
◊ I have perceived Frank's behavior as fitting my view of the concept of "stupidity."
◊ Therefore, I have concluded that Frank is stupid.

Notice that the words "I" and "me" enter in this analysis throughout. When I conclude that Frank is stupid, I am really talking about my own opinion. I've related these two things, Frank and stupidity. *I* have related them within my world of words. Whether or not they are related to objective reality remains unclear.

So, in essence, every opinion we offer is a statement about ourselves. This is so because:

◊ We can never say all there is we have to say about any topic, since this would take too long. Therefore . . .
◊ Those things we do choose to talk about and those that we choose to ignore involve a selection process on our part, based on our past experiences. Thus whereas . . .
◊ Each of us has had totally unique experiences and no two people have experienced the same things, and since . . .
◊ We have each created our own unique way of attaching words or labels to our world of experiences—therefore . . .
◊ When we combine several of these labels into a message, we are saying very little about objective reality and instead are describing something that is of great importance to us *personally*.

Thus to conclude that, "Frank is stupid," is to report on some word associations we have made. This statement doesn't really say much about Frank, but it does say some very interesting things about us.

A simple remedy for this problem of expression is by making clear that you recognize this process and by converting these opinions into facts. "*I think that* Frank is stupid," is a fact. Or, "I've observed Frank doing things *I consider stupid*," is a fact.

Although this changing of terms often results in additional effort and longer messages, the tradeoff results in greater accuracy and clarity of expression. Failure to so clarify what our message is can lead to considerable embarrassment, incorrect conclusions, and serious harm to our credibility. I suspect this potential breakdown was in S. I. Hayakawa's mind when he said that general semantics—that is, the study of language and its behavioral effects—could more accurately be described as the study of "how not to be a damn fool."

Another common problem in the way we structure language is the tendency to oversimplify the categories into which we mentally sort things. We deal with our life experiences in egg-carton fashion, neatly fitting each experience into one of several compartments.

THE EITHER–OR TEMPTATION

The problem with this practice is that people rely too heavily on polar terms, terms that force us to choose between extremes—like good or bad, weak or strong, big or little—and which tend to oversimplify and confuse the issues we are discussing. In reality, most things we encounter in life are more accurately described in terms of probabilities or fine variations among events or experiences than by an either-or categorization. In other words, our experiences represent some shade of gray, rather than black-or-white differentiations. To illustrate, simply ask yourself—and others—questions such as these:

> Are you rich or poor?
> Are you big or little?
> Are you handsome or ugly?
> Are you conservative or liberal?

The appropriate response, of course, to questions like these would be, "As compared to whom (or what)?" It can be very helpful to our communicative abilities to train our thinking away from over-simplified categorization, although this does take a more active intellectual effort to talk in terms of degrees or comparisons.

In an industrial organization, this process may mean avoiding the tendency to classify workers as "industrious" or "lazy" or as "productive" or "unproductive." In one company I've heard of, a sales manager actually had a big chart on his office wall with the names of all his salesmen boldly displayed under the headings "Heros" and "Bums."

The problem with this tendency is that when our language and thinking utilize such either-or logic, other possibilities are overlooked. If we only classify a manager as a "good leader" or "bad leader," we leave out a lot of other possibilities. Maybe he or she is effective in some dimensions of the job while ineffective in others.

Sales representatives and other persuaders often manipulate this either-or orientation to their advantage. "Would you like to take delivery immediately or next week?" attempts to preclude the option of not taking delivery at all. It's the old story of the ice cream shoppe operator who asked each customer whether they wanted one egg or two in their milkshakes. Few people said neither, and he charged extra for each egg, of course.

Another consideration is that our credibility can be seriously damaged when listeners recognize these kinds of oversimplified language structures. While there are legitimately dichotomous categories—such as male or female—most things don't fit so neatly into either-or slots. Or sometimes the categories themselves become so broad as to be meaningless. Whenever we hear ourselves or others sending either-or messages, it might be wise for us to consider:

Are all the options covered?
As compared to what (or whom)?

SELF-FULFILLING EXPECTATIONS

The manager who comes to actually see his subordinates as heros or bums is obviously not relating to reality. It is far more realistic and hopeful to think in terms of ever-changing individuals who can and will change their work performance. Today's hero may have been yesterday's bum—if we, as managers, have been able to avoid the related problem of self-fulfilling prophecies. Because we usually choose what perceptions we will pay attention to and then mesh these things into our views of reality, there is a strong tendency to only look for the pieces that fit.

Similarly, there are interactive effects between our perceptions and the ways we talk. What we see directly affects what we say. And what we say in turn affects what we see. The filters of our mind develop over time as we label our world of experiences, and these filters then determine what we select to perceive. When we can make no sense out of some thing or event—that is, if it doesn't fit our world view—we tend to reject it.

It can be quite disconcerting, for example, to find the worker we've labeled "rebellious" suddenly vigorously defending the status quo. It's also unsettling to find the "nice, pleasant" receptionist suddenly shouting angrily at a visitor. We'd prefer to reject or explain away such discrepancies because they just don't jibe with "the way things are" in our mental worlds. The way we label things lead to expectations of how the things will behave in the future.

Furthermore, expectations have a way of becoming self-fulfilling. The supervisor who labels a subordinate "lazy" will undoubtedly find more and more evidence to support the judgment. And in all likelihood, this supervisor's attitude will then be perceived by the worker, thus leading to suspicion and distrust. The overall result: a strong potential for miscommunication. So let's keep our labels—if we must use them—somewhat loose. Let's build into them some flexibility so that unanticipated changes in things, events, and people can be plugged into our mental worlds without throwing us off balance.

RECOGNIZING CHANGE

Now each time a person interacts with others, he or she is receiving feedback that either reinforces or modifies his or her view of the world. The development of self-image, stereotypes of others, and role expectations all result from this interactive process of communication.

Similarly, modern self-help techniques all begin with an important premise: *Each individual is unique and capable of change.* But problems of communication arise because although the world of experiences is dynamic and everchanging, the world of words is much less flexible. Language tends to change very slowly, leaving us with the problem of trying to describe fluctuating processes with words that stress consistencies.

People are also constantly in a process of change. (As George Bernard Shaw once said, "The only man who behaves sensibly is my tailor; he takes my measurements anew each time he sees me, whilst all the rest go on with their old measurements and expect them to fit me.") So failure to accept change leads to many communication difficulties. Psychologist Carl Rogers has suggested that, "If I accept the other person as something fixed, already diagnosed and classified, already shaped by his or her past, then I am doing my part to confirm this limited hypothesis. If I accept him or her as a process of becoming, then I am doing what I can to confirm or make real his or her potentialities." In other words, if I believe that the word labels I've attached to a person are not changeable, I cannot then cope with change vis-à-vis that person.

Before I leave this discussion of change, let me clarify one point. Language and word associations *do* change over time, but the changes in these labels are not necessarily logical. For example, consider these recent changes in slang expressions:

⋄ "Dude" used to mean an inexperienced cowboy. Now it more often describes a street-wise city dweller.
⋄ "Heavy" is no longer a measure of physical weight. It can now mean something of deep intellectual meaning or a half dozen other things.
⋄ "Coke" isn't just a cola beverage anymore.
⋄ "Righteous" doesn't necessarily mean one full of religious virtue.
⋄ "Bad" in some subcultures now means good.

NEED FOR CLEAR THINKING

To be credible as a message source, a person must be constantly aware of such things as the pervasiveness of change. In short, we need to think clearly and communicate clearly. When our ways of thinking become too rigid, we move away from paralleling reality.

In summary, we must remember that words do not have inherent meanings. They are simply labels that we attach in unique and individual ways to our world of experiences. And since labels trigger meanings in others, the degree to which we achieve true communication is determined in part by how accurate we are in relating these labels to reality. If we are inaccurate, we describe a world that is not there. Carried to the extreme, inappropriate language uses can affect our mental health. Our psychological and sociological well being can depend upon our being aware of the important ways in which language reflects and influences the way we think and communicate.

Many communication problems arise from a lack of awareness about "the way we word." In fact, when the many pitfalls of language processing are pointed out, it seems amazing that people can communicate at all.

Part Three

DOWN, UP, AND ACROSS

10

Communication in the Organization

Lois B. Hart

Leaders must improve their ability to communicate not only within their own work unit but also within the entire organization. Your own work unit does not function independently of the rest of the organization. Successful leaders learn about and utilize both the formal and informal communication channels.

Women are less familiar than men with the broad perspectives of an organization, though they are generally quite adept at taking care of the "home front." As women ascend the organization ladder, they must become more knowledgeable about the entire picture. The process is similar to the stages of growing up. Infants and young children are initially concerned only about themselves and, later, about their own family. As they begin to interact with other children, the world expands for them. The circle grows even wider as they become aware of their immediate community, then their nation, and finally the world. As adults, they are concerned about their own family circle as well as events that occur worldwide. The

From *Moving Up! Women and Leadership*, by Lois B. Hart. © 1980 Lois B. Hart. Published by AMACOM, a division of American Management Associations.

mature adult knows how much world events can affect her or his personal life. In a similar way, a developing leader must understand how the organization as a whole operates.

THE ORGANIZATIONAL PYRAMID

Most organizations are structured in a hierarchical pyramid. The majority of employees are at the bottom, a minority are in the middle, and a select few are at the top. Communication flows up and down definite lines within the pyramid. These lines can vary from organization to organization, as Figure 10-1 shows. The number of people at different levels of responsibility changes, but the structure, with its definite top and bottom, remains the same.

To analyze your own organization, obtain or draw a table that identifies formal roles in their hierarchical order and connects them to the formal lines of communication—that is, the ways used to relay policies, directives, and reports. Think of them as radio channels. A message goes along a specific channel with no deviation; it must pass point A before going to point B. Formal lines of communication are established to ensure orderliness and authority and tend to be quite rigid. Think about recent information you received in your organization. What parts were disseminated along formal lines? Was the information written or verbal, one to one or in groups?

Figure 10-1. Organizational structures.

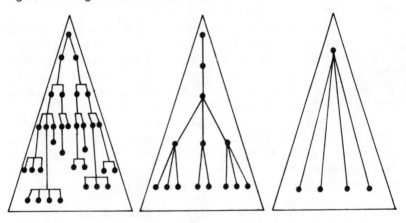

The responsibility for setting policy and determining the overall structures of the organization rests with the top managers, who also establish the communication climate for the organization. Middle managers are responsible for establishing networks or procedures to carry out the policy set by the top managers. As intermediaries in the organization, they serve as conduits of information to and from levels above and below them. They rely heavily on informal communication. Leaders at the lower levels are responsible for informing their subordinates of policies and communications they receive from higher levels.

Even if you are at the lower levels of your organization, you need to know how communication flows in the whole organization. There are several reasons for this. First, you need to be aware of how the whole system operates in order to understand your position relative to other positions. Second, if you know the communication networks, you can utilize them for your own needs. Third, you may not always be at the bottom of the hierarchy. If you plan to move up to the middle and top levels of management, you must understand the roles that higher-level leaders play in the total communication structure.

An effective leader learns how communication flows in the organization and systematically taps these flows. To do this, the leader must explore the informal methods of communication that develop in all organizations; it is often through these networks that crucial information is conveyed. The "old boy network," for example, is an informal system that has considerable power: If you're "in," you get the needed information; if you're "out," you are left in the dark. Ideas on how to get "in" are examined below.

The following exercise, based on a model used by Michael Korda, can help you understand how informal networks of communication work. Place a piece of tracing paper over the diagram you've obtained (or drawn) of your organization's formal structure. Think about the influence that different people in the organization possess. Draw circles of varying sizes to symbolize people's personal power. Obviously, the person with the most power will have the largest circle. As you continue, notice that you are adding circles that usually do not appear on the diagram. The additional circles may be for secretaries and custodians. Such people often have considerable power and influence and are an integral part of the informal communication network. Next, draw lines to connect the circles. Vary the width of the lines to symbolize the strength of the communication between individuals. When you finish the diagram, you will see that the lines of informal communication do not necessarily flow along the formal lines. The flow includes different people and channels.

INFORMAL NETWORKS

Informal networks of communication are active and changing in all organizations and supply a variety of information to their members, such as the latest gossip about interpersonal conflicts or affairs, inside information on job openings or terminations, information on relevant articles in professional journals, notices of conferences or workshops, and previews of organizational problems. Access to this information is crucial if a leader is to stay informed of the comings and goings of the organization and to take advantage of opportunities for professional growth.

How can you top this informal communication system? Take note of where influential people spend their informal time—that is, when they are not at their desks or in conference. When the boss takes a coffeebreak, where does she or he go? Does the boss roam around, stopping regularly at certain people's offices or work areas? Who spends time with the powerful people? Who rides to work together? Who goes to lunch together?

The first step, then, is to become an astute observer of powerful people, those who are most likely to have, hold, and pass along useful information. Observe their routine behavior for a few weeks. Next, gradually move into areas frequented by these people. For instance:

⋄ Take your coffeebreak at the same time they do.

⋄ Drop into their offices on any pretext.

⋄ As they walk by your office, call them in for a moment of conversation.

⋄ Invite yourself to lunch with the group. Say, "Where are you all having lunch? I'd like to go along today."

⋄ Get rides to and from work periodically, if not regularly, with them.

⋄ Join in the social events. Go to birthday parties, TGIFs, social hours, baseball games, bowling and golf leagues, and holiday parties.

Another way to ease yourself into informal networks is to tap the gossip system. As you mingle among the employees of your organization (and don't exclude the secretaries and custodians, who know more than managers ever imagine), listen to what they say. Repeat, *listen*. Don't embellish, substantiate, or challenge what is said. In other words, don't contribute to the gossip; just absorb and sift through the information for fact versus fiction. If possible, check the source of the gossip. Since you know the influential people and their relationships to others, you can probably trace the gossip back to the originator.

Suppose your boss's secretary casually mentions that Mr. Samuels, head of marketing, is looking for a new job. Is this fact or rumor? It's important to know the source of this information. You recall that the secretary giving you the tip and Mr. Samuels' secretary carpool to work together; thus it is likely that they have discussed this in the car. You can also assume that Mr. Samuels' secretary knows the content of phone calls and conferences that occur inside the boss's office. So through the two secretaries you may gain access to unofficial information. If this information is accurate, and you have your eye on Mr. Samuels' job, then you can prepare yourself for an upward move. If, however, you know that the secretary who is the source of the information loves to gossip or dislikes her boss and wishes he would leave, you better check the information out further.

Remember that the informal pipeline in the hierarchy works both ways, so that those at the lower levels pass up information as well. You can be sure that your actions, conflicts, and mistakes, as well as achievements, are being observed. If you are competent, that fact will most likely be passed along the informal channels. You may even receive feedback from someone several levels above you who says, "I've been hearing good things about you." If you know how the pipeline works, you can feed information about your aspirations and accomplishments into it so the right people will hear about you.

A third way to tap the informal communication system is through the written word. Read notices on all bulletin boards regularly. They contain a wealth of information, including job notices, announcements of educational opportunities and conferences, items for sale, and requests for information. You can also post notices on the bulletin board to get information you need and to keep visible. Bulletin boards often contain information that is available nowhere else. One saleswoman, for example, was trying to meet a potential client who had just been hired, but did not know her name. A habitual bulletin board reader, she happened upon a newspaper account of this woman that gave her not only the prospect's name but enough other information to make their first conference fruitful.

Get on the routing slips of important trade and professional journals. Notice which ones appear in the offices of influential people. Borrow their copies to determine what is useful to you. Ask them to add you to the list, emphasizing how anxious you are to keep informed. This expressed interest may spur them to put you higher up on the list so that you receive the current issue this month instead of next month. Ask these influential people to watch for certain articles for you in particular publications. This way, you may get a publication even before your name comes up on the routing slip.

One supervisor of five people has a system for determining the order in which she routes magazines, articles, reports, and conference notices. Those highest on her list are the people who have expressed an interest in increasing their professional knowledge and a willingness to read what she sends promptly. Their behavior has "trained" her to send them the information first. In a similar fashion, you can "train" others to keep you in mind when useful information comes across their desks.

Get copies of reports that are not normally or routinely distributed. When you hear that a certain report has been completed and think you would benefit from reading it, try to obtain a copy. If copies are not kept in an area accessible to all employees, ask someone diplomatically if you can borrow a copy. Don't be afraid to ask. The worst that can happen is that you will be told "no."

CREATE YOUR OWN COMMUNICATION SYSTEM

As a leader, you usually have the authority to develop some of your own mechanisms for communication within your work unit. What types of communication should you use?

One-Way or Two-Way?

Communication can be sent through one-way or two-way channels, both of which a leader should use. Recall a one-way communication sent to you, such as a memo instructing you to do something by a certain date or to obtain information and send it back to the requester. Similar one-way messages are given in PA announcements or in staff meetings when the boss announces a policy and allows no discussion.

Now recall a two-way communication in which the sender met face to face with you and was interested in your questions or requests for clarification. Recall a written two-way communication such as a memo asking you to respond through a phone call, a follow-up memo, or a conference.

Compare the two types of communication systems by completing the following:

	One-way Communication	Two-way Communication
1. Which is faster?		
2. Which appears to be more efficient?		
3. Which enhances morale?		
4. Which allows for initiation?		
5. Which is better for material that is:		
New, difficult, ambiguous?		
Familiar, previously understood?		
6. Which ensures greater accuracy?		

As you can see, both types of communication are useful in certain situations. When you need a fast, efficient method to convey information that is fairly familiar to the recipients, the one-way method is usually appropriate. The two-way method of communication is appropriate when you want to be sure that information has been understood thoroughly.

Each system has its advantages and disadvantages. The one-way method protects the sender's power, authority, and leadership status. Because no dialogue is possible, the sender is insulated from direct challenge or blame. However, frequent use of the one-way system can reduce employee morale and initiative. Employees like to be asked their opinions when they know the topic or problem and when they are personally affected. The two-way method involves employees directly and thus enhances morale and encourages initiation. However, this method is slower than one-way communication and leaves the sender vulnerable to challenge.

Which system should you use? Both. Determine your purpose and be selective. Ask yourself each time:

◊ Are speed and efficiency important?
◊ What will be the effect on employees?
◊ How difficult is the material?
◊ Am I overusing a particular method?

Individual or Group?

Messages can be conveyed to an individual or to a group. Once again, as a leader, you need to decide which method best serves your purpose. Here are some guidelines:

◊ Use one-to-one communication to discipline, to provide negative feedback, or to counsel an employee.
◊ Use group communication when information must be given to everyone. Cover only the points that are essential to all. Having employees listen to reports and discussions unrelated to their work is a waste of time, energy, and money.

Verbal or Written?

Communication can be verbal or written. As a leader, consider the advantages and disadvantages of both. Like one- and two-way communication, the appropriateness of verbal or written forms depends on the situation. Before you decide on a method to convey a particular message, review the questions listed above on one- and two-way communication.

Assess your abilities as a verbal and written communicator. In which are you stronger? In what ways are you stronger? How can you improve your skill in the other form? Check your clarity and accuracy in verbal and written communication with colleagues and employees. Emphasize your strengths and work on your weaknesses. Leaders should be skilled in both types of communication so they can function well in a variety of situations.

◇ Use one-to-one communication to issue instructions or hold discussions that are pertinent to only one employee.

◇ Use both one-to-one and group communication to praise people's work and behavior.

Communication Networks

Communication networks vary in kind, size, and purpose, as Figure 10-2 shows. Networks I and II operate without a designated leader. In I, communication flows from person to person, with eventual completion of the circle. In II, information is passed down the line, requiring those in the middle (B, C, and D) to serve as conduits. When the information reaches the end (A and E), communication flows in the other direction.

Networks of this type have certain disadvantages. In II, for example, the people at the ends sometimes never get the message; they are purposely or inadvertently left out. In both I and II, the absence of an identifiable leader can lead to inefficient and incomplete communication. When a task must be accomplished, a leader is needed to provide direction. In addition, only minimal interaction among group members takes place.

In the direct communication network (III), each employee communicates directly to the leader (L). This method works well when the number of employees is not large or when the leader needs to monitor the work of others closely. The indirect methods (IV and V) require the employee to report to an intermediary, who then reports to the leader. When the number of employees is large, this form of communication and supervision increases efficiency because it enables the leader to pursue other executive tasks and to delegate day-to-day operations to the intermediaries. This method, however, decreases the leader's direct contact with employees and allows greater opportunity for miscommunication.

In networks VI, VII, VIII, which can operate within the direct and indirect networks, communication flows both formally and informally among the members of the work group as well as toward the designated leader. The underlying assumption behind such an ar-

Figure 10-2. Communication networks.

Leaderless networks

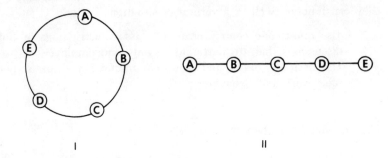

I

II

Direct versus indirect networks

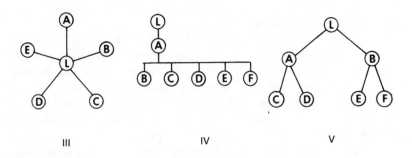

III

IV

V

Interrelated networks

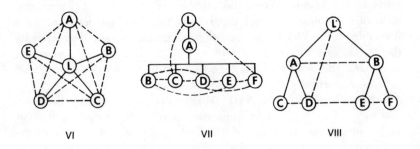

VI

VII

VIII

rangement is that group members can communicate directly what they know and what their problems are. Group members function as resources for one another. In order for the system to work, therefore, everyone must be interested in and committed to joint problem solving.

This knowledge of how different organizational networks work, informally and formally, can help you expand your own operating arena and build upon basic communication concepts to enhance your leadership skills.

11

Mastering the Techniques of Two-Way Communication

Philip Lesly

Communicating is something that everyone does. It's as universal as eating, sleeping, and loving, and as vital as any of these. Almost everyone goes through each day thinking that he or she is courting others—soliciting their support, seeking their love, currying their favor, or at least neutralizing their hostility. Yet most of us do it so poorly so much of the time that we seem to discommunicate rather than communicate, and we actually end up repelling those we court or reinforcing the antagonism of our opponents.

There are two major types of communication that the supervisor has to deal with on a day-to-day basis: upward and downward.

UPWARD COMMUNICATION

The following guidelines can avert discommunication when dealing with superiors in the organization and others who make decisions affecting the supervisor.

From *Supervisory Management*, November 1979.

• Analyze your audience. Most discommunication begins with failure on the supervisor's part to know and analyze the audience. Since there are so many different kinds of audiences, it's a mistake to set down rules as if they can apply to all or most situations. It is necessary to:

1. Consider the makeup of the audience. A single person calls for different treatment than a small group, and a large group requires still another approach to getting your message across. It's surprising how many capable managers frame their communications exactly the same way whether they're trying to reach one superior or an entire management committee.

2. Know as much as possible about what makes each member of the audience tick. Know each one's background in the company. The person who has always been in top management or in a level of authority will respond differently from one who worked up from the bottom. Other questions to ask: How well informed is he or she on the subject involved? What expectations is each individual bringing to the communication process? Is that person a figure of dominance in the group? If the latter is the case, your communication should be crafted toward winning that person over to your point of view.

3. Know the makeup of the group in relation to your subject. Is the group homogeneous—all executives at a certain level, with similar ideas—or mixed—including traditionalists and radicals, economic entrepreneurs and environmentalists, men and women, blacks and whites, and so on? If the group is homogeneous, it is easier for you to frame what you wish to communicate. However, homogeneity also accounts for the frequency of communication failure, for in this kind of group anything alien to the members' way of thinking is apt to be rejected outright.

4. Develop your communication—and the responses to be made afterward—specifically for the audience and that occasion. Never use formulas. Meet the audience's conditions. These include not only such matters as knowledge, prejudices, and politics, but timing. Victor Hugo said that "more powerful than armies is an idea whose time has come." But more impotent than a faded soldier is an idea whose time is past. Any message that is perceived as dealing with bygone interests is certain to cause discommunication.

• Decide on the true purpose of your communication. In general, it will be either to inform, to influence attitudes, or to motivate. Each of these is different. It may be necessary to inform and influence attitudes in order to motivate, but if motivation is your purpose, keep it clear to yourself that the other functions merely contribute to meeting that goal.

◆ Get active participation from the audience. Communication works best as a joint activity, not a lecture. Engage the self-interest of the members of your audience from the beginning. Make your words personal to them. Participation gives them a sense of contributing to the decision making and thereby your communication becomes more important. Try to guide them toward the conclusion you seek before you point it out to them. That will make it seem *their* conclusion, and one they are likely to hold on to.

◆ Be sure of your credibility. There are two sides to the balance of credibility: the inclination of the audience to believe and the acceptability of the source. The latter depends on the audience's experience with the source. In today's largely skeptical world, credibility of almost all sources is low when what is said is in the self-interest of the speakers. It is higher for those with a good track record. And it is highest for disinterested third parties speaking on behalf of management or about an idea from which they cannot benefit.

◆ Use multiple channels and repetition. One impression, no matter how intensive, is unlikely to have as much influence on the outcome of a meeting as the same message communicated through various sources or the same message repeated at different times. Remember that absorbing information or ideas is a cumulative process.

◆ Consider the rules of communication. In upward communication, it's most often best to follow this sequence (but be ready to break the sequence if judgment dictates):

1. State the question. Define and refine it to its essence.

2. Develop the relevant aspects in a logical sequence. Document, give examples, illustrate in words or graphics.

3. Present the answer, and how it is to be achieved, to your audience.

4. If there is disagreement among members of the audience, acknowledge opposing points of view and their weaknesses. Account for them; either counteract with information or put them into perspective against the weight of your knowledge.

5. Call for a specific result—approval or endorsement.

◆ Make your material as visually oriented as possible. This does not mean converting everything into audiovisuals; information and ideas can be made visible to an audience through the use of examples, testimonials, experiences, illustrations—especially if they are items already known to the audience or come from an individual or some organization they respect.

♦ Avoid your jargon and use theirs carefully. The only time jargon is justified is when it will bring a feeling of warm familiarity to the audience. If they say something like "impacts on the company" or "operationalize the plan," you may find it effective to use such terms. They're barbarisms, but they're *their* barbarisms. However, eliminate your jargon from your speech.

♦ Avoid using terms unfamiliar to your audience. You may be discussing a budget for installation of electronics equipment, but unless all the participants are versed in electronics terminology, translate everything into layman's terms.

DOWNWARD COMMUNICATION

Whenever other considerations obscure the human aspect of dealing with people, discommunication sets in. In dealing with subordinates the difference in status that automatically exists in the organization makes the employees especially sensitive to exertion of power. Approaches that seem to use status as a lever for imposing information tend to activate an already developed tendency to resist, jeopardizing the acceptability of the communication.

Effective downward communication in an organization cannot be a statement signed "The Management," but a transaction between adults participating equally.

THE NEED OF THE SUBORDINATE

In *Motivation and Personality,* Abraham Maslow stated that each individual has a hierarchy of needs. When the basic needs are met, those are taken for granted and higher or more subtle needs take their place. In the United States we are now at the stage where almost everyone is striving to meet his or her ego needs: a sense of worth, self-confidence, achievement, a sense of contributing, status, recognition, appreciation, respect, and expectation of improvement. Intended communication that assails or bypasses any of these creates resistance and resentment.

The need is to fulfill their egos—not yours. If the communication is used to make the communicator look good, feel big, or demonstrate superiority, it destroys its purpose. Concern for their feelings and aspirations makes possible a successful interchange; condescension prevents it.

So, again, the way toward curing discommunication with employees is knowing the audience. Know what its values are, what it takes for granted, what it aspires to, and what it wants to get out of its association with you. Each audience is made up of different people, and each individual brings a different background to the meeting.

MEET THE AUDIENCE'S CONDITIONS

People in accounting or data processing live and think in different ways from those in design and display, for example. Sometimes having to communicate simultaneously with both may be unavoidable; but it is far better to get as close to the background of each individual in the group and communicate to that person in his or her frame of reference.

Meeting with small, distinctive groups rather than large and diverse groups of employees has a number of advantages. First, the groups can be selected on the basis of their similar backgrounds and interests; second, the smaller group gives the individual a greater sense of participation. Finally, the meeting can be much closer to an equal exchange of ideas and opinions when each individual has the opportunity to be heard.

STATEMENT OF OBJECTIVES

There are three main objectives in communicating with employees: informing, influencing, and motivating. Clarity of meaning is impossible without clarity of purpose. Why are you communicating? What objective do you hope to gain? If that is clearly in mind, no meeting will break up with the various attendees having different impressions of the point you were trying to make.

One reason for failing to communicate one's purpose is having too many purposes. A single idea can be readily grasped by everyone. Each effort to add another idea reduces geometrically how well any of these ideas is remembered.

The communication process can be likened to a ladder, and the guidelines discussed in this article are its rungs. To be an effective supervisor, an individual should adhere to these guidelines. Using them, he or she can establish good channels of communication with those persons both high and low in the management hierarchy— individuals whose decisions and actions can greatly affect personal success. I do not believe that there is anything more important for the supervisor to master than the art of communication.

12

Opening the Channels of Upward Communication

Russell W. Driver

Problems relating to upward communication in organizations have recently been getting a good deal of press. It's not, however, because the problems are new ones. Years ago, Mao-Tse-Tung noted, "At the very highest level there is very little knowledge. They do not understand the opinion of the masses. They are very busy from morning until evening; but they do not examine people, and they do not investigate matters."

In business organizations, problems stemming from poor upward communication occur far too frequently. I doubt if any one of us with a few years of organizational experience has not seen management (whether ourselves or someone else) at some time become out of touch with the realities in the organization. When that occurs, it generally is the direct or indirect result of insufficient upward communication.

If problems in upward communication are not new, why then are they only now receiving major attention? The reason for the new interest in improving upward communication is simply that management has only recently been willing to deal with the issue.

From *Supervisory Management*, March 1980.

THE NECESSITY

There are four specific reasons for emphasizing good upward communication in organizations.

1. *Preventing managerial isolation.* Managerial isolation can be defined as losing contact with what is really happening in the organization. In these cases, lack of upward communication would seem to be a primary causal factor.

A fable relating to executive isolation is the classic tale of the ill-informed walrus. Although the old walrus's herd was deteriorating, his subordinates were afraid to tell him because he just could not bear to hear bad news. Daily, as he basked in the sun, his second-in-command would tell him how well things were going. Eventually, when only the second-in-command and the head walrus were left, the loyal aide told the head walrus that the herd was gone. "I can't understand it," the old walrus said. "And just when everything was going so well."

Upward communication will accomplish more than simply preventing a great degree of managerial isolation. Good communication fosters *esprit de corps* and makes a smooth-working team out of employees at all levels of the organization. It also helps management in getting adequate information to stay ahead of future needs and trends, keeping technological knowledge up to date, and heading off trouble before it occurs.

2. *The profit motive.* Perhaps closer to the core of the matter for most business enterprises is the effect that poor communication has on profits. There are at least four results of communication failures. These are from costly failures in downward, diagonal, and horizontal communication as well as in upward communication. The failures result in: (1) good ideas that are not sold and therefore not used, (2) improper actions due to errors in, or misinterpretation of, instructions, (3) a rise in employee turnover due to workers not having what they perceive to be adequate communication with their superiors in the organization, and (4) lack of sales due to misunderstandings.

3. *Need for feedback.* Top management is constantly sending information to the company's employees; but in order for it to be sure its messages are received, it needs employee feedback—or upward communication. For example, consider what happens when someone shoots an arrow at a target. To increase the probability of actually hitting the target, the archer must get feedback regarding his or her accuracy. Similarly, a communicator determines the effect

of the communication attempt by the feedback given and can adjust his or her behavior as a result. Are management's policies being understood by the workers? Only they can answer that.

Obviously, then, two-way (upward as well as downward) communication is more satisfactory than one-way (downward only) communication. Keep in mind, though, that it is not necessarily appropriate in *all* cases. There will certainly be times when speed is of the essence, and, at least temporarily, one-way communication will work better.

4. *Worker attitudes.* Young workers today want to know more and have more explanations made to them about their working environment. An increase in the level of education and the more permissive attitude that prevails today are at least two of the reasons that they feel quite free to request full explanations and make suggestions on matters concerning their work. This change in worker attitude has given rise to participative management, and it is under the umbrella of participative management that many of the techniques for communicating upward are found.

THE TECHNIQUES

Now that its advantages have been made clear, let's look at how an organization can improve its upward communication.

The techniques for upward communication described below have all been successfully put into practice. Also, all can be categorized as either participative management or feedback. However, since the two categories are not mutually exclusive, the techniques below can be discussed without making that distinction.

• Cracker barrel sessions. These are regular and periodic meetings between first-line supervisors and all or some of the workers who report to them. At these sessions, besides giving employees the information they want, a skillful supervisor can encourage them to increase the flow of information upward. The supervisor should use these sessions, also, to develop a closer identification of the individual employee with the organization, to identify training opportunities, to enhance the image of the foreman, to improve supervision generally, and to save time by giving information to the entire group rather than individually.

Certainly, the benefits could become detriments if these meetings are not handled in a professional and competent manner. Employees must be made to feel that these sessions are *theirs* to discuss on-the-job problems, raise questions, and make suggestions.

• Operational review. This approach has been used by American Telephone and Telegraph to overcome or prevent managerial isolation. The manager visits the floor operations for which he or she is responsible, and employees from that section review with him or her their phase of the operation. Special emphasis is put on identifying roadblocks and other problems.

Immediate removal of these hindrances is important to the success of this technique.

• Telephone messages. The popularity of this technique is apparent from its unusually high level of utilization. General Mills' version is called "FactFone," the United States Air Force in Europe (USAFE) called its an "open line program," and the Massachusetts area of New England Telephone referred to its as "private lines." In all cases, the employees may remain anonymous in phoning in ideas, complaints, congratulations, or anything else to the highest levels of the organization, and they expect prompt action and/or replies. In some cases the employees may get short but current and important recorded news messages about the organization from the same phone call. Thus downward communication may become part of this procedure.

• Suggestion box. Although somewhat archaic, this technique is still used and is the more traditional version of the above-mentioned telephone messages. A modification of this approach is the use of company-prepared forms that can be sent to a designated supervisor or manager in the organization.

• In-company educational courses. These can be designed with written homework assignments on topics that allow employees to express their thoughts and ideas to the instructors with the knowledge that the ideas will be passed along to appropriate sections of the organization for feasibility studies. The educational platform also allows for good face-to-face two-way communication. Needless to say, as with many of these techniques, a good deal of trust by employees is essential for this approach to work. There should be no fear of reprisal.

• Corporate grapevine. Although not normally thought of as a "channel" for corporate information, the corporate grapevine can be used as such. It need not be automatically thought of only in negative terms. Since research shows that 75 to 95 percent of grapevine information is correct, though incomplete, certainly it cannot be considered merely a gossip medium, and information from it should be considered by management.

• Task teams. These teams consist of nonmanagement employees who work in the same area. Employees volunteer to serve on a panel that spends a given number of hours of company time per project on identified problems. Their recommendations are sent to a management interdepartmental committee that has a specified number of days to respond.

• Management council or coordinating action teams. These consist of interdepartmental middle- or first-line manager volunteers who attack specific operating problems identified by higher management. The obvious problem with this is that the council could be redundant with regular management channels.

• Employee annual meeting. These meetings are conducted at about the same time and in about the same manner as the annual stockholders' meeting. The state of the company and future plans are reported to the employees by top management, and questions are solicited from them. Dana Corporation's recent TV commercials show that executives may be in a "hot seat" when conducting such an open meeting, and that fact should be considered, but such a meeting can be useful as an upward, as well as a downward, communication device.

• Nonmanagement task force. Issues that most concern the workforce are determined by both managers and employees. A group of nonmanagement people then attempt to solve the problems. This is a broader, more generalized version of the task teams discussed above.

• Junior board of directors. This is made up of middle managers and a cross section of others below that level. The junior board makes policy recommendations and presents them to the corporate board. In one company that uses this technique, 2,000 recommendations were produced by the junior board in a five-year period and only six were turned down by higher management.

• Corps of counselors or ombudsmen. The counselors are located throughout the organization so that they are readily accessible to employees. They can be appointed by management or elected by the workers. Their function is to act as liaisons through which grievances pass. In that way, they are somewhat analogous to union shop stewards.

• Use of existing mechanisms. These can be used for hearing complaints that are not normally within their jurisdiction. For instance, a safety committee may be more fully utilized if it is permitted to hear grievances and help settle employee/management disputes.

◆ Nominal grouping. When used in a communication context the goal of the nominal group (which is homogeneous in terms of rank and authority) is to arrive at a consensus regarding concerns that it wishes reviewed by management. The group is expected to provide any necessary information.

Upward communication in a noninteracting way with no superiors present depersonalizes individual inputs and reduces fear of reprisal by superiors. It is a vehicle for participative management as are other techniques listed above but it is unique in its approach because of its noninteracting aspect and the highly structured conduct of the sessions.

◆ Full-time coordinating staff. Such a staff is normally only necessary in very large organizations with programs that require it. This staff would handle coordination of all the communication techniques used in the organization in order to have a smooth running system.

A cursory examination of these techniques of communicating may lead one to believe that with the availability of such diverse means of communicating there should be no lack of upward communication in organizations. However, we know that is not the case. Just because the techniques are available is no assurance that they will be used properly.

IS THERE A BETTER WAY?

Yes, there is a better way to handle upward communication, but it is not an easier way. There is no simple single technique or method that will solve the communication problems of a large array of organizations.

It is most important to understand that there are two responses required from a communication system. The first is a need for information so that the individual may determine what is happening and why. The second is a need for action that will solve problems for the individual. Further, communication needs differ for different individuals and groups, and there can be a shift in needs as the situation changes. Each of the techniques mentioned represents only a fragmented, single-effort approach to the problem of upward communication, and it is far too complex to be dealt with in that manner.

When trying to find that "better way" to communicate, no better advice can be given than *caveat emptor* (let the user beware). Everyone claims to have *the* prescription to cure upward communication ills. Each must be studied carefully. It may have worked very well for a particular organization at a particular time; however, the same prescription may not be applicable to another organization under different circumstances. It is the duty of the specific organization to properly modify, combine, and apply the techniques to fit its own situation.

13

Performance Review: Pitfalls and Possibilities

Peter B. Olney, Jr.

During the past decade, the continued widespread adoption of employee performance-review plans by all types of organizations has demonstrated management's awareness of the importance of reviewing subordinates' job performance. But some have enthusiastically initiated a performance review plan only to discover that the plan does not work as anticipated. In some cases, organizations have tried to improve their program by changing policies and forms or by conducting supervisory training programs. These remedial measures may improve the program, but normally they are not aimed at the real problems inherent in most plans.

THREE BASIC PROBLEMS

Essentially there are three basic problems that can destroy the effectiveness of an otherwise well-conceived plan:

From *Supervisory Management*, July 1976.

Improper use of a factor-rating sheet.
Failure to separate performance appraisal from salary review.
The "monologue" appraisal interview.

1. *Improper use of a factor-rating sheet.* Many performance review programs are built around the factor-rating sheet that requires the supervisor to rate (using the terms *excellent, good, fair,* and *unsatisfactory*) his subordinates' performance on such factors as quality and quantity of work, judgment, and initiative. For years this method was accepted as an effective way to rate performance.

But there are major problems with this system. Often the rating sheet was completed by the supervisor, placed in the employee's personnel file, and never reviewed with the employee. This, of course, didn't do a thing to improve individual performance. Then it became clear to most employers that the rating sheet should be reviewed with the employee. Unfortunately, however, employees thought of the sheet as a report card, and they wanted to see exactly how it was filled out. They became disturbed when they were marked "unsatisfactory" or "below average." Often they asked and sometimes challenged their supervisor to cite specific examples of their unsatisfactory performance. Many supervisors were not prepared to handle the situation; some were hard pressed to explain their evaluations. To avoid this problem, supervisors tempered their appraisals. Before long, in many organizations, the performance of almost all employees was rated as *good* or *excellent.*

2. *Failure to separate performance appraisal from salary review.* In introducing performance review, many managements failed to recognize that the primary objective is to help employees *improve* their performance. Too many organizations felt that performance review was simply a method of determining which employees should receive merit increases. Obviously, using performance review to determine salary increase destroys the basic purpose of the program. Improvement of an employee's performance is of such importance that it should be the primary subject discussed at the time of the review. If salary review is conducted simultaneously with performance review, "dollar sign" considerations will normally overshadow a constructive discussion of performance. When an employee is waiting to hear "how much" and "when," comments from his supervisor about his performance normally go in one ear and out the other. Performance review may be conducted on a calendar or on an anniversary-date basis; salary review should occur at

any time during the year when the employee's performance or achievement warrants it.

Management should give supervisors the authority to recommend merit increases whenever employee performance warrants it—for several reasons. If, for example, salary reviews are on a fixed date, the employee tends to be very productive during the months immediately preceding his salary review but less so in the months after his review. When employees know that supervisors can initiate increases at any time during the year, they are more apt to be on their toes at all times, and they are motivated to achieve results that will warrant a merit increase. If the performance appraisal and salary review are not separated, the plan becomes "salary appraisal" and is used as the vehicle for getting merit increases approved by higher management.

3. *Monologue appraisal review.* All employees want to know what their supervisor thinks of the job they are doing. They may get indications of the supervisor's feeling through subtle comments, pats on the back, or facial expressions—but this type of feedback is not sufficient. An employee may feel that he is doing an outstanding job but wonders whether his boss is aware of it: Is his performance really appreciated? He may know he is performing many important duties that his supervisor is unaware of, and he would appreciate an opportunity to discuss these additional duties.

Surveys of employees show that while they want to know how they are doing, they are often critical of the way a review is handled. Almost all appraisal plans require the supervisor to sit down with the subordinate and discuss his progress, strengths, and weaknesses. Unfortunately, this interview is often conducted in such a cursory manner that the employee is not even aware he is actually having his performance review. Many supervisors avoid the interview altogether and simply send the review forms to the personnel department—hoping no one will ask if the results were discussed with the employee.

The kind of review form used during the discussion is not very important. In many situations, a single sheet of scratch paper would be more effective than a complicated form. However, without forms and ticklers, many supervisors would not get around to conducting an appraisal interview until a serious problem developed. The discussion interview must be candid—a "leveling session"—and the supervisor's primary role should be to listen. In practice, however, the policies, procedures, and forms of most performance review programs encourage the supervisor to conduct a patterned interview and do most of the talking. But a successful review plan must include policies and procedures designed to ensure that the interview will be a dialogue, not a monologue.

To develop and implement an effective review plan, management must recognize the importance of nonsupervisory employee involvement in the program. No amount of employee training or indoctrination can make a performance review program succeed if nonsupervisory employees don't feel that they are playing an active role in its administration. All employees must feel that they are *participating* in the program from the start and that they are playing as important a role as the supervisor. If an organization accepts the basic philosophy that "we are all in this together," an effective plan can be introduced and maintained.

The elements of the program outlined below should be included as essential requirements in a new plan. The policies and procedures of existing programs can normally be modified or revised to include these elements although, frequently, considerable retraining is required.

PERFORMANCE RATING FACTORS

The performance rating factors to be used must be made known to all employees. Some organizations have accomplished this by posting a sheet of factors on all bulletin boards. A more direct way is to give each employee a copy of the evaluation factors. New employees should be told—during their initial orientation—what factors their performance will be judged on. The factor rating sheet should include factors that management feels are particularly significant in evaluating its own employees. Rating factors normally vary from one organization to another, but generally include certain common factors that apply to all jobs. An example of a rating factor sheet is shown in Figure 13-1.

SELF-APPRAISAL SHEET

Each employee should be notified by his or her supervisor at least one week in advance of a scheduled performance review. At this time, the personal review form shown in Figure 13-2 should be

Figure 13-1. Rating factors.

Attitude

Does he speak and act for the good of the organization?

How well does he work with customers?

How cooperatively does he work with fellow employees?

How well does he accept direction from supervisors?

Initiative

Is the employee a "self-starter"?

How resourceful is he in meeting new situations?

Does he keep abreast of new techniques and developments in his field?

Does he contribute new ideas and suggestions?

Judgment

Does he recognize problems?

How well does he gather the information relating to a problem?

How well does he analyze the cause of a problem?

How realistic are his decisions or suggestions?

Self-expression

How well does he express his ideas orally?

How well does he express himself in writing?

Does he effectively represent the organization to customers?

Productivity

Does the employee meet the quantity of work expected for the position?

Does the employee meet the quality of work expected for the position?

given to the employee as a guide to the areas that will be discussed. The sheet can be filled out as extensively or as simply as the employee wishes. Self-appraisal enables the employee to review his accomplishments since the last review, to summarize personal strengths and weaknesses, and to prepare himself to discuss performance. Several organizations that use a personal review sheet have found that employees enjoy using the sheet and gain considerable insight from it into their strengths and weaknesses.

Figure 13-2. Personal review.

Your progress and accomplishments

Have you shown progress since your last review? Please explain.

Have you made contributions over and above basic position requirements? Be as specific as possible, using facts and figures as to quantity, quality, costs, and time, wherever possible.

_____

_____

_____

1. *What are your strengths?*
(Qualities that will aid your future growth)

_____

_____

2. *In what areas can you improve?*

_____

_____

3. *What are your plans for future development?*
Record any significant facts, opinions, constructive suggestions, and action contemplated.

_____

_____

SUPERVISOR'S WORKSHEET

The old-style performance rating sheet can be used effectively as a worksheet and thought starter for supervisors. A sample worksheet is shown in Figure 13-3. The worksheet is *not* brought to the appraisal discussion and does not become a part of the employee's permanent file. However, it is used to outline or profile areas of strengths and areas for improvement in the employee's performance. It should be used as a guide in completing the employee review sheet, which the supervisor discusses and reviews with his subordinate. This review sheet is similar to the personal review sheet and ensures that the supervisor and employee are using the same guidelines and preparing to discuss the same subject areas. The employee review sheet is shown in Figure 13-4.

DISCUSSION WITH THE EMPLOYEE

The performance review should be conducted privately with no interruptions. The personal review sheet, which the employee will have completed before the meeting, is designed to start the discussion. It permits the employee to discuss his accomplishments and strengths and delineate those other areas where he believes performance can be improved. This part of the discussion can be very enlightening to the supervisor, and he or she should encourage the employee to express opinions freely. If this procedure is followed, the monologue appraisal can easily be avoided.

After listening attentively to his subordinate and encouraging him to speak freely, the supervisor should discuss his evaluation of the subordinate's accomplishments and performance. The areas where improvements can be made should be thoroughly discussed. Often the employee identifies areas for improvement in his self-appraisal that the supervisor might not have brought up for fear of a strong negative reaction.

A mutually agreeable program for future growth should be outlined in the section entitled "Program for future development." This section should be completed during the interview and discussed with the employee. Lack of such planning greatly minimizes the benefits of the meeting. The plans should be realistic and within the employee's capabilities, thereby assuring a good chance for the suc-

Figure 13-3. Supervisor's worksheet.

Appraisal	Unsatisfactory	Meets Minimum Requirements	Fully Meets Requirements	Exceeds Requirements	Outstanding

Productivity

Does the employee meet the quantity of
work expected for this position?
(Disregard quality.)

Does the employee meet the quality of
work expected for this position?
(Disregard quantity.)

Initiative

Is the employee a "self-starter"?

How resourceful is the employee in
meeting new situations?

Does the employee keep abreast of new
techniques and developments
appropriate to the position?

Does the employee contribute new ideas
and suggestions?

Attitude

Does the employee speak and act for the
good of the company?

How well does the employee serve other
persons?

How cooperatively does the employee
work with fellow employees?

How well does the employee accept
direction from supervisor?

Analysis and Judgment

Does the employee recognize problems?

How well does the employee gather the
data relating to a problem?

How well does the employee analyze the
cause of a problem?

How realistic are the employee's decisions?

Figure 13-3. Supervisor's worksheet (continued).

	Appraisal	Unsatisfactory	Meets Minimum Requirements	Fully Meets Requirements	Exceeds Requirements	Outstanding

Planning

How effectively does he/she define
objectives for his/her activities?
How realistically does he/she establish
plans for carrying out each objective?
How well does he/she accomplish the
objective?

Training and Development

How effectively does he/she develop the
abilities and potential of his/her
subordinates?

Leadership

How well does he/she motivate
subordinates?
How effective an example does he/she set
for subordinates?
How sensitive is he/she to subordinates'
needs and interests?

Delegation

How well does he/she delegate
responsibility?
How well does he/she delegate authority?
How well does he/she follow up
delegation?

Self-Expression

How well does he/she express ideas orally?
How well does he/she express ideas in
writing?
How well does he/she communicate
company policy to other persons?

Figure 13-4. Employee review.

Progress and accomplishments
  Has the staff member shown progress since employment or since his/her last review? Please explain.
  Has the staff member made contributions over and above basic position requirements? Be specific, using facts, figures, and examples.

_____

_____

_____

What are the staff member's strengths?
  (Qualities that will aid his/her growth)

_____

_____

In what areas can improvements be made? Be specific.

_____

_____

Program for future development. Record any significant facts, opinions, constructive suggestions, action contemplated.

_____

_____

Staff member's comments. Record staff member's opinion of his/her performance and list his/her comments during the discussion interview.

_____

_____

_____

This review was discussed with me on _____
                                                    Date

                         (*Signed*)_____
                                          Staff Member

                         (*Signed*)_____
                                          Supervisor

cessful development of the individual involved. Any disagreements should be clearly noted for future discussion. Additional discussion scheduled after a definite time interval will clarify points not mutually agreed upon during the first discussion.

Harmonious cooperation should be the closing tone of the discussion. Any potential benefits will be undermined if the review ends on a tone of resentment, confusion, or general discontent. Plans for the employee's development will receive their greatest boost when the individual feels that he has been understood, helped, and respected. Dignity and concern are important.

Can employees' performance really be substantially improved by means of this kind of progress review? Certainly not everyone will benefit, but the majority can be motivated to use more of their potential on the job. To do this, supervisors must determine and understand such individual employee needs as group acceptance, self-esteem, and proper recognition. Once these needs have been ascertained, supervisor and employee can work out a sensible program that will satisfy the employee's needs and support management's objectives.

14

Communicating for Improved Motivation and Performance

Larry E. Penley
Brian L. Hawkins

The problem with so many of today's motivational theories is that they place too much emphasis on describing the motivational process. Such descriptions are important for the development of knowledge, but they do not address the problems of the practicing manager. These theories, on the whole, do not identify strategies for modifying and changing individual behavior, and these are what managers want. They want concrete, effective strategies for dealing with motivation.

Theorists often describe motivation as a process that occurs between the work environment and the individual's performance. Based on this concept of motivation, Douglas McGregor in *The Human Side of Enterprise* suggests that a manager cannot motivate

From *Advanced Management Journal*, Spring 1980.

another person. His contention is that a manager cannot *directly* affect the motives going on inside the employee's head. The manager can only indirectly affect these motives by manipulating the environment in which the employee exists.

What can a manager do to affect the environment of the employee? The answer lies in the communication that occurs between manager and employee.

To understand clearly the relationship between communication and motivation, let us briefly look at one well-received motivational model, that of Victor Vroom, and see how communication strategies can be integrated with it.

In his book *Work and Motivation,* Vroom suggests that three factors are important: (1) the "valence," or importance, of various outcomes in meeting an individual's needs, (2) the extent to which an individual perceives that his or her effort will result in the desired performance, and (3) the extent to which an individual believes that desired performances will be rewarded.

From what has been observed, the manager cannot directly affect what another person values; thus valence falls outside the realm of managerial strategy. A manager can, however, affect both the extent to which an employee believes he or she can perform a task and whether or not that performance will result in desired rewards.

Vroom refers to an employee's belief that he or she can perform the task as "expectancy." This belief that one can accomplish a task is affected by self-confidence, learned skills, and native abilities. The manager can increase an employee's confidence by coaching, encouraging, and being supportive of the employee who has low expectancy for a particular task. This may be the case for an employee who is new on the job or for one who has recently changed jobs. Further, the manager can train employees who have not learned the necessary skills, thus increasing expectancy.

The second variable from the model that can be modified by a manager's communication is called "instrumentality." Instrumentality is the employee's perception of the results of personal performance. In other words, it is the degree to which the employee believes that rewards are commensurate with successful performance. Does good performance result in merit pay? Does bad performance result in termination? The answers to both of these questions reflect the extent to which employees perceive that rewards or punishments are tied to performance.

What things can a manager do to affect these perceptions of expectancy and instrumentality? Are there contingency strategies that a manager can adopt to heighten these perceptions, thus encouraging better employee performance?

These questions were addressed in a survey of employee attitudes in a Southwestern financial institution. The balance of this article offers conclusions based on the findings of this study. (For details on study methodology, see the accompanying section, "The Nature of the Study.")

Receptivity and Responsiveness Are Key

Study results show that a supervisor's receptiveness or willingness to listen to subordinates' ideas, problems, and concerns will improve the motivation of subordinates. Through such receptiveness, supervisors develop knowledge of areas in which they need to provide additional training or explanation in order to build expectancy that the worker can perform tasks. A supervisor, however, must not only be receptive to the messages subordinates communicate, they must also respond to questions and problems. The study indicates that listening to the employee is not enough. If high levels of motivation are to be obtained, follow-up and communication of that follow-up are essential.

Praise Is More Than a Reward

Praise is a reward that many employees seek in organizations, both for its own sake and as a guidepost in directing their organizational behavior. More than that, however, praise also builds confidence in an employee that he or she can perform the task. This means that expectancy can be modified for an employee if a manager communicates praise, reducing employee anxiety as he or she moves toward success in task performance.

Effective Media Use Is Needed

Management can improve its communication of benefits and goals through more frequent communication and the use of varied media, including meetings, memoranda, bulletin boards, and orientation sessions. Management can also raise motivation through improving the clarity of written reports and instructions. Adapting written messages to the reader by writing at the reader's level and in terms of the needs or viewpoint of the reader means that employees will have greater understanding of what is expected of them as well as of what behavior will be rewarded by the organization.

Supervisors and management can also sharpen motivation by increasing the information that workers have on the reasons for doing a task, job procedures, specific goals of the job, how to do a job, the relationship of one job to another job, and organizational goals. The data from this study indicate that motivation and performance are higher for employees who can place their job in a "bigger picture."

Feedback Is Motivational

Adequate information concerning performance will improve the perception of the instrumental relationship between performance and rewards. By providing employees with information on performance and what is necessary to get a pay increase, management can help employees relate performance to reward. The net result should be higher motivation and performance.

Awareness of Career Options Helps

Employees who possess high expectancy describe themselves as having good information on career development. The communication of performance, followed up with information on the career "ladders" to positions in top management, may be an important key to employee motivation and performance.

Summing Up: The Big Five

Overall, this study suggests that managers need to examine closely their conduct in five areas: (1) their receptiveness and responsiveness to employees, (2) the clarity of their communication, (3) the adequacy of the performance-related information they give, (4) the adequacy of the task-related information they provide, and (5) the adequacy of information concerning career development they give. Based on the study, there is a clear justification for increasing management's emphasis on communication planning and on communication training for supervisors and managers.

THE NATURE OF THE STUDY

The conclusions drawn in this article are based on the findings of an employee survey conducted at a financial organization in the Southwest. Soliciting views on job communication, motivation, and performance, questionnaires were submitted to the firm's 354 employees, of whom some 75 percent responded. Supplementing this source of information, supervisors were surveyed and asked to evaluate employees' performance. A number of areas were investigated:

1. The quality of *supervisory communication* was measured with a scale formed of 11 items. The scale included items concerned with the responsiveness of the supervisor to subordinates' questions and problems, the degree to which the supervisor is receptive to the ideas of subordinates or listens to subordinates, and the degree to which the supervisor praises subordinates when they succeed.

2. The quality of *managerial communication* included items concerned with the degree to which upper management communicates information on benefits and goals, is sincere in its communication, is perceived to understand the employees, and clearly writes instructions and reports.

3. Three scales were developed to measure the degree of information adequacy that employees face concerning their performance, their career development, and their tasks. These scales were formed by asking respondents to rate how much information they *now* receive and how much information they *need* to receive in the three categories: *The adequacy of performance-related information* was determined by gauging responses to questions regarding the information employees now get on their job performance, and what they believe they must do to get a pay increase; the *adequacy of task-related information* was determined by evaluating the information employees reported receiving on task objectives, job procedures, task interrelationships, and organizational goals; the *adequacy of career-development information* was determined by assessing employees' knowledge as to how to get promoted and how to get additional training.

4. The measure of *expectancy* was formed by asking employees about their perceptions of the relationship between their effort and resultant performance.

5. The measure of *instrumentality* was formed by asking employees about their perceptions of the extent to which they are rewarded for performance by their supervisors.

6. As an additional element in assessing the effectiveness of communication, supervisors evaluated job performance of subordinates in terms of dependability, organizational ability, application of job knowledge, adaptability, initiative, interpersonal skills, leadership ability, and overall work performance.

7. The data for this study were analyzed using multiple regression techniques. These techniques allowed the researcher to determine whether motivation and performance were affected by communication, and they revealed that measures of communication affect motivation and performance.

15

The Power of Huddling

V. Dallas Merrell

Organizations don't work well normally. Everyone knows that. Throughout our lives virtually all of us confront perplexing, formalistic, phlegmatic organizations—hospitals, schools, governments, businesses, banks, postal services, unions, and so on. Yet some organizational workers manage to accomplish much more than others, to get results in spite of the formal organization. Sometimes we forget that organizations don't get results; people do! *People in huddles usually accomplish the most significant work in organizations.*

HUDDLING OBSERVED

Let's look briefly at how huddlers manage to get things done in organizations:

♦ A business executive is about to go into an important meeting with other company executives. He huddles for a few moments with a trusted assistant to make sure that everything is in order and that they are both up to date on what they are going to do. After the meeting two vice-presidents walk through the hall to their offices,

From *Huddling: The Informal Way to Management Success,* by V. Dallas Merrell. © 1979 AMACOM, a division of American Management Associations.

huddling informally to confirm the fact that a given proposal made in the meeting is contrary to their best interests.

 • A student sticks his head in a professor's door and in less than 30 seconds gets the professor to agree on what will happen in the next class. The student does this by making a suggestion and offering to do a task that will make it easy for the professor to implement the suggestion.

 • Government leaders are entertained by business contacts at a hunting lodge or country club. The casual setting provides an excellent opportunity for influence to be exercised, decisions to be made, information to be shared, and plans to be jelled.

 • A presidential candidate meets many people across the country in face-to-face encounters, discussing issues, sharing campaign plans, and soliciting their involvement. Subsequent exposure through television and other media solidify the campaign, but the extensive huddling beforehand paves the way for the campaign's success.

 • New farming practices are introduced into a community through "opinion leaders," those whose judgments are respected by other farmers. Discussions about new techniques take place through the informal interactions among farmers, and between farmers and suppliers. It is through these huddles that farmers share information and experiences, and obtain assurances from influential people that a new practice or a new piece of machinery is in their best interests.

HUDDLING DEFINED

A huddle is a temporary, intimate, work-oriented encounter between two or more people. Huddlers draw together informally and confer, "nestling" to get results where organizations fail. A huddle is the source of considerable information, the locus of significant decisions, the setting for power transactions, the place where many responsibilities get defined, and the impetus for motivating people to get things done. Huddles compensate for countless organizational ineptitudes.

COMMUNICATING IN HUDDLES

Top managers in one company made a confidential review of their field offices and concluded that several needed to be subdivided.

Because their decision would affect a considerable number of people, they agreed to keep it guarded until an official announcement was made. After making their disclosure, the managers learned that everybody concerned already knew about it.

These managers failed to take into account the power of informal communication channels in the organization. Informal communication patterns are natural streams and tributaries, unlike the "engineered channels" found in the formal organization. Left alone, communication will flow in natural patterns through areas of least resistance. Like a stream of water winding through a mountain valley, communication moves from person to person and huddle to huddle wherever the message can get through.

Huddlers provide an array of data important to the organization: facts, observations, opinions, and tidbits. Before you contribute any of this information, you should know the personality of the people involved and their habits of behavior. People are interested in different kinds of information relevant to any given task. The data you provide should be tailored to the needs and working habits of your fellow huddlers.

A management analyst confided in me: "The report was fine, but I figured a few things were best left out. They were a little personal and would only make a stink rather than help. At the right time when I had a minute to mention them privately to Joe, he thanked me and asked what I would do. After I made a few suggestions, he began to use me in some new ways. We have been working rather closely ever since."

Packaging Messages

Effective communicators in the informal organization know what things are important in communication and how they should be "packaged" or transmitted as messages. There are several approaches to packaging information. You can focus on facts and figures, technical or expert opinions, or the judgments of experienced participants in the organization. You can handle communication as an emotional appeal or as an objective, straightforward process.

Circumstances will dictate the manner in which information is best presented. In some cases it is wise to first convey background information and facts. In other cases it is advisable to present conclusions first and then discuss how the conclusions were developed and what facts you have to support them.

One executive I know insists that his people bring him solutions, not problems. Another executive will fire anyone who presumes to do his thinking for him. He prefers to be told about the problem, after which *he* will think about it and discuss it with you. Then he will give *you* the solution. Huddlers who ignore the personalities of decision makers will have short-lived impact.

Shorthand

Efficiency is imperative in huddles. Communication within the huddle is normally cogent, with on-target, shorthand vocabulary developed to meet the needs of those involved. Huddling shorthand develops over time as people work together. Previous experiences make it possible to communicate without extensive explanations, definitions, or justifications. That is what shop talk is all about.

Those who must have things "spelled out" for them will not be included in huddling for long. If you don't know what "You take it from here" means, you're on the outs—and the meaning of that phrase differs from huddle to huddle. This is all part of understanding the "street language" of huddle culture.

Vocabulary

What is the appropriate vocabulary to use in transmitting information? Again, appropriateness depends on the individual or group involved. Certain language that would communicate effectively to some people may be misunderstood by others. People react differently to the connotations of words. Awareness of personalities should help you judge the likely effect of your communications as you transact huddling business.

Regardless of whom you're communicating with, be certain to avoid gobbledygook—official language that fails to get ideas through. A sample of what to avoid comes from a government agency report about cutting down on paperwork: "In order to accomplish this initial consolidation the EIA must conduct detailed functional and user requirements analyses, systems analyses, programmatic and respondent impact studies and cost/benefit analyses, as well as program, document, and implement all cancellations, modifications, and consolidations."*

*National Journal, February 4, 1978.

Disclosures

Huddlers who have information need to decide what should be disclosed and whether disclosure should involve facts or opinions. In the interest of efficiency, you should avoid disclosing everything you know about a subject, unless you are in an extended huddle and full disclosure is called for. Huddlers must be sensitive to the types of information required by different individuals and should not disclose information when it would constitute a breach of confidentiality.

What is the proper timing of a disclosure? When should certain pieces of information be shared with others? In what sequence should matters be disclosed? With whom should information be shared—for whose "eyes or ears only"? How should confidentiality be handled? The answers to these questions usually call for judgment at the moment, but sometimes they can be determined beforehand, as you exchange information and observations with others.

Protecting Sources

"Here it is, but if you quote me I'll deny it" is a protective statement often voiced by huddlers. In some cases, it is essential for huddlers to shield their sources of information. If information has come from other huddles in a network, from individuals who are not acceptable to others in the current group, or from someone who is a confidential informant to huddlers in other discussions, it may be highly inadvisable to disclose the *source* of the information. Trust is not to be breached.

Some journalists have refused to disclose the sources of information used in their news articles. Since much of the information comes from huddles, to violate this trust would destroy access to these sources. In a similar vein, the inside sharing of information among organizational workers sometimes requires a measure of confidentiality that in the huddler's judgment will need to be exercised.

Readiness

Because huddling processes are somewhat unpredictable—arising to meet issues or problems on demand—huddlers must be ready at any time with information that is relevant to current or potential problems. If a huddler repeatedly lacks relevant information, his value to other participants is diminished. On the other hand, if he seems to have information readily at hand, his stock will go up with other huddlers.

16

Rumor Must Be Reckoned With!

Juliet M. Halford

Say! Have you heard?" True or false, it's all grist to the gossip mill, that seemingly built-in fixture of every office and plant. All other, more formal systems of communication occasionally break down; but the grapevine, it seems, can always be depended upon to operate speedily, efficiently—and without any particular regard for truth or consequences.

What's more, it is often said, there's nothing much you can do about it. You can't stop people from talking. Actually, that's beside the point. That people *will* talk we know. The question is, what do they say? Is the grapevine—as many managers believe—no more than a peddler of gossip, scandal, rumors, and half-truths? There is another school of thought which maintains that it has a legitimate function in the over-all communication process on the job. Its adherents say that a certain amount of informal shop talk and off-the-cuff exchange is not only inevitable but healthy—a sign that employees have a more than routine interest in their jobs, the people they work with, and the company they work for. Moreover, they point out, the grapevine is both fast and far-reaching. It's accessible. Why can't it be made to work *for* management instead of against it?

There is something to be said on both sides. That the grapevine *can* be invidious—a betrayer of company secrets, a poisoner of reputations, and a wrecker of morale—hardly need be argued; there is ample experience to prove it. Yet not all companies are bothered by their grapevines to the same extent. Some even go so far as to look upon them as a useful supplement to their formal channels of communication. Whether, in fact, you think of the grapevine as good or bad seems to depend pretty much on the kind of grapevine you happen to have. This may be a matter of luck, but the evidence is beginning to mount that there is nothing so fortuitous about it after all. We do not know completely as yet how the grapevine functions; but what we do know points to the practical conclusion that a company—or even a department within a company—usually gets the kind of grapevine that it deserves.

HOW THE WORD IS PASSED

To begin with, how much do we know about the way the grapevine operates—how the word is actually passed along? Does *A* tell *B*, *B* tell *C*, *C* tell *D*, and so on down the line? Or does *A* circulate at random, button-holing anybody who seems interested in listening? In an attempt to answer this type of question, Keith Davis, then associate professor of management at Indiana University, made a careful study of "informal" communication patterns in a leather-goods factory. Virtually the only kind of chain that existed there, he found, was what is known as "the cluster": One person told, say, three others, two of these merely received the information, the third passed it on to two more people, one of whom told somebody else, and so on. In other words, most people appear to be merely passive recipients of news, while a few make it their business to spread it around. In suggesting that the grapevine is kept going by what communication experts call "liaison individuals," this research substantiates what many of us have seen from our own observation: that some people in a work group are far more gossip-prone than others; similarly, certain people in a work group seem to exert considerable influence over the opinions of others and are particularly active in transmitting unofficial information or in stimulating conjecture about it.

In the case of the liaison individual who is primarily concerned with gossip, where this problem exists to a pronounced degree it can readily be recognized and can often be solved simply through disciplinary action. It is a matter, in other words, of dealing, in one way or another, with a problem employee. In the case of the opinion molder, the situation is somewhat more complex but has greater possibilities for being turned to good account. For liaison individuals who fall into this group are not necessarily antipathetic to management or to their fellow workers. They are, however, job-centered— that is, they are intensely interested in anything that may possibly affect their jobs or those of the people they work with; and they are quite vocal about it. Often they are the informal leaders of the group and have a reputation for being in the know about what is going on and what it may possibly mean. Obviously, it is important for the manager to make certain that such informal leaders are kept straight on the facts. This does not mean that he should discriminate against the others and take special pains to inform these leaders in advance or to give them more information. It simply means that he should be aware that liaison individuals can influence the opinion of others for better or worse; that he should know who they are and make sure, insofar as possible, that they have the right facts and attitudes.

WHY RUMORS SPREAD

The fundamental question, however, is not *who* is on the grapevine or *how* it moves. If one accepts the idea that the grapevine exists in most work groups—that the pattern may change as people come and go, are moved or transferred, but that the grapevine itself is virtually indestructible—then the larger question is this: *What* actually is being transmitted and *why*?

The grapevine doesn't buzz with stories that everyone knows to be patently false. If a rumor is going the rounds, it's something a fair number of people find both interesting and credible. Whether, in reality, it is true, half-true, or completely untrue is irrelevant. The question is, rather, why do people believe it? Why are they impelled to pass it on?

Psychologists who have studied rumor patterns say that they usually conform to a basic pattern. Rumor travels only when the story has *importance* for both the speaker and the hearer and when the true facts about it are shrouded in some kind of *ambiguity*. When news about matters that affect people's lives is not clearly reported, reaches them in conflicting versions, or is withheld altogether, some plausible explanation for this unintelligible situation has to be found. If people are anxious about the outcome, they will accept the version that serves to confirm their fears. If they are hoping for better things, they will snatch at anything that colors the world in a rosier hue. If they are resentful, they will be all the more receptive to ideas that fix the blame on a person or group whom they dislike.

In other words, rumor fulfills a double psychological purpose: On the one hand it caters to our need to make sense of the world around us, to know how things stand; and on the other it provides an outlet for our underlying emotional tensions. Any human situation can spark a rumor, but fear, hope, and hostility often supply the principal motivational power for passing it on. By and large, all rumors—other than those arising from mere curiosity—fall into one or another of these three categories.

Further, the psychologists point out, once the central theme of a rumor has been accepted, there is a tendency to distort subsequent news or events in order to make them consistent with the central theme. The farther the message spreads, the more likely it is to become garbled and twisted. Thus it can happen that what starts out as idle speculation in the toolroom may wind up wreaking general havoc in the organization; if the effects are not always as far-reaching as this, they can be serious and damaging enough. Rumors based on groundless fears ("They won't need any clerical help when they get the new computer") can cause employees to start looking around for other jobs. Rumors based on wishful thinking ("Have you heard? The Christmas bonus is going to be bigger this year") can cause morale to plummet when they turn out to be totally unfounded. Rumors based on prejudice and hate ("You know why he had to quit his last job?") can undermine authority and ruin reputations.

Hope, we are told, springs eternal in the human breast; so, to a greater or lesser degree, do hostility and fear. For this simple reason there seems to be little prospect that rumor mongering can ever be entirely rooted out. Nevertheless, if the rumor formula is true, it follows that many rumors would never have started if the full facts had been known in the first place. Supply the facts and you remove the element of ambiguity without which rumor cannot exist.

HOW RUMOR CAN BE CONTROLLED

For example, if people are ordered to do something whose purpose is not at all clear, their immediate reaction is, why? Further, if they aren't told, they conclude that somebody must have thought it better for them not to know. That's when the grapevine starts getting busy.

Most rumors that fly in the face of fact can be traced to a breakdown in communication between management and employees. Not everybody is able to figure out the annual report. Not all employees understand everything in the employee handbook. They expect *you* to be able to put them straight on general company policies and practices. It is you to whom they turn for the answers to such everyday questions as what the chances are of a raise, how changes in methods or machinery are likely to affect them, or whether they will be considered for the next vacancy up the line. If the answers are not forthcoming, the grapevine is only too happy to oblige.

Moreover, though you can't always prevent a fire from breaking out, you don't have to stand idly by until it burns down the plant. Listen to what your employees have to say; try to find out what is really on their minds.

If it turns out that the ideas aren't getting over too well after all, the remedy is in your hands. Keep yourself up to date on all the information that crosses your desk. See that it's passed on promptly: to all your men, if necessary; to your key people if it's something that they can safely be trusted to transmit to the rest of the group. When a rumor reaches your ears, take immediate steps to get at the facts. Merely to tag the story as a rumor doesn't help. From past experiences people know that a rumor may well turn out to be true. If the story has implications that extend beyond your own bailiwick, see that it's passed on to those who are in a position to take the necessary steps to counteract any harm it might do.

WHEN IT'S CONFIDENTIAL

Listen to what they say; tell them what they want to know; keep them informed. These precepts are familiar; we have all heard them a thousand times before. But in reality "Give them the facts" is often a good deal easier said than done. What, for example, if the boss says, "Better keep quiet about this"? What if the memo is labeled "confidential" but the subject matter is likely to leak out? How can you "communicate" and keep mum at the same time?

Many top management decisions and plans fall into this category, and often the individual manager is uncertain just how far he is supposed to go in the matter of passing on what he has been told. At such times, there's always the temptation to take refuge in those famous first words that seem to have an uncanny faculty for sparking the very blaze they are designed to prevent:

  ○ *"Sorry—no comment."* This one never fails to *provoke* comment.
  ○ *"I'm not saying 'yes' and I'm not saying 'no.' "* Aren't you? You may well be surprised when you find out later just what you have said.
  ○ *"I don't make the rules around here."* They know you don't make the rules, but they expect you to know why the rules have been made. If you're not telling, whose team are you on?
  ○ *"I just don't know."* Keep this up and you won't be troubled by too much traffic through the open door.

In the matter of handling news of major importance, Studebaker-Packard Corporation has this advice for its supervisors:

  1. *Contact higher levels of supervision.* Find out just what details can be made public. Discuss with the next line of management and your fellow managers the best approach to take. Questions are bound to come up. Be ready with the right answers.
  2. *Call in your key men.* Talk things over with them, find out their reactions, and see that they pass the right word along.
  3. *Get all your people together and explain the situation.* If the news means that some are going to be hurt, make sure that everybody understands why the decision was necessary.
  4. *Be reassuring as far as you can, but don't sugar-coat.* People can take bad news if you give it to them straight. Frankness with the facts, insofar as you're free to be frank, and honesty in communicating them are your best bets for winning confidence.
  5. *Never pass the buck.* If there are questions that you can't answer accurately, don't just guess or give the questioner the brush-off. Promise to get the information, and keep your word.

YOU MAY BE THE BOTTLENECK

Not all news that is classified as "confidential," however, falls under the heading of major importance. One of the commonest supervisory gripes is, in fact, the restricted handling of much information that could very well be released for general circulation without doing any particular harm. This may present a problem that, by and large, is beyond the power of the individual manager to solve. On the other hand, it is sometimes the manager himself who, through timidity or overcaution, is the real bottleneck. When the boss says, "Just keep it under your hat for the time being," you're obliged to respect his request so long as you acquiesce in it. But, as Standard Oil of California points out, it is always open to a manager to query his boss whether, in the circumstances, it's advisable or necessary to keep certain information under wraps.

IS "THE WORD" GOOD OR BAD?

In the larger context of over-all company operations, one manager's ill-considered remark may seem a somewhat trivial affair; yet it is upon such comparative trifles that the intangible thing called "confidence" primarily rests. It is not every day that you are called upon to break the big news or to clear up serious misunderstandings. But every day, in a dozen different, indefinable ways, what you say—or fail to say—shapes and colors your employees' opinions of you and of the company as a whole. *Every day, your words and actions determine what they talk about among themselves.* Is "the word" good or bad? In the final analysis, the answer is up to you.

Part Four

THE DAY-TO-DAY JOB

17

Nonverbal Communication and Business

Ken Cooper

It would be wonderful if a secret Eastern society existed to teach us the mysteries of effective communication. We might tear out a small coupon in the back of our favorite magazine, mail it with "only $2.99," and wait expectantly for the Ancient Wisdom Parchment.

Knowing help was on the way, we could endure our communications failures. At last, the scroll would be sure to save us. Opening the plain-wrapped package with nervous anticipation, we would finally have the answers to the most perplexing problems in human relationships. What would the message be?

Most likely, the parchment would not offer any deep secrets to successful communication—because there are none. Instead, it would probably contain certain commonly known communications basic⌐ that researchers in the field agree on.

From *Nonverbal Communication for Business Success*, by Ken Cooper. © 1979 Ken Cooper. Published by AMACOM, a division of American Management Associations.

COMMUNICATIONS BASICS

If we were holding that folded piece of paper, we would find four key concepts that can help us better understand any communications process. The first is that we communicate *with* someone, not *to* someone. Communication is not necessarily taking place just because one person is talking to another. We frequently assume that it is, until we find that our listener is a million miles away. In an article in *Reader's Digest* Carol Burnett tells such a story about a conversation with her seven-year-old daughter after a spanking:

> "At bedtime, she was still sniffling," Carol recalled. "So I went in and put my arms around her saying, 'Now, you know I love you very much.' And then I talked about character and what she did that was wrong, and she listened—never taking her eyes from my face. I began congratulating myself—boy, you are really getting through, she'll remember this when she's 40.

> "I talked for 20 minutes. She was spellbound; we were practically nose to nose. As I paused, searching for the clincher, she asked, 'Mommy, how many teeth do you have?'"

There's a punch, of course. The person who deserves to be punched in this type of story is frequently us. However, the humor fades when a raise is lost, a key employee quits, or a sale goes to a competitor. Communication is always a team effort between speaker and listener.

The second basic is that communication is separate from information. Communication is an *act;* information is the *content.* The medium is *not* the message, and expression of a message should not be confused with the message itself.

The third basic is that communication is nonrepeatable. There is never a chance for an identical second exchange after the first attempt. Even with writing or a film, readers or viewers change from day to day, from week to week, and are no longer the same people they were when the first exchange occurred. There is the added factor of the miscues in the first trial affecting the encore. A good example is the classic Unveiling the New Dress scene:

From the bedroom, the husband hears, "Close your eyes, hon, I want to show you something I picked up today."

If he's not thinking, the husband says, "Okay." If he's awake, he puts down his paper, mumbles a short prayer, and replies, "I'm ready!"

The rustle down the hall is punctuated by a Loretta Young swirl as the wife asks the surely dazzled husband, "How do you like it?"

Unmoving after a short, controlled pause, he states with hopeful enthusiasm, "I really like it!"

"You don't like it! I can tell."

"No, listen, it's really a dynamite dress."

"You hate it, Harold. Any time you say 'really,' I know you're not being truthful."

"Look, what do you want me to say, 'I worship the dress'?" he replies with a rising voice. "I *like* it. I wish we had been married in it. If there was another in the store in a smaller size, I would buy it for my mother. What more do you want, a notarized oath?"

"You don't have to get sarcastic, Harold. You don't like the dress and that's all there is to it. You're never satisfied with anything I do. And speaking of your mother and a smaller size—"

"Stop! Dear, go back in the room and come out again. I *do* like the dress and I'll do whatever you want me to do."

Poor Harold isn't living in the Twilight Zone, but he might wish he were so he could get another shot at commenting on his wife's new dress. That's because communication is not repeatable. Next time, he'll be ecstatic just to protect himself. If he fumbles that opportunity, he won't get another chance then either.

The fourth communications basic is that we should consider the total message whenever we speak. People who write about NVC often promote the idea that we are continually communicating "hidden nonverbal messages" that disagree with our verbal messages. This idea may sell a lot of books and seminars, but it just isn't true. Catchphrases like "What is your body *really* saying?" and "Are you missing the opportunities on those lonely business trips?" merely titillate us. In general, there are very few discrepancies between the overall communications message and NVC. Most people just aren't good enough actors and actresses to carry it off.

As an exercise in my college classes, I have students give a two-minute talk in which all their gestures and movements conflict with what they are saying. For example, they may stomp in, slam their books to the floor, and scream in agony, "I'm glad to be here!" I limit these talks to two minutes because it takes a great deal of practice to choreograph the movements to each phrase and coordinate them in a talk.

There is a danger in taking a single NVC sign out of context. I discovered this quite by accident when I made a call on one of my regular customers, a utility executive. I naturally had tried to observe his mannerisms for any useful information, and he had one habit that drove me to distraction. Whenever I presented an idea to him, either one on one or in a presentation, he always listened with his hand covering his mouth. All the NVC literature states that this is a strong sign of disapproval or disagreement. One day while we were having a casual discussion about a communications column I wrote for a local paper, he asked me if I "used" NVC on him and if I had noticed anything unusual.

"You know, Ken," he said, "I hope I haven't given the wrong impression when I listen to you fellows. Have you noticed anything unusual about me when I listen?"

Sensing I should dig more, I said, "No, Bob. Why would you ask?"

"I read a book that told me I shouldn't put my hand over my mouth when I'm listening. Have you noticed I do this?"

"I noticed it, Bob, but I wasn't sure what it meant," I said. It *had* been bothering me, but I wasn't about to let *him* know that.

"As you can see, my face is deeply lined," he began. "I was riding the bus one day and just happened to be sitting in a seat where the large convex mirror by the rear door shot my reflection right back at me. I glanced up and saw my face looking grotesque and distorted, glaring back with an enormous frown. The lines on my face made me look terribly negative. It left such an impression on me that I decided to be certain I didn't accidentally make someone think I was angry or unhappy when I was really just listening. Now I always cover my mouth when I listen so that I won't turn the other person off."

That little confession made me breathe a sigh of sales relief. It also taught me a valuable lesson, and unlike most valuable lessons, it came relatively cheap: *No single NVC sign can be read accurately out of the context of the entire communications process.*

Nonverbal communication consists of three steps: reading, evaluating, and controlling body signals. Accurate and timely reading of nonverbal information is necessary because of the nonrepeatability of the communications process. There is no second chance. Evaluation is necessary to separate information from expression and to better identify the total message. Controlling NVC is necessary because communication is an active process, whether people are listening or speaking.

THE CHECKLIST APPROACH

As a firm believer in effective time management, I have written this book to be efficient and practical in its presentation of ideas. Special emphasis is given to "checklists" of nonverbal signals to help you observe and apply them in social situations. Up to now there has been no structured approach to NVC, much less to NVC in business. Yet NVC can play a major role in improving your business image and increasing your chances of success.

A Winner with NVC—Joe B.

Joe B. is a prime example of how people can be winners with NVC. Before his recent retirement, Joe was one of the foremost architects in a large Midwestern city. Extremely talented, he was known as a supersalesman who always won competitive bids. This success was especially remarkable in view of the way organizations select architects. When a company decides to go out for bids, it will schedule marathon sessions during which any qualified architect, solicited or otherwise, is allowed to present ideas. On the appointed day the architects assemble outside the conference room like a bevy of shotputters, flexing their muscles and trying to psyche out their opponents. They sit with their drawings rolled up under their arms and nervously wait their turn.

Joe's success was so legendary that when he merely walked into the waiting area, half the architects immediately got up and left without presenting. Joe was an exceptional architect, but he was not that far ahead of his rivals in technical skills. What gave Joe the edge was his superiority in communications skills. He was so superior, in fact, that his competitors began to assume he would win.

In a long conversation with Joe one sunny afternoon, I asked him about his secret. He had a very simple method. "When I go into the room," he said, "I look for two people. The first is the Star, the big boss. He is the key decision maker. I make certain I sell to him and get his commitment. I also look for the Heel. This is the negative guy, the one who will make trouble for me when I present and when I'm out of the room. I make sure I either put him in his place or draw out his criticisms so I can respond to them before I leave."

"It all sounds simple enough," I commented, eager for some juicy tips, "but how do you tell who is the Heel or Star?"

Giving the answer I feared, he responded, "Oh, you can just tell."

Therein lies the excitement of NVC—and the frustration. NVC can increase your chances of business success, but only if you have a systematic technique for learning its vocabulary and applying it in business. The NVC checklists in the first three chapters of this book will give you a framework for learning the vocabulary you need. The three NVC checklists follow the standard pattern of observation: where you put your body, its appearance and what you put around it, and what you do with it once it is there. The remaining chapters will help you gain fluency.

1. Body Position and Status
     Territorial space
     Height might
     Tread spread
     Size prize
     Seating dynamics
     Office etiquette

2. Indicators
     Personal
     Shared
     Public

3. Body Movement
     Center
     Head
     Posture
     Hands
     Legs

With practice, you will be able to make these NVC scans automatically, taking only a few moments to size up a new person or situation. The time is always available, even if you are speaking. Scientists estimate the speed of conversational thought at 750 words per minute; yet average speech is only 150 words per minute. This leaves you with 80 percent of your mental capacity to do other things. Frequently, you may daydream or plan your next response with this time. What you ought to do is become a better "listener" with your eyes.

NVC IN BUSINESS

You may be curious about how much information you will gain if your eyes do become better listeners. Albert Mehrabian conducted a series of tests to determine how much body, voice, and words contributed to the communication of attitudes. Take a moment to fill in your estimates of the proper percentages. (Remember, the percentages should reflect the communication of *attitudes*, not ideas.)

BODY	%
VOICE	%
WORDS	%
	100%

The results of Mehrabian's research were body, 55 percent; voice, 38 percent; and words, 7 percent. The percentages are, of course, highly dependent on the situation measured. After asking my audiences this question for seven years, I obtained the following averages: body, 60 percent; voice, 30 percent; and words, 10 percent. Our attitudes are communicated silently. This is the message that most people miss.

If you don't agree with my percentages—if you believe that words are far more important—you can do a little research on your own. Try this experiment when you come home from work tomorrow. As you walk in, tell your loved ones that you do, indeed, love them. Run over to them, shake your fist, and sweetly say, "I love you!" Then walk away snarling, with a horrible grimace on your face, while you clench and unclench your fists. If words are truly more important than gestures, your loved ones will come over to you with outstretched arms and sweetly respond, "Why, thank you, honey. What a nice surprise. We love you too."

If you survived that experiment, you can follow up with a test on words versus tone of voice. When you come home from work *two* days from now, wait for your loved one to ask, "How was your day, dear?" Then walk over, maintaining as pleasant an expression as possible, and say in a loud voice, "I had just a wonderful day!" with as much sarcasm as you can muster. Once again, if the response is anything other than "That's nice, dear," voice is the dominant factor. Your experiments will have to stop here if you don't want your loved one to develop a nervous tic when you arrive home. If the responses were calm and oriented solely to your words, you can forget this book. You've somehow landed Mr. Spock from *Star Trek*.

President Franklin Roosevelt was particularly aware of NVC. Standing in a boring receiving line one evening, he decided to have a little fun. As each guest came up and said, "Good evening, Mr. President, how are you, sir?" he responded warmly with a pleasant smile, "Fine, thank you, I just murdered, my mother-in-law." Not one person going through the receiving line reacted to his comment. It's doubtful people even heard it.

You are now ready to flex your communications muscles at the office. As you walk down the hall tomorrow, try an FDR. When you're asked, "Howya doin'?" cheerfully bubble, "Pretty bad, and you?" Keep count of how many of your fellow workers even hear your words. If *anybody* hears them, he or she is unusually attentive. Most of those you meet will be paying attention only to your nonverbals.

Obviously, words are important and necessary for conveying *ideas* or detailed information. If that weren't true, this book might be a film. (Not a bad idea!) In general, your body is the best indicator of *purpose* and your voice is the best indicator of *importance*.

NVC and Success

NVC has an important impact on all of us. Every President since John F. Kennedy has been tutored in NVC. These politicians realized the tremendous effect of NVC on people's perception of a candidate and on their voting decisions. Your NVC can drastically affect the decisions of your voters—those people in authority who hold your career in their hands.

The animal kingdom, dealing with its human masters, is much more successful than most of us are in using NVC. Even the youngest members are quite adept at seeing into us. If you have ever trained a puppy, you've seen an advanced NVC-reading organism at work.

When you train a puppy, sooner or later you find a "mistake of the second kind" (solid). As you're kneeling there in resigned disgust, your nice canine bumbles by. You call it, using your kindest, sweetest doggy voice. "Here, Thorndyke! Come here, sweet puppykins. Your faithful and kind owner wants to pet your lovable doggy hide."

Does Thorndyke come? Of course not! He knows full well that you plan to beat the daylights out of him with today's news, slam his nose in what he did, and throw him out in the cold, lonely backyard. He knows because he can read your NVC even though you were trying to appear as kind and nice as possible. You even reinforced his feelings by carrying the paper in your hand.

The first recorded NVC professional was not even human. He was a wizard by the name of Clever Hans who could perform *any* mathematical computation at all. Hans was a horse who lived in Germany in the early 1900s, touring the countryside and giving sellout performances at each stop. He would answer any question from the audience that could be represented by the tapping of a hoof. For a year and a half, audiences were baffled, swearing that there had to be a trick. The show conditions got tougher and tougher, but Hans never missed a question.

Then, after 18 months of success, Hans flopped for the first time. He missed a question that was asked by someone out of his line of sight and kept secret from his trainer. Clever Hans's hoof tapped right past the correct answer. For the first time in his career, Clever Hans was no longer clever.

The reason was simple. On his own, Hans had learned that if he stopped tapping his hoof at a certain point, he would get a reward. Hans was nothing more than a psychologist's rat responding to a stimulus. The stimulus Hans responded to was the tension in his trainer! He found that if he stopped tapping just as the tension eased—that is, just when he had tapped out the answer—he was rewarded. When the question was given to him from someone out of his sight, and kept secret from the trainer, there was no tension to "read."

18

When and How to Argue

William A. Delaney

As in any other form of human relationship, people at work get upset, angry, frustrated, and depressed. During such times, many of us have damaged our careers by inadvertent or deliberate remarks made to superiors, peers, or subordinates, responses that we regretted later on.

If such blunders occur frequently, then serious personal attitude and behavior problems are present that far transcend the job. Professional guidance is called for, and the problem probably isn't job-related, so the remainder of this article is not concerned with these chronic cases. I want to discuss situations that occur occasionally, or even rarely, when you want to (or have to) argue for one reason or another.

In such cases, irreparable damage can be done to one's career for the momentary satisfaction of putting down someone who has been bothering you for years. Before you argue, I suggest you consider what the consequences will be and decide what you have to gain or lose.

From *Supervisory Management*, December 1979.

RULES TO FOLLOW

Even in warfare many countries attempt, through the Geneva Convention, to make the whole terrible affair more "humane" by setting certain rules and regulations. Procedures have been agreed to, right down to whether or not to allow a soldier to use a "silencer" on his rifle, or what type of bullet could explode on impact and what type could not. It's O.K. to execute spies, but not O.K. if the person is in uniform when captured. You can shoot him dead while he is shooting at you, but if he drops his weapon and raises his hands, you are supposed to capture him alive, feed him, and protect his life, as you would your own comrade.

The point I'm trying to make is, even in as senseless and barbarous an activity as warfare, people try to make and observe rules on how and how not to fight.

In everyday work, fortunately, no one is ever deliberately killed or injured. So it should be even easier for us to make up a set of guidelines to follow before we fight or argue and rules on how to conduct the argument, if it is deemed necessary.

It is best to think out clearly and objectively before you argue what you plan to say. With emotions aroused, we say too much, or say the wrong things, to the wrong person, at the wrong time, and injure a career or hurt someone else needlessly.

There are three conditions that should exist before you argue at work. They are:

1. The problem should be a permanent one.
2. The problem should be serious.
3. You should have a real chance to win.

Some examples are in order here, to prove each point.

1. *If the problem is temporary, don't argue. Save yourself for more important matters.* If your secretary, who is your right hand, goes on vacation and is replaced for two or three weeks by someone who comes in late, leaves early, types sloppy letters, and has a bad attitude, it may be better to grit your teeth and await the return of your pride and joy than to have an argument with the person over a problem that time will solve.

If on occasion the boss is "out of sorts" and difficult to approach, it's best just to avoid him or her for a few days. If it happens more often or does not go away, then that's another matter. It must then be faced, and, hopefully, resolved.

2. *The problem must be serious.* No one should argue or "make noise" over trivia. If the coffee machine doesn't work, forget it. Bring in your own pot; don't argue and fuss over an insignificant point. Even if you win, what do you win? You get better coffee and a reputation as a chronic complainer. It's just not worth it, is it? Arguments at work should concern only such matters as promotions, raises, job assignments, future opportunities, and the like.

At one of my former places of employment, one senior manager didn't like the food in the company cafeteria. He complained repeatedly to higher management about it, and he even formed a committee and went around getting signatures to back up his claim. He eventually won. The cafeteria was closed. Cooks, cleaners, and food servers lost their jobs, and we had to go outside to get lunch. Most of us had found the food to be acceptable, but one chronic complainer got his way. He won nothing and gained a reputation that still persists, because he really was, and still is, a chronic complainer. He could have eaten elsewhere, but he chose to argue instead.

3. *Finally, and most importantly, you must see an opportunity to win your case before you start the argument.* If you can't see a reasonable opportunity to win, then don't argue. It's pointless.

If you complain to the manager that his son or daughter who is working for the company during school vacation is a problem and not working hard enough, you won't win. Even if the boss secretly agrees with you and removes his son or daughter, the boss will remember that you complained about it. Parents love their children. You do, too; remember that. You can't win such an argument, ever.

If you are passed over for a promotion, it is reasonable to ask why. When you are given a reason, if you don't like what you've heard, don't argue; remember you are not going to change the boss's mind at this point. To argue or complain that it wasn't fair won't gain you anything and may cost you your job. The time to argue this point is *before*, not after, the promotion is announced. You can't win by arguing or complaining in such situations. You can't change the score after the game ends.

If you consider the three conditions that should exist before you argue at work (or anywhere else for that matter), you will find that the majority of issues most people argue about do not pass the test. Especially at work, one should be more careful about when and with whom one argues. At home, you have people who love you, know you very well, and may not mind listening to you, periodically, when you want to free yourself of your frustration, anger, or depression by a long talk, discussion, or argument. This is not necessarily true at work. If one tries this sort of behavior at the office or factory, it can, and generally will, adversely affect one's career. Higher management does not, in general, promote people from the ranks of those who "have problems" of one sort or another. Generally, a history or record of having a "hot temper," or of arguing a great deal about small or unimportant items, can, and generally will, slow down or stop a budding career.

It's a question of judgment, as it is with most things in life. The human "door mat" who never speaks up, no matter what happens, will be taken advantage of sooner or later and will be judged by superiors as one who lacks the moral fiber to assert himself or herself, even when justified. Leaders and top managers are never "door mats." But one must be selective about picking arguments. Also, an argument doesn't have to be a shouting match. This generally accomplishes nothing except to arouse emotions, create resentment, embarrass, or humiliate the initiator and recipient. What is meant here by arguing is presenting an opposite, alternative, or different viewpoint to whatever situation you are in at the time and the reasons for your opinion.

THE ART OF ARGUING

Now that we have discussed when to argue, the next item to discuss is how. Again, we can list some concerns to consider in advance when you find yourself in an argument and emotions are starting to get "hot." It's much like training in sports or in the military. The theory is (and it does work) if you train and rehearse well enough, certain actions then become almost automatic. You will then react properly even when under stress later on—in real-life situations of high emotion, strain, anger, or even fear.

Assuming, again, that the three conditions for having an argument exist, then how do we argue our point? Below are tactics or methods to use to win one's point. Some of these may appear obvious, but they bear repetition because many people don't use them, or they use them improperly.

1. Don't get personal; that is, don't criticize or hurt someone else in order to gain your point. Whether you win or not, by using personal attacks, you gain an enemy for life at work if you hurt

someone else or prove him or her wrong before others. It is better to say, "I have a different conclusion," than to say, "You are wrong."

2. Always give your opponent an honorable way to retreat or admit you are right. Don't overkill. Be gracious if you are winning; you can afford it. Try to let the other person "off the hook," unless he or she is a repeater.

3. Stick to the issue at hand. Don't go back into the past and bring up other problems you want to argue about. Don't save them up for occasional outbursts all at once.

4. Be sure you are talking to the person who is able to give you what you want. This is a common mistake many people make. They tell everybody what the problem is and how they feel, but they don't talk to the one person who can do anything about it. This person is usually your boss, and he or she does not like to hear about your arguments or complaints second hand. Tell your boss first and no one else.

5. Try to see the other person's situation before you argue. You may not agree with it; but in trying to put yourself in his or her position, you can, many times, be better able to present your argument in a manner more acceptable to that individual.

Remember you have to convince the person to do it your way, and anger, noise, and name calling won't do it. Calm, reasonable, logical presentations are much more likely to help you gain your point or win your argument.

6. During your argument, be sure you state exactly what you want. Many times people will come in and present a case, yet fail to state what they want done. It may be obvious to them, but it may not be to others. They may need to be told in plain words. Don't assume that they will come to the same conclusion or solution that you have reached. They may not, and you can't go back again if you win your argument but disagree with the solution to the problem because you left that to others to decide.

Think it through before you start. In the past, I have listened to arguments or problems, and when I asked the person what he wanted me to do about it, he didn't know. He just wanted to go on with his "presentation" with no recommended solution. He just wanted to gripe. This is pointless.

What most managers do in these situations is to let the person talk himself out and then quietly say, "Is that all?" or, "Do you feel better now?" If any boss has ever said anything like that to you, be careful. That's what psychiatrists do with disturbed patients. It's a form of therapy. And bosses don't promote people who need therapy, do they?

7. Be prepared to listen as well as talk. Rehearse your presentation and give time for your "opponent" to respond. Rushing in, having your say, then rushing out accomplishes nothing, except to convince your boss that you get upset, sound off, then run away. We hardly consider such people for promotions.

8. Don't keep going back over the same issue. Remember, there are two possible outcomes to an argument: You win or lose. If you lose, either accept it or leave; don't keep harping on it. You can't win that way, and you may be removed involuntarily, as a result. You may be "right" in your argument, but it becomes a moot point if you lose your job over it.

In summary, don't argue unless the three conditions for having an argument exist. If they do, then prepare your tactics and present your argument in the best way to win it. Don't "crow" about it when you win, and be gracious and accept the decision if you lose. It's easy to be a good winner, but losers tend to moan and gripe about it. A famous football coach once said, "Winners win. Losers quote statistics." I agree.

Remember your long-range goals. Don't win the battle and lose the war. There are times in every person's career when one has to argue, or be ignored and lose by default. A well-thought-out and well-presented argument can do wonders for one's career but the opposite can ruin it, so be careful about how you argue, with whom, and about what issues. Harsh words said can never be withdrawn. You can only apologize. The pain may leave, but the scar remains forever. Those who inflict scars on others, either deliberately or thoughtlessly, will, in general, receive the same in return and very probably from someone else. Think carefully before you "sound off," and I venture a guess that, if you do, you'll find in 90 percent of the situations that it's not worth the trouble for what you can possibly gain in return.

19

Memo to Interviewers

Larry E. McDougle

On August 1, 1977, an issue of *The Chronicle of Higher Education* presented a feature article that dealt with issues of current concern to personnel officers all across America. The article was entitled, "Business Graduates Find it Helps to be Female or Black—or Both."

The central theme of the article was that "job recruiters were out in full force on campuses all spring with a new brand of super-sophisticated hard sell that was designed to sign up as much new talent as possible—preferably from groups that had been under-represented in the past," namely women and minority group members.

I use this article as an example of today's employment conditions, which can be so competitive that recruiters are forced to utilize "super-sophisticated hard sell" techniques to attract new employees who are qualified and who meet government requirements. But what about the *interview process* itself? What sophisticated techniques should interviewers be ready to use once the recruiters have done their job?

From *Supervisory Management*, May 1978.

I am of the opinion that the interview process itself still contains several fundamental techniques that cannot be improved upon, no matter how sophisticated the hiring system has become. Many might call these "common sense" techniques, but it is still worthwhile to list them periodically. The ten techniques are:

Know your objectives. Identify in advance what you hope to gain from the interview, and continue to focus on these objectives throughout the interview.

Avoid interruptions. Plan ahead to insure that you and the applicant will not be interrupted during the interview. Interruptions can be quite disconcerting to the person being interviewed, and these can also create serious doubts in the individual's mind about how serious you are in hiring him or her.

Communicate. To get the best results from an interview, talk on the individual's level. Use language that he or she can understand. Ask questions skillfully and carefully, and similarly answer questions completely and honestly. Don't put words in the individual's mouth. And, of course, avoid personal references; the applicant will have plenty of time to hear about you after he or she is hired.

Listen carefully. Concentrate on what the interviewee is saying. Beware of monopolizing the conversation yourself. Give the interviewee an opportunity to impress you, rather than vice versa. Avoid becoming preoccupied with tangential or unimportant details.

Observe nonverbal behavior. It is your responsibility to make the individual feel at ease. Read the nonverbal clues that the applicant is giving you. Recognize the "danger signals" that tell you you are about to lose the applicant's interest or spontaneity. Remember also that you can often learn as much from how a person behaves as from what he or she says. Note behavior patterns throughout the interview.

Allow sufficient time. Don't rush the interview. Any person worthy of being interviewed is worthy of being given sufficient time to satisfy all the objectives of the interview. If circumstances require that the interview be terminated prematurely, take steps immediately to reschedule it at the earliest time convenient for both parties.

Ask each candidate the same questions. Establish a standard question-asking procedure that can be applied uniformly to everyone you interview. Similarly, it is helpful to have the same people interview all the candidates for the same position. Prepare in advance a list of standard questions to be asked. Although the questions will vary from situation to situation, such a list will likely include the following queries:

Why are you attracted to this position?

What are your qualifications, both in terms of formal education and experience?

What contributions do you feel you could make to the organization by accepting this position?

When would you be available to begin work?

What are your salary requirements?

How does your spouse (if the applicant has one) feel about your applying for this position?

What are your career objectives?

How do you see this position fitting into your overall career pattern?

How well do you function under pressure or in a crisis situation? (This question may be more appropriate for high-risk positions such as policeman, fireman, or top-level executive.)

Why are you leaving your present position?

How much are you willing to travel?

Are you willing to relocate? (In some firms, relocation may be necessary for promotion and advancement.)

What are your personal interests and hobbies? How do you enjoy spending your leisure time?

Remain objective. Do not ridicule or criticize comments being made by the person being interviewed, and attempt to remain nonjudgmental during the interview. Feel free to take notes as needed, but try not to allow this to interfere with the interview by making the applicant feel ill at ease.

Maintain control of the interview. Take charge of the interview in a firm and positive manner, and do not allow the interview to stray from its stated purpose. Indicate at the outset the amount of time available and continue to focus on the desired objectives. If the interview is being conducted by a team, do not allow any one team member to dominate the discussion.

Terminate the interview on a positive note. Provide your genuine attention to the very end. Treat the individual with respect and courtesy, and summarize all agreements—if any—that have been reached during the course of the interview. Provide the individual with a tentative timetable concerning your own decision-making process and suggest when he or she can expect to hear from you.

20

What's Wrong with Meetings

Richard J. Dunsing

I used to ponder the meaning of the expression, "Nero fiddled while Rome burned." Now, after 20 years of managing and helping others manage, I have a good idea.

Nero was in a *meeting*.

Instead of rallying their energies to put out the fire, Nero and his staff chose to gather around a table and follow a meeting agenda planned several days before the fire started. True, the fire was a more pressing topic—but in the way of bureaucrats then and now, the agenda could not be changed.

They turned their attention to such matters as:

The tax problem.
The tardiness of underlings.
What time wine-break was.
The disrespectful, even surly attitudes of young people.
A new organization chart for city services (including fire control).

From *Supervisory Management*, September 1976.

At the end of the six-hour staff meeting, two people had stomach cramps and three more had stiff knees from being in the same position for so long. Although the wine-break had been held, none of the other agenda items were resolved. All the items under "old business" were either taken under advisement or consigned to a subcommittee for further study. Under "new business," three members were assigned to study the growing red glow in the sky and given instructions to report back in two weeks at the next regularly scheduled staff meeting. Because the chariots were already waiting at the gate, the group voted against studying the steadily increasing odor of smoke in the air or the mounting piles of ash that drifted through the doors and windows.

A FEELING OF *DÉJÀ VU*?

If you have been to many organizational meetings, this imaginative one probably struck a responsive chord in you. In fact, it may even have given you a feeling of *déjà vu*.

Déjà vu is that eerie feeling that people get now and then that something has happened this way before, and that, in fact, they are witnessing themselves in some previous scene. Most meetings in organizations seem to be an endless stream of *déjà vu*—except that the other feelings they inspire fall far short of wonder, awe, and surprise.

The actual feelings to be found in organizational meetings are typically restlessness, disgruntlement, and raw boredom. Even so, it's safe to bet two things: First, although the leader is clearly not pleased with the way the meeting goes, he has no idea that the atmosphere is thick with such negative feelings and would scarcely credit their intensity if he did have some idea. Second, no one in the room is going to do anything to correct or alleviate what is going on.

If you want a choice between being trapped in an endless succession of such meetings and changing things for the better, read on. What follows is designed to arm the suffering "meeting-lifer" to:

Understand what is going on and why.

See how meetings act out the management life-style of participants.

Determine what options are available, along with their risks and benefits.

Start developing some skills to make change in meetings possible.

Make meetings work and at the same time be fulfilling to participants.

Before we get into ways of changing our meeting lives, let's
take a closer look at meetings themselves.

WHAT KIND OF MEETINGS?

Meetings come in all shapes and sizes, from the monstrosity called a
political convention to a quick huddle in an office hallway. Here, we
will be concerned with small working meetings—with groups that
have a job to do requiring the energy, commitment, and talents of
those who participate. Such groups want to get some kind of result
out of their time together: such as solving problems, setting goals or
priorities, or simply defining with each other some mutual needs
and fears and hopes. At its best, such a group knows what it is
about, knows and utilizes the strengths of individual members, and
openly shares their emotional and intellectual selves. In doing so,
they feel good about themselves and their efforts because they get
visible results.

The working meeting rarely consists of more than 8 to 10 people. Unfortunately, however, in the name of "participative" management or in line with a tradition of "touching base with everyone,"
some groups that are supposed to be working groups grow to assemblies of 20, 30, or even 40 people. But though they're billed as
"working" meetings, their size alone makes them barely able to
function at all.

We're not going to discuss conventions, assemblies, or other
large gatherings that require public-address systems, podiums, thea-
ter screens, ushers, panels, and the like. Neither will we be concerned with the legally constituted meeting that must observe the
pomposities of Robert's Rules of Order. The high structure imposed
severely handicaps the flow of energy and ideas in an operating
group. We *will* be concerned with the operating meeting that agrees
to manage itself fairly, courteously, and efficiently—as a matter of
choice.

The small working meeting is found everywhere in organizations. Its dimensions are few: It has a group of people, three or
more; it has a purpose; and it has a function to perform that will

contribute to the mission of the organization. Such meetings are found in all kinds of organizations—large, small, professional, volunteer, for-profit, and not-for-profit. The concepts and approaches we'll discuss are valid in all these settings.

Meetings are not, of course, inevitable—they are the result of a management or leadership choice. The issues central to a meeting could have been handled without a "getting together"—by phone, perhaps, or memo. The recognition of this choice is one of the keys to improving the quality of meeting life—and we'll discuss it more fully later on.

But when the choice to meet is made, the operating meeting by definition requires the involvement and commitment of members. People who sit through an entire meeting without becoming involved might just as well not have come to it at all. Such a group must understand its peculiar needs, resources, tasks, and dispositions so that members can act quickly and effectively—and, in the process, feel good about themselves.

MEETINGS AS REFLECTIONS OF ORGANIZATIONAL VALUES

Every meeting is a microcosm, a condensed version of the values and style of the organization. If the meeting leader is also the boss, the relationships in the meeting will be those he permits or encourages, the tone and style like his own everyday style, its sense of organization like his, too. Regardless of his pledges and promises, his pep talks and slogans, every member of the meeting can "read" the boss's *behavior* and will act accordingly. More than anything else, the boss is a model whom his people emulate—at least in his presence.

If the meeting leader is not the boss, he or she tends to use the prevailing norms and attitudes of officials in the organization. Because of this tendency, a pattern develops in meetings throughout the organization, from those at the highest echelon to those at the first-line level of supervision.

In working toward a change for the better, then, meetings defy separate treatment because they are all contaminated by the organization's basic values and styles. They cannot, for example, force motion onto an organization in which the overriding purpose is to preserve in perpetuity jobs, status, and the world in general as they are. Meetings are only a single instrument of the total organization.

THE MEASURES OF A MEETING

Therefore, the measures of a meeting are the measures of organization style. Business, church, government, and other organizations can be measured by the way they focus on goals rather than by their activities and motion. They can be measured by their use of rules and regulations to control people or else to give maximum latitude within a framework of limits. On the one hand, an organization's leaders can give attention to testing reality, to hearing both good and bad news and dealing with it objectively. On the other, they can be defensively protective and cloud the issue by spouting slogans or glossing things over with vague assertions and generalizations.

The members of a meeting are more likely to show high trust and openness if their boss is able to encourage and handle such behavior. Similarly, the boss will be able to supply positive strokes (give positive feedback on good work performance) if his boss in turn models that behavior or if it is a norm throughout the organization. And it follows that the use of power and authority in a meeting will tend to mimic their use generally in the organization.

Meetings, then, are clearly linked to all the other aspects of management in the organization. Yet pointing this out should not be taken for a disclaimer to the effect that meeting improvement awaits the complete renewal of the organization (and thus, perhaps, awaits the millenium). Not at all. It is simply a recognition that factors affecting the organization's total management approach and those affecting its meetings are the same. Making internal changes in meetings will require some change outside the meeting. In fact, internal changes made in a meeting may begin to affect other areas of the organization.

Of course, some organizations are so tradition-bound and so highly structured that there is little likelihood of changing their meetings very much. But there are many more organizations in which it is possible to breathe life into meetings regardless of how narrow the organization's traditional approach has become. In fact, the dedicated meeting leader with a stimulated group can give hope and new skills to those all around him, and in an inductive way bring new processes and values to the wider organization.

The point is clear: If you are about to try to change a meeting, you can get many significant clues by looking at the way things are done in the organization as a whole.

COMPLAINTS ABOUT MEETINGS

If you want to change a boring or flagging conversation to a lively one in record time, all you need do is drop the question, "Say, have any of you been to any good meetings lately?" You'll be inundated with "You've got to be kidding" and "Gawd, ain't it awful" comments, "Poor me" stories, and a chorus of groans and head-shakings. However, this flush of excitement is soon converted into a quiet sadness and stoic bravery as all admit, in one way or another, that that's just the way things are.

People who run meetings or participate in them take nonachievement and nonenjoyment of meetings as a part of "the way things are." It seems to be an unwritten rule that all meetings are conceived to drone painfully on to dismal results.

There is not enough room in this, or perhaps any, publication to catalog a total shopping list of meeting faults. The possibilities are as endless as our ability to find new ways of stumbling over one another. The start of another meeting is the best source of information. A fly on the wall might hear something like this:

"Would you believe that this is my fourth meeting this week?"

"Does anyone know what the boss wants this time?"

"We're scheduled to go at 12:30. He'll fill it all."

"Don't forget Floyd. He'll give the boss a break with one of his self-aggrandizing success stories."

"Why don't you tell the boss to shut Floyd up?"

"After you, friend. You know as well as I do that he's the boss's pet. I'll watch while you tell him, though."

"What I can't stand is that pile of call-backs my phone is collecting while I'm in here holding down this seat."

"Don't complain. You know the boss is dedicated to 'touching base' with everyone."

"Know all, see all, be informed."

"And be out of action. Things will be going wrong—and even though I can't be there to handle it, I'll get flak about it."

"At the next 'evaluation meeting,' of course."

"Say, he even has an agenda."

"Same as last time, so don't be too happy. Look, you can even see where the date has been changed."

"Let's see, sixteen items. Where were we when we got sidetracked last time, George?"

"Well into item one, if I remember correctly."

"One remark is enough to trigger several pet peeves here."

"Why can't we get started?"

"Because his Lordship isn't here, and he isn't here because he doesn't want to deal with the five people who come in a half-hour late every time."

"Alice, give me some paper and a pencil. I've got to write a few memos during this."

Enter others. Far too many others for the unclear purpose of this gathering of expensive talent. Throats clear, and another exercise in endless discussion is under way. Although it is called a meeting, and is held in the name of managing, it bears little relationship to either. Instead, it is a collection of busy people who are frustrated because they have no clear relationship in this setting to each other or to the issues listed on the so-called agenda. It will end as it began, in quiet anger or resignation, after little achievement.

THE COST OF IT ALL

Although this pervasive sense of helplessness in itself needs handling, it gives rise to an even more deadly effect. A tremendous ripple effect is caused by holding large numbers of meetings with little result. To be sure, meetings are costly in terms of the time and salaries of participants. But the ripple costs go much farther. A major additional cost lies in having managers unavailable where the action is going on. Tying key people up (or down) in meetings becomes quite costly when others (below, above, or alongside them) are unable to reach them. People outside the organization, too, are blocked from engaging the time and talents of the professional "meeting goers."

Another major cost lies in the effect meetings have on the quality of life of the individual at the meeting. Meetings inevitably either add something to a person's life or take something away. For most people, unfortunately, meetings take something away. When the meeting is over, there are rarely any "good" feelings (except relief that it is over).

THE RIPPLE OF NONACTIVITY

Let's drift down the hall, away from the nonevent taking place in the "conference room." Imagine all the empty offices of the people who went to the meeting.

So if they are not there, what is going on? Could it be nothing? No. That would be relatively inexpensive. What *is* going on is worse than nothing because it is, in effect, make-work.

Like: subordinates and peers, peering into the offices and asking the secretaries, "Is he (or she) in? Will he (or she) be back today? When?" and other businesslike questions.

Like: mail, reports, and other documents moving from mailroom to in-basket. Once in place, such items begin what an industrial engineer would call "storage time." Others call it "delay" or "backlog of things to do."

And: secretaries talking to people on the phone. "I'm sorry, he's not here; he's in a meeting (or in conference, or unavailable, or out of the office)." Whatever the precise wording, the effect is clear: a blocked discussion. The person has been frustrated and he may or may not leave a call-back message.

After the meeting, a tired manager returns to his office to find a pile of things in his in-basket, a stack of call-back slips, and a line of people who say things like, "Got to catch you for just a minute."

The manager becomes angry because he knows all these need attention, and he can't do justice to any of them. Least appealing is the stack of call-backs, because when he returns the calls he may very well hear, "I'm sorry, he's not available—he's in a meeting."

If the manager has job insecurities, this series of events will reassure him because he knows that tomorrow he can start it all over again—earning money by filling time and never ever running out of anything to do.

When you accept poor meetings as a fact of life, you are in collusion with many others doing the same thing. In effect, you are aiding and abetting them in clogging the system and in eroding the quality of working life. Managing means changing things that aren't what they need to be. Surprisingly often, it is merely the management of the obvious.

Before considering corrective measures, let's look more specifically at factors that make meetings ineffective and intolerable.

THE OPEN-HOUSE MEETING

Some meetings, much like an open-house party, last for hours without being able to boast of a single half-hour during which all participants are present. Those who arrive late stagger themselves sufficiently so that the confusion of stragglers goes over the halfway mark. Others claim a need to leave early or nip out for a spell, thus forcing a rejuggling of the agenda. This distresses other members, who see their pet items moved further and further down on the agenda.

The boss doesn't stay put, either. He takes a "must" long-distance call, which wears on some 25 minutes, smack in the middle of things—thus breaking any rhythm or serious accomplishment that might have been under way.

Skilled old-timers train their secretaries to pull them out for two or three calls during the meeting. This lets them achieve two things: They reinforce their importance and they are able to take a break from the monotony of the meeting.

THE NONEVENT MEETING

In the "nonevent" meeting, there may be a kind of activity on the part of at least some participants. But the activity tends to be random, irrelevant, and self-serving. Great energy might be expended, but none in the service of reaching a goal.

Nonevent meetings have special characteristics. For one thing, everyone present wonders why he or she is there—but no one *asks* why. (The norm in the organization is to lie low—under no circumstances to ask questions or otherwise rock the boat.) For another, silence is greatly feared. Participants are divided into "actives" and "passives." The actives agree to rescue the leader from that frightening experience of silence. The passives deeply resent domination by the actives, but prefer it to sticking their necks out on anything. The actives most often have some axe to grind.

The passives are always entertained by at least one "warrier bull" who can be counted on to charge at the leader or some other "big hitter" who takes a strong position on an issue. A firm stand—any firm stand—serves as the red flag. These warrier bulls love to do battle regardless of the odds. They are always repulsed and they always sustain gaping wounds—but they never understand why.

Passives and actives alike help the warrier bull salve his wounds later on. They applaud his courage. They urge him on. They never point out the futility—not to mention stupidity—of his foolhardy charges.

Nonevent meetings, then, have high entertainment value. The

warrier bull offers drama, just as the meeting clown offers diversion. Most of the meeting, however, is given over to a series of unfunny zaps leveled at each other by members of competing factions. Such zapping is not pointless: It is part of the managerial philosophy of the meeting leader and others in the organization and thus reflects the reward system in effect *inside their departments*. Although the leader and other managers often give lip service to "teamwork," they rarely reward sharing or caring behavior among individuals—either within a single department or from different departments. Such leaders actually, if unwittingly, encourage members to work each other over. The leaders become referees. Although real blows are not thrown, a good deal of psychological damage is done as participants work to embarrass, discount, and put down their enemies (everybody else, that is):

> "Do they *really* pay you for what you do in your department?"
> "That's not a bad idea—for an engineer."
> "Well, we could buy it for $200 or have maintenance make it for $800."
> "The number-fumblers in accounting have finally got some figures for us."
> "Let's go over that marketing 'goof list' again."
> "I know you don't have time to do it right, but you'll find time to do it over."

Very entertaining. Very risky. Very much unfunny after a while. Challenged about this kind of behavior, participants usually give the same answer: "Oh, we just kid around a lot." Most of all, each is kidding himself or herself.

Of course, this kind of behavior would be O.K.—if that's how you get your kicks—at a party, a card game, or a picnic. But not at *my* meeting, if you please. There's too much work to accomplish for such nonsense.

Personal attack isn't the only kind of behavior exhibited at the nonevent meeting. The nonevent is also made possible by the way in which participants engage in discussion. "Process watching" is a relatively simple skill that involves watching *patterns* of conversation. What is the content of one person's input and to whom is it directed? Real meaning can be blocked in several ways: First, the input may be so fuzzy and undirected that *no one* can respond, and the leader won't press for more meaning. Or the recipient may clearly understand the meaning, but simply won't respond. Or he may relate his response not to the input but to his own pet idea, which he was in fact mulling over while pretending to be listening. In the highest state of this non-art, the intended target knows he or she can depend on someone else to respond—with something only vaguely related to the point.

Meetings that operate on this merry-go-round principle are doomed to an endless circle of unrelated speeches and commentary. Typically, there is never any *closure*. Everything is opened up, nothing is ever closed. All issues get a few words, nothing gets pinpointed or acted upon. When the meeting ends, some have had a kind of catharsis and all have avoided responsibility. Again, nothing has really happened, nor is it likely to.

ALTERNATIVES TO HOLDING A MEETING

A manager is often defined as someone who gets results through other people. There are several media through which the manager can influence those others—whether they are above him, below him, or alongside him. Meetings are only one of several communication vehicles that include:

Statistical data and reports.
Memos, letters, and other forms of the written word.
Telephone conversations.
Meetings.
Face-to-face conversation with one individual.

While all of the above may be used to influence a group of people, only in the meeting are the members of that group brought together in the same room at the same time. The dynamics of a meeting distinguish it from all the others. But the meeting has both advantages and disadvantages; it is not always the right answer to a communication or "need-to-influence" problem. Part of the solution to a "meeting problem," then, is an understanding of the alternatives available to the manager.

Each is most preferable under certain circumstances though, oddly enough, the circumstances and the alternative are often mismatched. Say that in a particular circumstance, the intensity of human contact becomes paramount. In such a case, the appropriate medium would be the one listed *last* above (the list is in the order of least to greatest contact).

Reports and memos are ways of managing at arm's length. While they have a certain tangible, even scientific character at times, they are by nature one-way streets. Arriving at the receiver's desk, they are left solely to his or her interpretation. (Indeed, some informal meetings are convened simply to share various interpretations of the boss's latest memo.)

Communication of certain kinds of information—the complex or lengthy, for example—demand written treatment. This treatment is most effective, however, when followed periodically by person-to-person contact. The telephone is often the only practical way to achieve such contact, particularly when receivers are out of town. Phone contact has the advantage of being two-way, allowing for give and take, questions and answers. It also allows for the sharing of subtle signals "sent" by vocal tones and inflections. What it lacks, of course, is the ability to transmit the facial and body language that always accompanies oral exchanges.

The most intense—and therefore sometimes most effective way to communicate—is face to face with one person at a time. This is best accomplished in an office with the door closed or somewhere else that's reasonably quiet and uninterruptable. Such a setting facilitates communication on both the rational and the feeling level. Of course, this method has some disadvantages. Such sessions require time, for example, and lots of it. The manager must postpone a number of managerial activities to give first priority to this personal contact.

There is yet another kind of disadvantage—or risk, if you will— in using person-to-person contact or the small meeting. It entails being reachable, vulnerable, and challengable (unless, of course, the manager hides behind a lot of structure and formality).

It's obvious, then, that when the manager decides to call a meeting (or to continue with a regularly scheduled one), he is making a choice. If he understands the purpose of the meeting, the talents of the people involved, and his own management style, he may make sound choices of when to hold and when not to hold a meeting. If he doesn't understand all of that, he may well make the wrong choices—and find himself trapped in a series of painful meetings that don't get off the ground.

LET'S NOT HAVE ONE AT ALL!

So the easiest answer to the problem, "You and I Have Simply Got to Stop Meeting This Way," could well be just to stop—not to have one at all. You win some, you lose some, and some are rained out. And some are never scheduled!

Cancelling meetings doesn't solve everything, however. If the manager means to manage, then he must conduct the business of his operation in some other way. He must do more memo writing, have more personal contact, get on the phone more often. And if his competence is also under-developed in these areas, he is truly in a dilemma. Avoiding a bad meeting won't mean much if it is replaced by a bad one-to-one session with a key subordinate.

The meeting leader can try another way to avoid a bad meeting: He may call it and yet not run it. He may choose to delegate its leadership to a subordinate or associate who has shown some promise in group leadership. Before the meeting, he can help clarify goals of the meeting with his substitute, explain the limits he is to work within, and then let him have at it. In organizations where authoritarianism is a big hang-up, this approach may be successful simply because "the big cheese" is not there inhibiting the action. This works—if the big cheese's ego can take it.

And so, on our meeting decision-tree, we have come to Junction Number One, and the choice may be to choose nonmeeting routes. You may decide to conduct your business in some other way—and meet not at all or infrequently. If you are a meeting participant and not calling the meeting, you may approach the leader with some of these options and try to negotiate more effective ways to get on with things.

21

Feedback on Feedback

Philip L. Quaglieri

How am I doing? It's a question each of us has asked. Everyone needs reassurance now and then that they are succeeding in the job for which they are paid. But feedback's use extends beyond this.

WHAT IS FEEDBACK?

Job performance feedback is information that may be used by an individual in order to determine how well he or she is meeting organizational and personal goals. It can provide instructional information, and it can motivate individuals to exert greater effort. These are typically referred to as the directive and incentive functions of feedback. From a management standpoint, feedback is a critical component in both motivating and training employees. And management literature tells us that to be effective, feedback should be specific, frequent, direct, and constructive.

Unfortunately, managers who follow the above rules when providing feedback have no guarantee that the desired changes in performance will occur. Why? Employees have many sources of

From *Supervisory Management*, May 1978.

feedback that provide them with information about their performance; the supervisor is only one of them. Other possible sources of
feedback include co-workers, the task itself, the employment section
of the newspaper (which indicates other organizations' requirements
and rewards for jobs similar to the one examined), the company
through its performance appraisal system, and an individual's own
feelings about how well he or she is performing the task. While all
these sources may provide information, it must be recognized that
individuals come to value or trust different sources of information
more than others. Feedback from a particular source may be ignored if, for example, the individual feels that its supplier does not
possess the necessary expertise or experience to judge him or her
adequately. Whether this or any other feeling or perception about
the source is accurate or inaccurate is unimportant. Feedback influences performance or learning only to the extent that the individual
uses the information provided. The impact of feedback is increased
or lessened, then, according to the recipient's perceptions of the
information's usefulness.

In order to evaluate individuals' perceptions about the feedback
they receive from various sources, two questionnaires were developed. Each was distributed to 95 clerical employees of a large eastern insurance company. The first questionnaire involved the
frequency with which individuals received feedback from various
sources (the day-to-day comments of the supervisor and co-workers,
the company through its performance appraisal system, watching
others, self-evaluation, and newspaper advertisements about the requirements of similar jobs in other organizations). The second asked
individuals for their opinions on the usefulness of the information
provided them from each of the five sources.

Participants in this survey were first asked their reaction to the
question "How frequently do you receive information about your job
performance from the following sources?" Frequency ratings were
made on a five-point scale (5—very often, 3—occasionally, 1—
never). Subsequently, participants were asked their reaction to the
question "To what degree is the information provided you from each
of the following sources useful?" This question was also answered
using a five-point scale (5—extremely useful, 3—moderately useful,
1—completely useless).

Figure 21-1 shows the major results of this study.

The results indicated that feedback from co-workers and from
one's own feelings about work occur more frequently than feedback

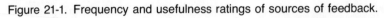

Figure 21-1. Frequency and usefulness ratings of sources of feedback.

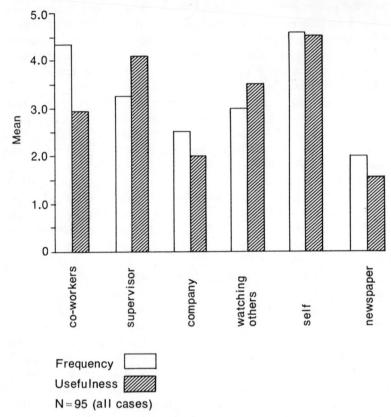

Frequency ☐
Usefulness ▨
N = 95 (all cases)

from any other source. Further, feedback from the supervisor and comparisons made by watching others occur only occasionally, while feedback from newspapers and the company's reward system are the least frequent. The results of this part of the survey are not surprising. The reason for the greater frequency of feedback from one's own self is evident. Further, it seems natural to expect a greater exchange of feedback among co-workers than between subordinate and supervisor. Finally, the company provides little feedback because its opportunities for doing so are limited.

More interesting is the portion of the graph dealing with the individuals' perceptions about the usefulness of the information provided them from the various sources.

For instance, while feedback that is exchanged among co-workers occurs extremely often, it was viewed as only moderately useful, whereas feedback from oneself and feedback from one's superior as to the quality of job performance were described as the most useful. It should be emphasized at this point, however, that supervisory feedback, while extremely useful, typically occurs less frequently than self-feedback. Newspaper and company feedback were described as the least useful of all the sources of feedback.

Two recommendations may be drawn from this survey of employee attitudes. First, it appears that individuals to a large extent depend upon themselves for feedback about how well they're doing in their jobs. Since this type of feedback is constant, supervisors should attempt to "check out" its accuracy. This suggests that supervisors should discuss with subordinates in very specific, task-related terms how they feel they are doing in their jobs. Any differences between the individual's and supervisor's evaluations of performance should be immediately reconciled.

Second, while the infrequency of company feedback is understandable, its lack of usefulness, as described by the participants in this survey, is not. The performance appraisal can be used to provide the individual, in very specific terms, with information about his or her potential for development. This kind of information reduces employee uncertainty about one's role in the organization and ultimately contributes to more efficient human resource management.

22

Quality Control: A Communications Function

Harry E. Williams

New challenges for all levels of management are currently being experienced in almost every field. In one specific area, namely quality control, some dramatic changes are taking place. Of these, the most significant is its transition from an inspection orientation to that of a monitoring, fact-finding, and reporting activity.

Many factors have contributed to this evolution. Among them, consumer legislation, inflation, reduced profits, OSHA, and Ralph Nader.

With the dramatic increase in product liability lawsuits, management is looking to quality control for the information it needs to improve product reliability. Today, a successful quality control manager not only must possess the necessary technical expertise but must also be more proficient in the art of dealing with people. These skills encompass not only the employer—employee relationships but also the interface with many levels of management, cus-

From *Advanced Management Journal,* Winter 1979.

tomer representatives, and such personnel who may visit the company or organization as subcontractors, suppliers, or vendors.

It is the quality manager's responsibility to assure top management that quality control is being managed, not that the job is managing him. This entails that each of the basic elements of the typical quality system be evaluated in terms of effective communications in order to ascertain that accurate information is being consistently collected, tabulated, analyzed, and translated into clear, concise reports so that personnel outside the quality organization can understand exactly what the data indicate.

In order to approach the quality-system evaluation in an orderly way, the activities should be separated into three categories: subcontracting, facility, and field.

SUBCONTRACTING

The category of subcontracting consists of all of the quality activities associated with the purchasing of parts, materials, components, assemblies, and services. It also includes the receiving-inspection service, since this is an integral part of the procurement function.

The selection of a supplier is a process that is dependent upon the type of quality system in effect. Commercial, consumer, military, or aerospace suppliers will all have different contractual requirements that have a significant impact upon recordkeeping and the associated documentation necessary to the system. Military and aerospace contracts, for example, generally require an in-depth survey of the candidate, not only from a quality-control point of view, but also from a capability and financial perspective.

After selection has occurred, various contractual documents are transmitted to the supplier that are the legal communications defining what is being purchased, the applicable criteria, terms, conditions, price, and delivery.

Sometimes a sample item is requested for evaluation in advance of the stated deliveries. This represents a vital stage in the communications link between the two parties, and all the variable data should be recorded and exchanged in addition to the actual item itself. The exchange of recorded variable data will usually minimize the chance of drawing misinterpretations and clarify any inaccuracies in measurement methods or instrumentation.

Other communications that are contractual in nature cover compliance or conformance, design-change order approvals, periodic destructive/non-destructive testing, design reviews and approvals, process-change control, source inspection, configuration-change approval, and supplier-performance ratings.

For years personnel in the business of dealing with suppliers have tried to devise a simple, viable rating system that would accurately and fairly evaluate a supplier's performance. The introduction of electronic data processing made it possible to include compliance data on the product, cost variances, delivery slips, advance shipments, and latent failures when failures could be identified as a specific supplier's responsibility.

Less attention has been directed to properly communicating the results of the rating system to the substandard supplier so he is motivated to improve his overall performance, thus in turn reducing cost and eliminating rejections. One constructive method that has been used with success is to arrange a meeting with the supplier's president or general manager, the appropriate buyer, and a representative of the organization who is familiar with the product or service. In achieving the end objective or improved performance, attendance is crucial, and a benign, relatively informal atmosphere should be created. In this way, person-to-person rather than company-to-company communications can prevail, engendering a feeling of mutual trust and understanding.

This approach to the problem of poor supplier performance may appear at first to be excessively permissive and mawkish, but the key objective in these meetings is *not* to communicate dissatisfaction, but to minimize the customer-supplier relationship and emphasize the infectious attitude of "let's solve our mutual problem." Out of this environment should come a heightened desire for finding realistic solutions. The supplier may well express his wish to fulfill the necessary tasks in order to improve his performance. The meeting should be closed on a friendly note without a review of commitments. The point must be tactfully made, however, that it is the result that is the end objective and not the effort.

Clearly, this approach to problem solving concerns itself with communication and motivation, but with different emphasis and meanings attached to these terms. Communication is as much the means of changing attitudes toward problems in general as it is the method of determining the cause of the problems. Motivation, with its specific measure of performance rather than effort, creates less need for future meetings once a supplier understands that only his success is being questioned, not his intentions and efforts to perform.

Many experts agree that one of the most difficult elements of the quality system is the control of suppliers, subcontractors, or vendors. In a recent publication, a leading aerospace company commented that out of 96 in-depth surveys and audits of its suppliers, there was one predominant weakness found in all of the quality systems. That was the lack of control of its subsuppliers! Perhaps another more subtle example reflecting the difficulties in supplier control can be found in the government's comments concerning the validity of its official qualified products list: "Approval only signifies that at one time the manufacturer made a product that met specification requirements."

It may be concluded that the control of supplier performance is indeed a difficult task, requiring highly specialized and trained personnel in order to assure success. Intensive communications at all levels of management may be the key to achieving it. Since feedback is a prerequisite to behavior modification, it appears logical that feedback through meaningful communications with a supplier is critical to improved supplier performance.

FACILITY

The second category is the facility, which includes all quality activities inhouse—from stockroom to shipping dock. The communications involved in this system are of a different type from those previously described. Here an effective control system must include a formal communications network. Informal networks, because of their inherent unreliability, are useful only as supplements to the formal networks. Where formal networks are nonexistent or in some cases ineffective (as manifested, for example, by the loss of a key employee), a state of incipient chaos prevails, with the quality organization responding to an endless succession of fire drills and crises.

The theory of formal organization is, in itself, quite simple. It holds that throughout the organization there is a strict definition of authority and responsibility. Similarly, there is a definition of the function of every department. Free communications flow from every part of the organization to every other part. Every action is guided by the principle of what is best for the organization as a whole. Although this theory must be considered utopian, it is valuable because it identifies the three prerequisites to a viable control system: strict delineation of authority and responsibility, precise definition of the function of every department, and free and accurate communications. It must be understood that these prerequisites are closely interrelated. In particular, communications in order to be effective must be accepted as authoritative. And communications can only be considered authoritative within a well-defined structure of authority, responsibility, and function.

People will accept a communication as authoritative only when four conditions occur simultaneously: They understand the communication, they believe that the communication is consistent with the purpose of the organization, they believe it to be compatible with their own personal interest as a whole, and they are mentally and physically able to comply with it. These conditions are significant because they point out the necessity for all instructions to originate at the top of the organization in the form of policy statements that are shaped into procedures of increasing detail as the responsibility for implementing these policies is delegated throughout the organization.

There will be diversity in the form and content of instructions, since there is great diversity among employees and the tasks they perform. In order to better appreciate this diversity of personnel and responsibilities and to become familiar with the requirements that various work instructions must satisfy, we should consider, in turn, each of the three basic types of instructions: management instructions, technical and administrative instructions, and specific work instructions.

Management Instructions

Policies aid the process of managing a company in a number of ways. With policies understood, a busy executive can delegate duties to subordinates with confidence that these duties will be carried out along the general lines specified. Since each executive also knows how the other will act, coordination is easier to achieve. As a result, there will be a consistency in actions taken by different members of the firm.

Policy statements are management's work instructions. Of all the various types of instructions, policy statements are the most difficult to write. They must be specific enough to assure the appropriate management decision yet general enough to allow freedom of action, too.

Policy should meet the following requirements in order to be useful:

1. Policy must be comprehensive. Every task, whether required by contract or merely an element of a common-sense business system, must be within the purview of a policy statement.
2. Overall policy is generally extensive, so each individual policy requirement should be identified for easy reference. Also, all policy requirements and a complex index of their contents should be assembled under one cover.
3. Policy must be unambiguous. Each policy statement must clearly define what is to be done and by whom.
4. Policy must include a requirement for control of its implementation, whether by audit or by other positive means.

Technical and Administrative Instructions

Operating procedures are the work instructions of technical and administrative employees. They define how policy requirements are to be implemented in terms definitive enough to be clearly understood by these employees, yet general enough to encourage professional approaches to assigned tasks. In order for operating procedures to be useful elements in the control system, they should meet these requirements.

1. Procedures must be inclusive. Each of the policy statements should be implemented by a procedure.
2. Each procedure must be unmistakable to those who are responsible for carrying it out. Each procedure must define what is to be done and by whom. The actions at group interfaces must also be clearly described.
3. Each procedure must be directly traceable, by cross-reference, to the policy that it implements.
4. Where a procedure contains technical requirements, as engineering specifications do, these parameters must be expressed in a form capable of translation into the nontechnical language of work instructions. Such translation is necessary in order to assure that the employees who manufacture a

product do so with a clear understanding of the applicable engineering requirements.

Specific Work Instructions

These are the detailed, specific directions at the work station where the job is being performed. The guidelines for initiating the directions are:

1. Instructions should contain simple verbs and nontechnical terms.
2. They should utilize sketches and pictures whenever possible, in addition to the narrative.
3. The type size should be suitable for easy reading at about four feet.
4. The instructions should be uniquely identified to assure the proper implementation of revisions.

Freedom and flexibility at this level are not advisable, and marking up the instructions or verbal deviations should not be permitted under any circumstances.

FIELD

The third category, the field, consists of the quality activity and product performance from the start of the warranty period to the conclusion of the product's life or warranty, or whichever comes first. The communications required for this system are dependent on the customer providing feedback to the manufacturer. Often this does not happen on a timely basis, and generally information is in terms that are not easily translated into meaningful data to identify the cause(s) of the problem. Field service personnel and/or field sales engineers provide one solution to this communications problem; but again, mutual understanding is essential in order to achieve the desired result of problem resolution.

The term "quality" means different things to different individuals. If it is thought of as meaning only compliance, then it becomes obvious that compliance has several interpretations also. To some, compliance means that the item is in every sense 100 percent in accordance with the documentation that defines it. To others, compliance means that the item fits and will function as it was intended.

In addition to these interpretations, there is a difference in perspective between the buyer and the seller. Each will see the same item from an entirely different point of view. The solutions to these types of problems can only be reached through straightforward, regular communications at as many levels of the respective organizations as possible.

CONCLUSION

Even if subcontracting, facility, and field activities are performed well, quality control's success will ultimately be determined by the timeliness, effectiveness, and durability of its efforts against the causes of poor quality. The three factors affecting its success in these areas are (1) speed and accuracy in identifying these causes, (2) determination of responsibility, and (3) implementation of correction. It is interesting to note that the one common element in this entire process is effective communications!

23

Fighting Business Gobbledygook: How to Say It in Plain English

Alan Siegel

Figure 23-1 shows three examples of business gobbledygook. All come from documents used until recently by major American companies. They are prime examples of the insensitivity, impersonality, and incomprehensibility that are all too common in corporate forms, manuals, and customer correspondence—in fact, in business communications of all kinds.

At the three companies where these examples were uncovered, management soon realized that the problem was more pervasive than they had thought. So they began a review of all their corporate communications, internal as well as external. In doing so they joined the growing number of executives who are committed to clarifying and simplifying the documents used by their companies.

A major force behind this change has been the growing public interest in plain English. While this interest focuses primarily on

From *Management Review*, November 1979.

Figure 23-1. Examples of business gobbledygook.

INSENSITIVITY

Dear _____ .

We were indeed sorry to learn of the death of your wife, and we appreciate your taking the time to notify us.

Naturally the Charge Card account in her name is cancelled, and we suggest that all Cards issued under the account be destroyed at once.

As some one [*sic*] who has enjoyed the many benefits of a Charge Card, it occurs to us that you may now want one in your own name. Accordingly, we have enclosed a simple form for your use.

You'll find that the Charge Card is a most effective way to manage money. Virtually everytime [*sic*] you use the Card, you'll receive a charge record that shows where, when and how much you charged. Then, each month you'll get an itemized statement, plus a duplicate copy of the charge record for double checking. You'll have a convenient, accurate record of spending, without complicated record-keeping . . . one card, one bill, one check.

Of course, you'll always have the convenience, security and emergency financial protection that is automatically yours with the Charge Card. . . .

INCOMPREHENSIBILITY

Corporate Policy Manual: Incentive Compensation of Sales Volume

The critical element in this general principle of relating the past year to the current year compensation opportunity is that the selling task requires equivalent effort for attainment of goals. Consideration must be given to the condition of the market, price increases, etc. From this reference point sales volume bracket levels would be the entering point for incentive earnings. The highest bracket level above the reference point would represent the sales objective. . . . The total compensation control limit and base salary range provide for flexibility as to the incentive portion of total compensation.

Figure 23-1. *(continued)*..

IMPERSONALITY

NOTICE—TERMINATION OF AUTOMOBILE INSURANCE

(Applicable paragraphs marked X)

☐ You have been notified herewith that this company is cancelling your above numbered Automobile Policy, effective on the date shown above.

☐ You are hereby notified that the above numbered Automobile Policy, which expires on the date shown above, will not be renewed or continued.

☐ Termination is due to your failure to discharge when due your obligations in connection with payment of premiums on the above numbered policy or an installment thereof, whether payable directly to this company or indirectly under any premium finance plan or extension of credit.

☐ You may request that the Company give you a written explanation of its reasons for terminating, provided your written request for such explanation is mailed or delivered not less than _____ days prior to the effective date of termination specified above. . . .

---

legal documents used in the consumer marketplace—such as leases, loan notes, and insurance policies—simplifying these has made executives much more aware of the wide range of documents they deal with every day. Many businesses are now simplifying everything from corporate reports and policy manuals to the humble memo.

SIMPLIFYING LEGALESE

Traditionally, business's legal documents have been prepared by lawyers—for other lawyers. The focus of their efforts was narrow—to conform to regulations and protect the institution from its customers. As new laws, court decisions, and regulations emerged, new boilerplate was added for protection. The result is the popular stereotype of the incomprehensible fine-print contract that the customer is handed with the order: "Sign here."

Now the rules have been changed; consumers no longer are willing to sign on blind faith. They want to know what they are buying, and what the words printed on contracts or other documents really say.

The first significant sign of this came in the results of a 1974 Louis Harris poll for the Sentry Insurance Company of Wisconsin. The consumer's desire to know what common legal documents say is now widely recognized as a right, and court opinions have made language—and its visual presentation—fundamental elements of a contract. Federal legislation such as the Moss-Magnuson Act covering warranties specifically requires businesses to produce documents that consumers can understand.

More than half the states are now considering legislation calling for plain English contracts. Last year New York became the first to enact such a law. It requires that all written agreements for personal purposes involving less than $50,000 be:

1. Written in a clear and coherent manner using words with common and everyday meanings.
2. Appropriately divided and captioned by its various sections.

ST. PAUL'S COMPREHENSIVE APPROACH

Perhaps the most ambitious simplification program so far has been that undertaken by the St. Paul Fire and Marine Insurance Company, of St. Paul, Minnesota. In 1975 it became one of the first large insurers to begin simplifying their policies. As a pilot project, the company produced a simple and easy-to-read "personal liability catastrophe policy." Here's an example of what was done:

Before

> The Company will indemnify the Insured for all sums which the Insured shall be legally obligated to pay as damages and expenses, all as more fully defined by the term 'Ultimate Net Loss'. . . .

After

> We've designed this policy to give you and your family extra liability protection above and beyond the coverage of your present auto, homeowners, and other policies. . . .

Say you have a standard auto policy that covers you up to a $300,000 liability limit for bodily injury for each accident. With this policy you're covered even if a jury says you have to pay $1,300,000. . . .

In addition to such simplified language, with frequent use of examples, the policy was completely reorganized and redesigned.

The success of this project led St. Paul to commit itself to a full-scale simplification effort. This has since been extended to applications, billing statements, agent manuals, customer correspondence, and other items. Last year St. Paul finished revising all 366 policy forms in its commercial business package, reducing the number to 150 in the process. The company's plans call for most of its commercial insurance policies to be rewritten and reprinted in a more readable format by 1982. St. Paul management also recently embarked on another ground-breaking project by simplifying the notes to the financial statement in the company's 1978 annual report; next year it plans to simplify the entire report.

What motivates a company to undertake such a massive task? "Senior management became convinced it was the right thing to do," according to Kent Shamblin, senior communications officer at St. Paul. "Consumers' interest in what they are buying extends to insurance policies as well. Our product is words on paper." Once in use, the simplified policies received favorable reactions from customers, agents, and employees, who found them easier to understand and explain. Shamblin is convinced that the effort was worthwhile: "It's enhanced our standing among our customers and regulators, because it shows we're willing to invest time and money in serving the consumer."

HANDLING SIMPLIFICATION

That investment can be considerable when the approach is as broad as St. Paul's. But producing even a single plain English document demands commitment, because this kind of project is more than just a cosmetic rewrite. Rather than reworking old material, simplification demands starting from scratch, analyzing what must be said and then organizing, writing, and designing a document that says it clearly. In dealing with large and complex customer correspondence systems, for instance, we've discovered that trying to figure out the old letters' meanings and purposes is more time-consuming than building a new system from the ground up.

The same principle applies to rewriting a consumer contract. Rather than just translating what's already there, the plain English drafter starts by analyzing the substance of the agreement. For example, the default section of Citibank N.A.'s old consumer loan note read as indicated in Figure 23-2. It contrasts sharply with the simplified version introduced in 1975.

The difference between the two isn't just the number of words; it lies in an analysis of the bank's actual policy and experience. "We were able to eliminate provisions that were out-dated or rarely used," says Citibank vice-president and consumer credit counsel Carl Felsenfeld. So simplification projects offer the promise—and the challenge—of bringing documents into line with today's corporate policy and legal requirements.

Having made a commitment to simplifying documents, management should insist on adherence to two principles:

Writing must be tailored to the audience. The tone and character of the language and its degree of simplicity and informality can be adjusted for the reader's sophistication and knowledge of the material. A directive detailing accounting practices to CPAs should be written differently from a companywide brochure on health benefits; these should be written differently from an annual report addressed to investors.

In more subtle ways, too, documents should be written with the reader in mind, taking into account the pitfalls of impersonality and insensitivity. Customers can't be expected, for example, to be happy about having their insurance policies cancelled or their credit-worthiness questioned. In such instances, letters should avoid threatening coldness; instead, they should project responsiveness to readers' feelings.

A document's structure, as well as its language, must be shaped for the ease of the reader. Just as each sentence should be clearly written, the organization of the entire document should make its contents clear and more accessible.

Exactly what this means depends on the document and its use. Take a firm's summary plan description of its employee benefits, for instance. These booklets usually suffer from being organized strictly for compliance with federal ERISA regulations. That is, they put the required information in the same order the regulations do in the *Federal Register*. But the organization used for regulations is not the

Figure 23-2. How to tell a customer, "You're in default."

Old way:

In the event of default in the payment of this or any other Obligation or the performance or observance of any term or covenant contained herein or in any note or other contract or agreement evidencing or relating to any Obligation or any Collateral on the Borrower's part to be performed or observed; or the undersigned Borrower shall die; or any of the undersigned become insolvent or make an assignment for the benefit of creditors; or a petition shall be filed by or against any of the undersigned under any provision of the Bankruptcy Act; or any money, securities or property of the undersigned now or hereafter on deposit with or in the possession or under the control of the Bank shall be attached or become subject to distraint proceedings or any order or process of any court; or the Bank shall deem itself to be insecure, then and in any such event, the Bank shall have the right (at its option), without demand or notice of any kind, to declare all or any part of the Obligations to be immediately due and payable, whereupon such Obligations shall become and be immediately due and payable, and the Bank shall have the right to exercise all the rights and remedies available to a secured party upon default under the Uniform Commercial Code (the "Code") in effect in New York at the time, and such other rights and remedies as may otherwise be provided by law. Each of the undersigned agrees (for purposes of the "Code") that written notice of any proposed sale of, or the Bank's

---

best order for an informative brochure addressed to employees. This approach seems to emphasize administrative details, giving the typical benefit booklet a stilted, legalistic tone. To find out what they really want to know, readers are forced to wade through information that's unlikely to be of interest.

Experience shows that the benefit booklet will be read under two circumstances: first for general information about benefits, when the employee receives it; and later, when benefits become payable, for specific details. The most logical structure for such a booklet then, would be something like this:

1. General introduction defining the benefit and giving some idea of how much the participant will get.
2. Detailed section on benefits (who's eligible, what they are, and what happens to them when the employee leaves the company).

Figure 23-2. *(continued)*

---

election to retain, Collateral mailed to the undersigned Borrower
(who is hereby appointed agent of each of the undersigned for such
purpose) by first class mail, postage prepaid, at the address of the
undersigned Borrower indicated below three business days prior to
such sale or election shall be deemed reasonable notification thereof.
The remedies of the Bank hereunder are cumulative and may be
exercised concurrently or separately. If any provision of this paragraph shall conflict with any remedial provision contained in any
security agreement or collateral receipt covering any Collateral, the
provisions of such security agreement or collateral receipt shall control.

In plain English:

I'll be in default:
1. If I don't pay an installment on time; or
2. If any other creditor tries by legal process to take any money of
   mine in your possession.

You can then demand immediate payment of the balance of this
note, minus the part of the **finance charge** which hasn't been
earned figured by the rule of 78. You will also have other legal
rights, for instance, the right to repossess, sell and apply security to
the payments under this note and any other debts I may then owe
you.

---

3. Administrative information on claiming benefits, rights of appeal, and regulatory "housekeeping" details.

Once a logical structure has been set up, the document can be made
even more useful by wise use of headings, tables of contents, indexes, and related devices.

SIMPLICITY IS CLARITY

Putting these principles into practice requires thought. Simplicity in
communications does not mean simple-mindedness. Simplified documents are clarified documents, in which the basic elements have
been clearly defined by the writer and expressed in terms the
reader can understand.

Every aspect of the document should be clear; along with the words, appearance is also important. Visual simplicity is a crucial characteristic of simplified documents, for simple language can be defeating if it looks confusing. Layout and typography, even the colors of ink and paper, should be carefully selected for readability.

AREAS FOR IMPROVEMENT

In addition to consumer contracts and corporate policy manuals, simplification projects hold particular promise in these three other areas.

1. *Employee benefits.* Clarified communications help employees appreciate their benefits and use them more easily. This makes the benefits more valuable to both employees and employers. Better organization of a summary plan description, as discussed above, is one example of how to be more helpful to people in real situations. But companies are also learning that simplified benefit booklets aren't enough. Additional materials such as posters and pay envelope "stuffers" are being used to reinforce messages about benefits and to focus on special questions. Many companies are issuing annual reports to employees describing the value of their benefits. Union Pacific's report, for example, includes a section called the "Hidden Paycheck," which tells how much the company pays for employee benefits. Of course, simplification represents a threat to companies whose benefit plans sound inadequate when described in plain English.

2. *Customer correspondence.* Word processing machines now offer even the largest companies the chance to respond quickly and accurately to a wide variety of customer complaints, inquiries, and predicaments. But the hardware isn't enough; boilerplate invades customer correspondence as well as warranties, insurance policies, and the like. For example, here's one company's response to a letter asking what a "scheduled airline" is:

> As stated in the Description of Insurance, a Scheduled Airline is a) an Airline of United States registry holding a certificate of Public Convenience and Necessity issued by the Civil Aeronautics Board of the United States or its successors; b) an airline of United States registry operating intrastate and maintaining regular published schedules which is licensed for the transportation of passengers by the duly constituted authority having jurisdiction over Civil Aviation in the state in which it operates; or c) an airline of foreign registry maintaining regular pub-

lished schedules which is licensed for the transportation of passengers by the duly constituted authority having jurisdiction over civil aviation in the country of its registry.

Thank you for giving us the opportunity to explain this. . . .

A reply like that makes you sorry you ever asked. Simplified, the same information reads like this:

A 'scheduled airline' meets these standards:

⋄ It maintains a regular published flight schedule.
⋄ It is licensed for the transportation of passengers by the government agency responsible for civil aviation in the state or country where it is registered.

It's clear that correspondence systems in many firms aren't systems at all, but agglomerations of form responses that have grown in *ad hoc* fashion. Greater demand for communication from customers resulted in the institutionalization of what was once a casual process. Letters improvised to meet a situation became fossilized forms after 10 or 20 years.

This was the case at one large consumer services company, where analysis showed 2,000 different form letters in use, covering about 850 situations. The use of "pattern paragraphs" led to composite letters that were choppy and confusing. Some letters were indirect, condescending, and even downright insulting. This was particularly ironic for a company well-known for its high-quality marketing. Look at these examples:

Unfortunately, we have been unable to develop sufficient information to enable us to properly appraise your application. Therefore, we must cancel your application.

You obviously did not retain the Purchaser's Application Form provided as a record for the purchaser's convenience at the time of sale which would have been helpful. Accordingly, we can only hope that you can provide us with some other specific evidence based on which we can favorably entertain your request.

If you cannot reconcile your account with the information provided, we suggest you have an accountant explain it to you.

Management recognized the problem and called for a new approach, whose goal was an integrated correspondence system compatible with the company's image. Once considerable research had been conducted to determine what letters were needed, they were written in a flowing, conversational style. To bring the letters' appearance into line with their simple, direct language, their layout and graphic standards were improved.

It's possible to produce clear, informative, personalized form letters. But analysis is as much a prerequisite for this as for any other form of written communication. And although legal advice is often necessary, lawyers shouldn't be the ones to do the writing.

3. *Internal memos and reports.* Many executives believe these documents are ripe for simplification. CEOs and managers complain constantly about the quality of written communications that their own people send them.

At the Connecticut Mutual Insurance Company, members of senior management realized that memos could and should be less time-consuming to read.

Connecticut Mutual President Denis Mullane and Vice-President for Communications Peter Moore decided to attack the problem on a companywide basis. Early in 1979 they authorized the development of a program that included a colorful booklet, an accompanying videotape, and special stationery to get people in the habit of writing short, clear memos. The focus was on four points:

Identify your subject.
Tell what action you expect.
Number your points.
Keep to one page only.

In a day-long series of sessions less than half an hour each, executives received the booklets and saw the videotape. President Mullane opened each session, pointing out how paperwork was strangling productivity. His commentary gave weight and credibility to the entire program. The sessions closed with remarks by an outside expert in written communications.

One striking and effective feature of the program, was its lighthearted tone, set by the booklet "Being Brief," which features the "gremlins of gobbledygook"—Rambling Rose, P. R. Prattle, Jargon Jack, and Technical Tim. The humor kept readers from feeling defensive, while dramatically illustrating common shortcomings in their writing.

Now, instead of memos, the new "Brief" forms are used. Their very name, as well as their layout, helps keep writers to the point.

Three- and four-page memos are a rarity now, and thanks to the "ACTION:" line at the top, readers can quickly decide whether the message demands immediate attention. The message itself is more likely to be written in plain English than in managerial jargon.

The fight against insensitivity, impersonality, and incomprehensibility is no longer just a concern of consumers. Obfuscation is everyone's enemy. Executives feel the need for plain English in their own lives: It's as close to them as the pile of papers on their desks. When it comes to paperwork, many of us are producers—and we are all consumers.

24

Corporate Speech Making: It's Not Like Selling Soap

Norman Wasserman

It is almost axiomatic in the marketplace that when demand picks up dramatically for a previously moderately popular product or service, an ersatz element will be hastily engineered to meet the new demand. Strangely, this also applies to the surge of corporate speech giving in recent times.

The phenomenon of the business speech is certainly not new. Executives have been making speeches for a long time in America. Fifty years ago, speakers mainly addressed groups of their own kind. They talked about tariffs, keeping labor in line, and the early signs of government interference. Their speeches were private, infrequent, and low-key.

A BROADER ROLE FOR SPEECH MAKERS

Over the years, however, dramatic advances in transportation have resulted in a greatly increased demand for business executives to

From *Management Review*, November 1979.

address large and widespread audiences. Today, companies and associations arrange and conduct close to one million meetings annually.

Moreover, businessmen are no longer talking only to businessmen, and even when they do talk to their peers, their subject matter is no longer strictly business. Furthermore, their views on a wide variety of current topics are being sought aggressively by groups for whom business per se holds little interest.

Perhaps the greatest stimulus for executives to mount the speaker's rostrum has been the drive toward fuller and more open corporate disclosure. While at first the goal was to learn more about the balance sheet and related facts, the movement soon was expanded by diverse groups to include more or less total exposure of the corporation and its officers vis-à-vis virtually every contemporary financial, socioeconomic, ethical, and political question.

Disclosure has now reached a new level that management should acknowledge and respond to with far greater earnestness than it has in the past. This new level reflects the public's desire to witness a personification of leadership on the part of America's corporate executives. Watergate, illegal payoffs, business frauds, inflation, unemployment, the high salaries of some top management, and other factors have combined to undermine confidence in the nation's corporate echelons. Yet the new large audiences for executive speeches today may not be all that critical; rather, they may be seeking a degree of reassurance that there *are* high-caliber business leaders in control of America's corporations.

Shareholders, employees, customers, suppliers, and investors, as well as consumers, students, professionals, government officials, and other groups, are, in effect, asking corporate executives to project and personalize their operations and their own styles, their opinions in addition to their products, their philosophy along with their fiscal results, and the nature and depth of their interaction within the community, the nation, and the world.

Has the corporate response been adequate? Yes and no. Yes, in terms of quantity: Increasing numbers of corporate executives are making themselves available to diverse groups. But no in terms of quality and content. It is one thing to seek out or accept a speaking forum; it is a different and more difficult matter to honestly come to grips with an issue and communicate it in a way that strengthens credibility instead of further eroding it.

If polls were conducted among shareholders, employees, consumers, the financial community, and other groups to gauge the credibility of business executives, there is a strong possibility that they would point to deficiencies in the corporate profile—and perhaps motivate executives to make themselves better known among their various publics.

SPEECHES AREN'T JUST PRODUCTS

When it comes to addressing external audiences, many corporate speeches have a distinctly "canned" flavor. To be sure, the speakers take their audiences seriously. But they appear not to take themselves and their positions seriously enough.

Business has responded to the accelerated interest in corporate speaking engagements as if this were an increased demand for some product or another. Management has "geared up" for it by setting into motion the operations for producing and delivering more of those products, by assigning personnel and devised budgets, and by purchasing all kinds of speaking aids and speech-enhancing services. The response has been businesslike, mechanical, and—with noteworthy exceptions—wholly inadequate.

The trouble can be traced to the diluted motivation of top management. In recent years, various middle-level corporate personnel, as well as external specialists, have been delegated the task of dealing with the new environment of disclosure and the concomitant demand for corporate speakers. The result has been a growing number of business speeches—professionally produced and presented, but generally lacking in corporate personality and the heartfelt ideas and commitment that can only come from a truly involved upper-echelon management.

Something has gone awry between the awareness of the demand and the final delivery. For one thing, the nature of the demand has not been properly understood. Furthermore, the deeper insights that often come through intuition and the direct involvement of top management have not surfaced to any significant extent. Rather, the demand has been treated as if it could be satisfied by a new pretty package, some merchandising hype, and a few "big name" spokespeople.

Audiences today are viewing the results of a dazzling array of technology and techniques devised to polish the public speaking demeanor of America's CEOs. A plethora of speech coaches offers instant TV playback in full color, picture-drawing speech making, simulated interview situations along with hot-and-heavy question-and-answer periods for practice, voice projection and tonal modulation, pointers on posture, sartorial secrets, eye-to-eye audience contact, the rehearsed spontaneous gesture and ad-lib remark, as well as multimedia audiovisual extravaganzas that virtually eliminate the spoken word and human personality.

Such aids are useful if applied judiciously. But the risk is that a glossy veneer will outshine the real purpose of the event. Many CEOs and other top executives are unaccustomed to public interaction. They frequently suffer from the feeling that speakers must be glib, that everything has to go just right, that the audience is a delicate mechanism—upset by the slightest thing.

Granted, audiences react favorably to a smooth, effective delivery. But when form overwhelms substance, there is a tinny ring to the entire occasion. Audiences are canny; they react more favorably to a speaker who is genuine and perhaps a bit awkward than to one who is polished and superficial.

EXECUTIVES MUST GET INVOLVED

It is time for the pendulum to swing back to a point where important, honest information becomes the real core of the corporate speech. CEOs must also accept their additional contemporary role of "chief impacting officer" (CIO). They can no longer afford to serve as mere functionaries of speech counselors, cadres of aides, and even speech-writers. They, along with other corporate officers who address external audiences, must insist that speeches prepared by themselves or others bear their own imprimaturs and convey their own personal, incisive corporate viewpoints. And there is no way that this will come about without the personal in-depth participation of the person planning to speak. Rather than casually accepting a speaking date, the executive must summon forth a genuine willingness to communicate to his or her audience in a meaningful way—through content.

One of the most common complaints of businessmen is the tremendous time pressures they face. Some of the new burdens of CEOs and others can be reasonably delegated without any serious loss in efficiency. But when it comes to personal appearance and in-person communications that reflect the corporation's outlook and personality, there can be no substitute for direct, creative participation.

And, in fact, participation doesn't take much time. It does require an understanding of the real value of the speech. The event is both an opportunity and an obligation to spell out a meaningful corporate position. It proves that the speaker is willing and eager to make the effort to involve himself in establishing a real rapport with the audience. And the effort is worth it in terms of impacting audiences with the clear identification and personality of the corporation through the medium of one of its key managers.

Once this attitude is firmly rooted, everything else falls into place—and it is surprising how little time is required to prepare an effective speech. Real motivation at the top tends to generate efficiency at all levels. Here are some hints and guidelines to consider:

1. *Whether you have actively solicited a place at a particular forum or are being invited to speak "out of the blue," carefully consider the general topic.* If you are not comfortable with it, and cannot modify it after conferring with the sponsors of the program, it may be best not to participate at all. In actuality, most speaking forums allow for considerable flexibility. Corporations should be able to relate in some way to almost any contemporary issue.

2. *Once the speaking topic has been decided upon and narrowed, give it your personal attention.* You may have already begun to think about the speech during the process of determining the topic. This is an important phase in the evolution of a speech. In essence, it is a personal way of tapping your knowledge and creative thinking.

There are two tried and true methods to achieve the desired results. First, set aside no more than an hour (sometimes much less time is needed), during which you don't accept calls or allow any other interruption. By speaking into a tape recorder and/or taking notes, you can record your spontaneous thoughts about the topic and the speech. Rambling is permitted and is even advantageous. Remember, this is the first go-round; the idea is to identify some parameters, focus in on some meaty directions, and come up with blocks of thought for later development.

The second method proceeds from the first. Now that you have extracted the nucleus of the speech, however vague, you will subsequently at odd times—at home, during meetings, while commuting, even at the pool or playing golf—come up with ideas for possible inclusion in the speech. Don't ignore these flashes. Note taking is a must at this stage.

3. *Distribute a brief memo to a select handful of associates—just three or four will do—asking them to give some thought to your speech ideas and to gather whatever preliminary written materials are readily available.* Set up a meeting with the speechwriter present.

This meeting—usually no more than an hour or so is needed—is a crucial input and synthesizing session. A tape recorder can be very useful. You and your associates should present and explore ideas within the framework of the speech topic and the previously issued memo. The discussion should be free-wheeling. Everything that is said is grist for your speechwriter. All questions and suggestions by the speechwriter should be carefully considered. An experienced speechwriter will get a feel for your personality at this meeting, as well as for the direction he or she is to take, the available material, and the over-all tone of the speech.

4. *Assign one of your associates present at the meeting to furnish the speechwriter with all the research and related materials he or she may need.* Occasionally, it will be necessary for the speechwriter to interview other department heads. Usually, any indication of this will surface at the brainstorming session.

5. *Don't isolate the speechwriter.* Make yourself directly available to answer any inquiries. An experienced professional speechwriter will not bug you with needless questions. Also, you should feel free to contact the speechwriter with any additional ideas that come to you.

6. *Set a reasonable deadline for receipt of a first draft.* Under normal circumstances, speaking engagements are arranged long in advance, allowing ample time for preparation and review. A first draft generally should be submitted 3-4 weeks following the meeting and ideally no later than 5-6 weeks before the actual speaking date.

Is an outline necessary? Usually not. A good speechwriter will be able to fit in the blocks of material in a logically unfolding and dramatic sequence as he or she proceeds, thereby achieving an effective flow. However, if you feel more comfortable viewing an outline first, this should not be a problem. In actuality, a generalized sequence of development may emerge from the meeting, eliminating the need for a formal outline, or making it easy to prepare one if required.

7. *Reading the first draft calls for a special perspective.* In many respects, it is like reading an original playscript. You should rehearse as you review the manuscript and try to imagine the nature of your audience. Remember that the speech is really an informative monologue. At this stage, don't allow yourself to get bogged down in the details of sentences and possible inaccuracies. Get a feel for the development and sweep of the speech, while determining that all the major points you wanted included are adequately covered and given the proportionate emphasis they deserve. You should be especially sensitive to the tone of the speech.

Don't react to the draft until you have read it twice. Inevitably, in the first reading, you will be bothered by certain sentence structures and phrases that seem awkward; you will come across things you "would never say in that way." Remember that a speech is not a formal treatise. Many executives find it hard to adjust to the frame of mind required to read a first speech draft.

Redrafting, reorganization if necessary, and polishing will follow. Any initial draft, regardless of how sound, will need revisions. If the first draft is 75 percent on target, the rest should be easy.

8. *Distribute copies of the first draft to a small trusted group of associates—probably the same people who attended the brainstorming meeting.* Solicit their comments, and ask one of them to centralize all comments on one master draft. Review these comments carefully, but *you* must be the final judge as to what is important to include, delete, change, and add.

From this point on, redrafting—which may include a second or third or more drafts—should proceed fairly swiftly if everyone has done his or her work. After a final draft is approved, professional speech coaching can help to make the delivery more effective.

Conventional considerations of cost effectiveness tend to weaken the executive motivation needed for top-level speech making. Part of the problem is the apparent inability of many corporate managers to perceive the real value of the potential returns. They are conditioned to evaluate every effort in terms of its hard and direct contribution to profits. This is unfortunate—where credibility and a deeper and more universal rapport are the goals, the balance sheet and improved profit margins are not the best criteria.

Related to cost-effectiveness is the size of audience for any particular address. Modern public relations "merchandising" techniques are capable of generating a vast additional audience of readers. By stimulating media interest before and after the event, and by reprinting the speech and distributing copies both within the company and to key groups outside the company, exposure can be multiplied many times. And there is a lasting record of fundamental corporate views that will always be available for reference.

Part Five

THE WRITTEN WORD

25

Johnny, the Grad
You Hired Last Week,
Can't Write

Joseph A. Rice

Johnny, who recently graduated from _____ High School or University, is a functional illiterate—and *you* hired him. And it looks as though you'll have to live with him. That means *you* have to teach him to write.

Here's the situation with Johnny, that fresh-out-of-school youngster you put on the payroll last week: Johnny sees himself as an *accountant* (or *engineer* or *marketer* or whatever). Johnny thinks he doesn't need to write/spell/paragraph letters/memos/reports.

Where did he get such notions? Well . . . maybe from his experiences in our public schools/colleges/universities. Everything Johnny has learned in the educational system has prepared him to expect to earn his living in—there's no better term for it—a "multiple-choice world." He thinks he will be able to satisfy every need of the job for which you have hired him by blocking in "A" or "B" or "C" or "None of the above."

From *Supervisory Management*, September 1976.

Indeed, scratch Johnny and just under the surface you'll find a firm layer of belief that the written language is moribund—about to pass into history like the steam locomotive. Johnny has accepted a position with your progressive company because his sensitive antennae tell his pulsating brain that you will be among the first to do away with written communication. You'll lead the way in replacing the memo, the report, the letter with tapes, cassettes, television sets. Entirely. When will this dramatic switch to totally oral communication take place? "Soon," the vibes tell him, "very soon." Maybe you'll announce the good news Wednesday: *No more writing! Ever!*

Of course, that's not what you'll do Wednesday. What you *will* do Wednesday is spend the morning deciphering one of Johnny's memos. And the afternoon working up your own multiple-choice list:

1. Dribble Johnny down the hall like a basketball.
2. Fire him.
3. Demote him.
4. Transfer him into the department of your worst enemy.

FACE THE PROBLEM SQUARELY

Restrain yourself. Face the problem squarely, like the good manager that you are. Consider the situation realistically:

◇ You hired Johnny and Johnny can't write. But neither can the other candidates you interviewed.
◇ Johnny is, if anything, a bit more highly motivated than the others. He's quick. He respects you. He wants to keep his job.
◇ The buck has been passed right down the line. And you're at the end of it. You'll have to teach Johnny to write because nobody else did and nobody else will.

Now for the good news:

◇ Since Johnny can't write, he will have less to unlearn. That may be more of a plus than you might think.
◇ There's something called the "language acquisition mechanism" which gets turned on when a young new-hire goes to work at his first career job. Because of the language acquisition mechanism (L.A.M.), Johnny will absorb a formidably

large array of technical and jargon terms over the next few months. He will never again learn so much so quickly—and that's another plus.

◦ You're better prepared to teach Johnny than you might think. If Johnny is a hunk of raw granite, you're . . . Michelangelo. And that's the biggest plus of all—as I'm about to show you.

From the top, then. If Johnny had been taught how to write, he would probably have learned writing-through-literature (because that's what 98.7 percent of the teachers in the schools know). By coincidence, writing-through-literature is 98.7 percent oriented to a pretechnology world. It is writing out of the past. It has virtually 0 percent to do with the writing Johnny must produce from now until the day he retires. If Johnny had paid attention, he would have learned writing as a "subjective outpouring of innermost feelings" or some such—a concept that generally results in an outpouring replete with woolly lambs, fleecy clouds, springy grass, and the like.

The door is open for you to introduce Johnny to a new concept: *Writing is the single most effective method for objectively recording and storing and sharing complex information.*

A CLEAN SLATE

If Johnny doesn't have to unlearn writing-as-imaginative-outpouring, you're miles ahead. The woolly-lamb, fleecy-cloud, springy-grass guys have delivered to you a pure specimen. Not because they wanted to. Because they weren't able to get him to go along for the ride.

Now, about the L.A.M. (not to be confused with woolly lambs). Psycholinguists, scholars of language, note that small children acquire linguistic concepts at a phenomenal rate. Every observant parent has reached a similar conclusion. And parents who have lived abroad note that their children absorb a foreign language much more readily than they, the adults, are able to.

It is possible to show a parallel (though less dramatic) language acquisition ability in the young adult world. The young adult, the recent grad, experiencing the fascinating career-world after years of boredom in school, is as alert as he will ever be. His L.A.M. is turned up full force.

Hit him now and hit him hard.

What follows is a memo you might hand to Johnny—as a subtle reminder that writing is as important as his academically acquired accounting (or other) skills. I would recommend that you place the memo in Johnny's hand at the same time you hand him his gate pass.

YOU'RE THE EXPERT

And one more thing, before we review that important memo-to-Johnny: There's not a reason in the world why you shouldn't be an effective writing teacher for Johnny. You don't know the difference between a gerund and a present participle? So what? You know the most important thing—how written communications work in your organization. Share that with Johnny and everybody benefits for as long as there's a you or a Johnny or a corporation.

Here's the memo you hand Johnny with his parking sticker:

JOHNNY, THE SUBJECT IS WRITING

REMEMBER:

1. You nearly always write for two purposes—
   To communicate.
   To document.
2. Your written message goes in one or more of these directions—
   Up.
   Down.
   Laterally.
   Out.
3. Your most common sin is probably dullness from material that is—
   Redundant.
   Extraneous.
   Irrelevant.
4. The most costly sin you'll ever commit is—
   Taking a caustic tone.
5. Your most overlooked aid to good communication is—
   Layout.
6. Finally, Johnny, I know you can't spell. You should know that I expect you to learn—on your own. English is full of non-

phonetic words, variants, exceptions, oddities. You have no choice but to memorize 'em one by one.

Johnny won't read the memo, of course. He may even lose it. So the next move is yours. Start walking Johnny through that memo point by point. A few minutes a day. An hour a week. Whatever is necessary until it's covered. Maybe you can start by drawing him a picture . . . a triangle.

TO COMMUNICATE AND DOCUMENT

Johnny (you might begin), organize your writing into a triangle. Know why you do that? Because you're just about always writing for two purposes. Know what those are? To communicate is the first one. To document is the second.

Up at the top of the triangle, at the beginning of your memo, you're making a recommendation or stating a conclusion or answering a boss's question. That's where you are doing your most important communicating. Know the single biggest mistake you can make when you're communicating with a boss? To put something in his way that he doesn't need to read.

As you work down the triangle, as it gets broader, give the reasons behind your recommendation. Itemize these when you can. Know why you do that? So that the reader can refer back quickly. It saves time if he or she can say: "I buy everything except item number three, Johnny," instead of "In the section of your report where you examine imported trichlorethylene over the next five-year period. . . . "

The boss will appreciate it if you'll give him some tables, or "pictures," of your data wherever possible—so that he won't have to dig it out of long paragraphs.

Finally, Johnny, you have to keep in mind that the boss who assigned you that report won't always be around. Your main job is to write to him, of course. And in doing so, you must keep in mind how busy he is. But you should also keep in mind that the report goes into the files. In a year or 18 months it may be read by who knows who for who knows what reasons. Keep that mystery-reader in mind as you write. Document everything you can. Provide all the data. Lock it together with the best judgment you've got.

Okay, Johnny, have you got the first lesson? Communicate

quickly for the first reader. Document thoroughly for the down-the-line reader.

UPWARD DEFENSIVENESS

Now let's go to lesson number two:

Johnny, a message going up has different problems from one going down, laterally, or out. Here's what I mean by that. Suppose you could look at every memo ever written by an employee to his boss—or his boss's boss. What problem would you find over and over? You'd find defensiveness. Over-caution. You'd find hidden recommendations. Evasive language. Why? Because a lot of people have figured out that you don't get fired as quickly for pulling your neck in as you do for sticking it out too far.

I'll make a bargain with you, Johnny. I won't fire you for sticking your neck out. The other side of that bargain is that I'll raise hell every time you hide your recommendation from me in the middle of a fat paragraph or at the bottom of a wordy memo loaded with inflated words.

Now, Johnny, you make a bargain with me. Any time you can collect data, conduct a survey, show hard facts to beef up your recommendation, be sure and do it. In other words, Johnny, don't say:

"I feel that we should . . ."   (Sounds too subjective.)
"It is recommended that . . ."   (Who recommends?)
"I recommend that . . ."   (Did you collect any *data*?)

Say this whenever you can: "After collecting the data and studying it, I recommend that . . . "

What goes wrong with messages going down? Let's draw another picture. (Begin drawing a picture of a STOP sign.) Can you tell me what word goes in that picture? Sure. "*Stop.*" That's an example of what semanticists call a "directive" message. A stop sign doesn't ask. It doesn't persuade. It doesn't give options. It doesn't suggest alternatives. It doesn't provide for feedback. The shape of it, the size of it, the color and location all simply shout a command: STOP! The message is about as "directive" as anything could be.

On the other hand, an "affective" message, to continue using the semanticist's terms, uses persuasion to communicate. This kind of message forms part of a "loop" and calls for feedback.

THE BIGGEST ERROR

The biggest error in downward communication lies in being too directive. The second biggest error lies in using jargon words or professional terms that won't be understood by the person out in the plant. If you are an accountant, Johnny, and you write a memo to a lathe operator the way you'd write it to another accountant, you insult that lathe operator.

What's that, Johnny? You say that there's *no way* a lathe operator can understand the new federal regulations about profit-sharing benefits? You have no choice but to state the regs as written?

Maybe. But let me tell you what you should also do:

◇ Give some examples.
◇ Draw some pictures.
◇ Set up an oral communication exchange. Speaking is always more persuasive than writing, Johnny. Set up a loop. Give the lathe operator a number to call. A person to talk to. An office to visit.

In short, Johnny, use a little imagination. Put your back into it. Frankly, a good lathe operator is worth more to us than an accountant, anyway. Exercise a little humility.

Now, what can go wrong laterally, when you communicate with somebody of your own rank in another department? Well, we have these procedures, these standard ways of doing things. Walls, some people call 'em. After a while you'll get a feel for the territory. You'll sense when you'd better go up before you go across. You'll know when you can get away with a "blind carbon." This will come with practice.

What can go wrong when you communicate out? When you're writing a letter to a customer or contractor or subsidiary or anybody else out there in the world who does some kind of business with us?

I think the mistake I notice most often, Johnny, is simply not saying what it is you want the reader to *do*. There's an ancient letter-writing formula called A.I.D.A.—short for *Attention, Interest, Desire, Action*. "Get the reader's Attention in the first paragraph . . ." and so forth.

AN ACCENT ON ACTION

Okay. You write that formula this way, Johnny: A.I.D.A. But don't think you have to put that big "A-for-Action" last. In a letter, as opposed to a memo, you may not want to put the Action right up front. But *say it*, Johnny—say what you want the reader to do, and don't hide it when you do.

Johnny, you need to know some new words: *redundant, extraneous, irrelevant.* Why did I choose those three words—and how are they different from each other?

Let's use an example, Johnny. Let's say that I could make a million-dollar decision if you'd collect data on a certain subject and give me the information I needed about three factors relating to that subject. Let's call those factors A, B, and C.

You're redundant, Johnny, if you tell me: ABC—ABBCCAB AACB. You're spinning around, digging a hole. You probably do that because you feel you haven't made the point clear the first time you said it. Redundancy is a common mistake in corporate writing.

I said I could make a decision based on factors ABC. If you told me ABC—DEFGHIJKLMN, you'd be committing the error of loading your communication with extraneous material. This is not quite so common a failing as redundancy, and it is a harder one to pin down. Here's where judgment comes into play. One logical mind might say that the decision could be made on factors AB. Another, equally logical, might say ABC. Another, ABCD. Just to be sure, you might include all the back-up factors that seem the least bit important—in the supporting, or bottom, section of your communication. Like this:

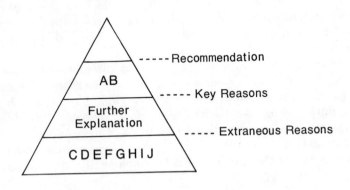

What is irrelevant? If I can make a decision based on factors AB as they relate to a certain product, and if you get into things that don't relate to the problem I've set up for you—things that are completely off the subject—you've gotten irrelevant, Johnny: AB & % + @. It's the second most heinous sin and can get your name on the "bump" list.

The most deadly sin is a caustic tone—and don't you forget it! What could cause you to be caustic-cutting-bitter-biting in a written message, Johnny? I can give you a raft of causes:

Rude customers.
Unrealistic federal regulations.
Shutdowns.
Bad weather.
Pressure.
Lack of support.
Shoddy workmanship.
Errors.

Sometimes, Johnny, you'll get mad and the anger will come out subconsciously. It will creep between the lines of the message. Know how to prevent this?

Don't put off writing until the last minute.
Let it cool and revise it.
Let a colleague look it over.
Talk about it.

Don't ever write a caustic message, Johnny. Even though your reader files it away somewhere, it can come back to haunt you years later. Besides, if word gets back to me, it's an automatic bump.

Nobody has ever taught you anything about layout, Johnny? You don't want to get cute. You don't want your memo or report to look like a real-estate promotion. But *help* your reader every way you can, Johnny.

Set off important information.
Write in short paragraphs.
Use white spaces.
Don't do this: !!!

Mostly, Johnny, you want to *be conservative* with layout and punctuation. But be conservative in a way that helps your reader.

Johnny, nothing you do here is worth a dime until you communicate it. Do it willingly, not reluctantly. Do it as soon as you can. Don't put it off. Revise it. Show it around. Let me give you one last thought, Johnny, before I send you out into the corporation on your own:

You explain something to somebody because *you* benefit. Every time you put it into words for somebody else—spoken words or written words—it gets just a bit clearer in your own head. There's a reverse spin on communication, Johnny. Take advantage of it. And good luck. We think the company's fortunate to have you with us.

26

A Systems Approach to Business Writing

Robert F. DeGise

Many business people struggle to put their thoughts in writing. It's a fearsome encounter between paper and pencil, and the result is often interminable procrastination.

Can business writing be done with less torment? Yes. You can alleviate the pressure by using a system that provides a framework for your words, yet is flexible enough to accommodate any subject. The system can also help to start your words flowing, the beginning is usually the most difficult part. Believe it or not, achieving these benefits easily is *not* an elusive hope or unattainable goal, if you follow the system.

Here, then, is the systematic, functional four-step approach you can use to make writing easier: (1) Be reader-oriented. (2) Open with a contact statement. (3) Concentrate on paragraph development. (4) Use transitional bridges.

From *Supervisory Management*, October 1979.

STEP 1: READER ORIENTATION

Effective business writing begins with an awareness of the reader. He or she should have a considerable influence on the content of your message and the way you phrase it. The more you know about him or her, the better equipped you are to communicate to that individual successfully.

Knowing as much as you can about the reader will also, in a sense, protect you from the "error of subjectivity." You make this error when you are satisfied that you know what *you* mean and want to say; but you forget about the reader and let that individual interpret your message as he or she understands it, *not as you want it understood.*

Some general information about a reader that might be helpful might include interests, values, background, experience, motivation, and attitude. Specific information that works to your advantage includes the reader's position, what he or she needs and wants to know, how much detail is appropriate, whether that message will go to one or multiple receivers, how the information will be used, and what action is desired.

Two areas that merit further comment are the reader's familiarity with the subject, and the reader's impression of the writer.

• *Familiarity with subject.* A common pitfall for writers is to erroneously assume that their reader's knowledge is equal to their own, causing them to omit essential facts. If you know how informed your reader is about a subject, you are in a better position to give him or her all the detail needed. When unsure of your receiver's knowledge, it is better to risk boring him or her with too many details than to leave the individual with gaps in understanding.

• *Impression of writer.* It is advantageous for you to have a good business relationship with your reader. Even if you don't know the receiver personally, the group you represent should have a favorable image in your reader's mind. In this positive climate, a reader is more inclined to see the soundness of your ideas. If the individual has a negative attitude toward you or your organization, he or she is more likely to resist your communication, to look for flaws in it, or to find real or imagined reasons for rejecting its content.

When writing business memos, it is particularly important to be aware of how you are likely to be received by the reader, and to adjust your writing accordingly. If you detect some hostility, work extra hard at selling the ideas that you have, and not at selling yourself.

STEP 2: CONTACT STATEMENT

Once you've identified your audience, the next step is to develop your contact statement. This is simply a specialized topic sentence. Its principal purpose is to open a memo or report—to accurately reveal the essence of your message. Topic sentences, explicit or implied, introduce subsequent paragraphs. If a topic sentence is used, a reader should be able to easily grasp the paragraph's point.

The contact statement establishes a frame of reference for your reader. In a sentence or more, the individual's attention is channeled into the text, and he or she is given a quick overview of the entire message. The effectiveness of a contact statement lies in its structure; it tells in advance what is coming, so your reader can comprehend the details that follow.

A contact statement is analogous to a newspaper story lead: that is, one or more sentences at the beginning of an article covering the four Ws—who, what, where, and when. Contact statements, however, have a somewhat different purpose; they are designed to help readers anticipate the ensuing message, rather than to tell all that lies ahead.

At least one, or ideally all three, of the following should be done by a well-written contact statement:

- ◇ Prepare—focus on content of message, put reader in receptive frame of mind.
- ◇ Point the way—direct receiver's attention, imply need and/or importance of information.
- ◇ Pique—stimulate reader's interest in message, suggest benefits.

Here is an example of a contact statement that might open a memo or report:

One-day service is now possible on all your short letters, memos, and reports—one page or less—from the word processing center. Additional equipment and two full-time typists will ensure fast response to urgent typing requests if the following procedure is carefully observed.

Note how each phrase is designed to enlist the cooperation of the reader:

One-day service (*stimulates reader acceptance and heightens interest*) is now possible on all your short letters, memos, and reports—one page or less—from the word processing center (*directs attention*). Additional equipment (*implies need*) and two full-time typists (*importance*) will ensure fast response (*benefit*) to urgent typing requests if the following procedure (*focus on content*) is carefully observed.

STEP 3: PARAGRAPH DEVELOPMENT

The major function of a paragraph is to group sentences around the same idea so they form a cohesive unit. As long as it covers only one thought, a paragraph can be any length—a single short sentence or six or more sentences.

Although all sentences in a paragraph should relate to one idea, this does *not* mean that all sentences relating to one idea *must* be in the same paragraph. Properly divided, successive paragraphs can cover various aspects of the same idea. Moreover, a memo or report need not always be divided into paragraphs if the subject is treated concisely, is uncomplicated, or is concerned with a single thought.

In general, good paragraphing is governed by logic and visual impact. Massive blocks of type are uninviting and make it difficult for the reader to discern organization. Conversely, too many short paragraphs in sequence are distracting; they hinder readers from perceiving relationships essential for a clear understanding of your communication.

To help you paragraph effectively, mentally identify the main point of each paragraph before starting to write, then determine what to tell your reader to support, explain, or clarify that point. This will give you a feel for how much each paragraph should cover. As a further aid, consider the following uses of paragraphs and their effect on your writing style. Check your paragraphs with these functions in mind. A paragraph should:

  ⋄ Keep together thoughts or statements that are closely related.
  ⋄ Separate thoughts or statements that belong to different parts of the subject.
  ⋄ Break up blocks of words into easily absorbed thoughts for readability.

⋄ Vary reading pace to hold interest.
⋄ Provide inviting thought groups for eyes and mind.
⋄ Show a change of direction in thought.
⋄ Improve reader's comprehension.
⋄ Convey a sense of order and coherence.

This final point on paragraphs may be the most cogent: *If a paragraph covers more than one major idea, it is too long. If two successive paragraphs cover the same idea, they are too short.*

STEP 4: TRANSITIONAL BRIDGES

Transitions help to relate units of thought. When these units are connected so that one thought group leads the reader to anticipate the next group, comprehension and clarity improve. Careful use of transitions move a reader from thought to thought so there is no doubt about meaning.

To effectively bridge the gap between two paragraphs, you should have the transitional phrase open the second of two paragraphs, rather than close the first. By such positioning, you do not weaken the first paragraph, and you help to introduce the subject of the second.

Transitions in thought are achieved in one of four ways:

⋄ Repeating a key word or phrase occurring in a previous paragraph.
⋄ Using a reference word—for example, this, that, those, and such—at the beginning of the second paragraph.
⋄ Inserting within the first sentence of the second paragraph a transitional expression. Some examples: also, however, therefore, consequently, thus, but, yet, nevertheless, moreover, furthermore, in addition, equally important, to this end, and on the other hand.
⋄ Writing succinct subheads that accurately identify the core ideas of clusters of paragraphs.

The use of subheads requires elaboration. Besides the desirable characteristic of helping to smooth and ease connections between the end of one major topic and the beginning of the next, they allow quick selection of topics for review and reference and provide relief from monotonous blocks of type. The number you should use is not determined by hard and fast rules. As a guide, however, note the frequency of subheads in this article and in other material where they are used to improve the organization of a subject. Your objective should be to insert subheads close enough to keep your receiver constantly aware of what is being covered, but not so close as to disrupt the continuity of the text.

IN CONCLUSION

Your writing task can be eased considerably if you use the four-step system described. Its key elements provide checkpoints as you develop the content of your memos and reports. And, perhaps most important, the system will help you get started because you know how to begin.

You now have a framework. Your thoughts can flow freely while they conform to a template for effective communication. At the very least, this system's approach to business writing diminishes your reluctance to put your ideas into words and enables you to get them the attention they deserve.

27

Fear of the Blank Page . . . and How to Overcome It

Allen Weiss

Early in our seminars in business writing, my partner Maureen O'Connor asks participants what their writing problems are. Invariably, several people say they have trouble getting started.

There are other problems, too, of course. Some participants say their memos are too long, and they want to acquire a less wordy style. Some feel they aren't persuasive enough. Some are bothered by technical language. Some can't meet deadlines. Some are unsure of themselves when called on to edit their writing. Still, a sizable number report a fear of the blank page. That concern seems to be widespread. However, there are steps that can be taken to overcome the problem—and they are helpful in correcting other problems as well.

Actually, trouble in putting those first words on paper is only a symptom of deeper problems—but it is a symptom easily recognized. In describing it, people may talk about their inertia, hesitancy, or procrastination as often as they mention difficulty in getting started or fear of the blank page. The way people perceive

From *Advanced Management Journal,* Autumn 1978.

the problem differs, but the problem is the same. If it happens to be a problem of yours, too, cheer up. No matter what form it takes, you can beat it with a systematic approach to writing.

START-UP METHODS

The first thing to understand is that your problem is not with the unsullied purity of the blank page but rather with your inadequate preparation for the work that lies ahead. There are several preparatory stages to go through before you can set about writing. Skipping any one of them can lead to trouble.

The stages emphasize, respectively, your audience, your material, a suitable structure, and an appropriate opening. Each of these planning stages has a methodology of its own, and it will be worth your while to become skilled in the whole methodology.

Audience

Before writing a memo, letter, or report, you must define your audience in broad terms. In doing this, include not only the addressees but also those who are likely to be given copies to read.

There are certain assumptions you can make about the people in your audience. They are not strangers from Mars, unfamiliar with your subject, your company, or the English language. They are more likely to be educated people who read extensively, have a reasonably good vocabulary, and know something about the topics you will be writing about.

Describe your audience as accurately as you can—in terms of their background, interest, prior knowledge of the subject, probable misconceptions, and use of words (including technical jargon).

It will help to select a representative reader or, for a heterogeneous audience, perhaps several readers who represent specific segments. Your boss is a candidate for inclusion, especially if he will review your report before it goes out, although it's unlikely that he's representative of the rest of your audience.

When you're selecting the limited number of readers to write to, don't be overly concerned with details or idiosyncracies peculiar to them. Remember that your purpose is to acquire a reader-oriented approach that will suit a cross section of the audience.

That reader-oriented approach is essential to good business

writing, just as a market-oriented approach is essential to good product promotion. When you write, after all, you are trying to sell your ideas—and yourself. Let no one tell you that the purpose of writing is "to express and not to impress." That is a myth to be exploded. With your writing you make an impression, and you must be concerned with making a favorable one. You want to present yourself as a person with sound ideas who knows how to get them across to the readers. To that end, your best starting point is an awareness of your audience's characteristics.

The reader-oriented approach doesn't pander to preconceived notions or bizarre tastes. It picks the readers up where the writer finds them, and then proceeds to carry them along to where he wants them to be. Reader orientation avoids talking down to people just as carefully as it avoids talking over their heads. Present what you have to say, and put it in a way that your audience will be able to follow.

Material

A knowledge of your audience will help in gathering and selecting the material to put before it. Additionally, the nature of your memo or report, the circumstances surrounding its issuance, and your own previously acquired knowledge of the subject will determine how much material you will need and how you will go about gathering it.

For a short piece, it may suffice to collect your thoughts, decide what you want to say, and cull the material you will include. In preparing a brief report, begin by listing your thoughts as they occur to you, without regard to orderliness. Find a quiet place for reflecting, and relax while you jot down whatever ideas present themselves. After one or more such solo brainstorming sessions, group your notes rationally, bringing together those that relate to a common theme. Then establish a logical sequence of themes, taking care to follow their order of importance.

If you will be reporting at length on a study instead of writing a short memo, then more formal procedures will serve you better. One suggestion is to classify data as the study progresses, using a tentative outline adopted for the purpose. Better still, assign each item to at least two categories according to classification schemes determined by the study.

Each note should be written on a separate sheet of paper or an index card and coded for ease in sorting and re-sorting while looking for logical relationships and testing sequential arrangements. When the notes have been arranged satisfactorily, you are ready to take the next step: structuring the memo or report in outline form.

Structure

Everything you write, regardless of length, should be outlined before you begin a first draft. For long pieces, several outlines should be prepared independently as you experiment with a number of approaches. After completing several outlines, select the best one and rework it until you are completely satisfied. Always allow time for constructing and revising an outline: It will not be wasted. Don't be taken in by another myth, "write as you go." That's the road to anxiety, frustration, rewriting under pressure, and wasted time.

Why should you prepare an outline? First, it establishes the logic of your presentation so that ideas will follow a proper sequence. Second, it avoids cut-and-paste revisions of your draft and the time-consuming task of writing new transitions that would not otherwise have to be written. Third, an outline protects you from losing your train of thought when interrupted in the work by others. Fourth, if a new idea presents itself while you are writing, you will be able to insert it in the outline and put it out of your mind while you proceed with your work in an orderly manner. You needn't be distracted for more than a minute or two.

All good writers use outlines to guide them in systematically getting a piece written with fewest problems and least delay. The more thorough an outline, the easier it will be for the writer to get on with the job of writing when the time comes.

In a detailed outline, a topic caption should be assigned every paragraph. If no one else is going to see your outline, the captions need not follow a consistent form: Words, phrases, and sentences may all be used randomly. If a topic sentence occurs to you while you're preparing your outline, capture it in your outline. Otherwise, a brief reminder—even a single word—will do for a caption and also for a heading and subheading.

When the time comes to write, treat each heading and subheading as a reminder to write a transition paragraph. Ask yourself, "How should I pick up from what has been said and carry forward to what will be said?" Transitions guide the reader; without them, he may get lost.

Openings

Once you have completed your outline, do one more thing before setting it aside: Write a tentative opening. The best time to turn to the opener is while you have the contents of your memo, letter, or report firmly in mind. Don't let that opportunity slip by!

Your opener must tell the reader what the subject is. An opener for an article should help the reader to answer the question, "Should I read on?" Reports and correspondence must also announce at the beginning what their subjects are or where they are picking up previous memos or letters.

In all your business writing, avoid trick openers, for they cheat readers by leading them to expect something other than what they are offering. Readers will not thank you for having wasted their time when they discover that they have been misled. Also, by using trick openings, you run the risk of losing your proper audience at the outset.

In writing your tentative opener, in short, simply state what you are writing about: don't bother to polish the opener at this time. Jot something down about a subject that is quite fresh in your mind now that you have just completed your outline. Polishing can come later—perhaps when you edit your completed draft. At that time, getting started will no longer be a problem to overcome.

If you can afford to wait, it is best to put your outline and tentative opener away for a day. On returning to them, you will be ready to write. You will have an audience in mind, represented by selected persons whose characteristics you have analyzed. You will have your material gathered and organized. You will have a structure—an outline. And you will have an opening sentence or paragraph to provide a launching pad. There are no mysteries and no tricks. Starting to write is a matter of methodically pursuing the job step by step. Fortunately, that isn't hard to do.

BEYOND START-UP METHODS

Although a sound method can get you started, it would be foolish to suppose that confidence in yourself as a writer is of no consequence in tackling the job. The more confident you are of your writing skills, the less fear you will have of writing that report or memo.

Writing is a combination of skills, each of which needs to be developed. Don't become discouraged if you have concentrated on improving one of the writing skills and you still are not satisfied with your output. Work at each skill in turn, and when you put them all together, you will be writing better than you might have expected. These skills include:

Logical Planning

The skill that produces an outline is logical planning. It is also the skill that turns out a good paragraph. In moving down your outline and converting each caption to a paragraph, you have more planning to do. A paragraph has a structure of its own, a topic sentence, and a method of development. These elements should not be thrown together haphazardly; they should be planned.

Paragraphing

In business writing, the favored structure puts the topic sentence first in the paragraph, chiefly to help scanners find their way easily. But if the topic sentence is not placed first, then it should go immediately after a transition sentence, which should be short.

Not all readers are scanners, of course. Some readers will take time to read your report carefully, and they, too, deserve help. Fortunately, they will also appreciate a paragraph that addresses its topics at the outset. Business readers, like others, like to know where they are headed.

The topic sentence is no different from other sentences in form. Its purpose is to express the central thought of its paragraph. At each point, your outline contains a heading that tells what you are going to write about next; it remains for you to decide precisely what you are going to say about your subject and how you're going to say it. Both topic sentence and method of development should flow from those decisions.

The paragraph must be developed in a way that supports the topic sentence. In other words, a planned effort should unify the paragraph and make it whole. Of the many methods of development—including defining, explaining, illustrating, enumerating causes or effects, describing temporal or geographical relationships, and delimiting the scope—one or more are chosen. If several methods are to be combined in the same paragraph, they must be compatible. For example, a definition may be followed by illustrations and limits. Neither conflicting methods nor extraneous thoughts can be allowed to confuse readers or detract from the force of the paragraph's central thought or its presentation. Give each idea a paragraph of its own.

Sentence Writing

Planning will work for outlines and paragraphs, but sentences should be played with and rearranged until they express your thoughts in a readable style. Many sentence problems can be overcome simply by switching words around. In particular, relative pronouns (like the pronouns *he*, *she* and *it*) can often be brought closer to their antecedents by changing the order of clauses within sentences.

In writing sentences, introduce variety. Most of your sentences should be in the active voice, but a passive verb now and then provides relief. Most of your sentences should also be in the declarative mood, but occasional use of a question, a command, or an exclamation can add the spice of life to your writing. And by all means vary the length of your sentences, interspersing short ones among the long.

The blanket proscription of long sentences is another myth to disregard. Complex sentences are quite necessary to express complex thoughts. However, sheer verbiage must be avoided. For best results from your writing, try a lean style. Go through each sentence trying to eliminate unnecessary words. Any word you can do without should be stricken; it doesn't deserve a place in your writing. A lot of adjectives, adverbs, articles (*the*, *a* or *an*) and intensives (*very*, *extremely*) can be excised with neither pain nor loss. But remember that pleasantries serve a useful purpose, as do connecting words between sentences, and words that improve the rhythm.

Word Selection

Good writers have in common a love of words. In odd moments, for instance, they will track down derivations, and that pursuit can provide interesting surprises. Try tracing *garble* and *discern* to the same root, which means *to sift*. Find out how left-handedness is perceived in different cultures, as indicated by the words *sinister* and *gauche*. Even a casual study of words can become an enjoyable pastime and one that will be useful to you as a writer.

Participants in seminars ask how they can improve their vocabularies. Our advice to them can help you, too. Try starting with words you already know. Look them up in a dictionary, studying in particular the fine distinctions between synonyms. Too many people ignore altogether the highly informative paragraphs headed *synonyms* and the references that read, "See synonyms at _____ ." Making more precise use of your present vocabulary is beyond any doubt the most productive single step you can take in equipping yourself with more words to express your exact meaning; and precision in use begins with respect for the distinctions your dictionary explains.

Another myth would strike all long words from your vocabulary. Actually, a far more useful touchstone of reader recognition than length is familiarity. And a more reliable test of readability is the rhythm of the sentence. Conduct your own research among associates and find out how many people know the meaning of *feral* as compared with the number who can instantly recognize *undomesticated*. To acquire rhythm, try reading your sentences aloud. They should flow freely off the tongue. Rearrangement of words can improve rhythm, but the selection of a particular word should be governed by the need to be precise.

Even jargon has its place when it promotes precision. The problem with technical jargon is that it is so often abused. It should never become a means of obscuring your meaning beyond recognition by the uninitiated in your audience. They are entitled to be presented with your thoughts in a style that is understandable to them. Neither should jargon be used to show off familiarity with a technical field. Pompous writing only causes resentment.

There is a simple cure for pomposity in writing, and it lies in adopting a courteous, respectful attitude toward your readers. When you edit your manuscript (or someone else's) before sending it on its way, consider the tribulations it may impose on readers because of unexplained jargon, unfamiliar words strung out as though they were pearls, verbiage, and bombast. Have mercy on your fellow human beings!

There are more skills and attributes to acquire than have been mentioned here, and there is, in truth, more to be said about those that have been discussed. Nevertheless, the methodical approach, along with accessory skills, has proved successful in conquering the fear of the blank page that bedevils many people.

It hardly needs to be said that other writing problems, too, are amenable to treatment along similar lines. Or that the effort you put into learning to write and speak well will be repaid over and over. The best advice is to get started promptly, so that you will have a longer time to reap the rewards.

28

Targeting Your Vocabulary

Allen Weiss

It is important for both the business writer and the business speaker to remember that written and oral communications are verbal— which is to say they use words to convey meaning. Pictures may be added for illustration and gestures and facial expressions may help a speaker get a point across, but the essential elements of speaking and writing are words. Hence the audience-directed approach requires that a writer's selection of words should be geared to appeal to his audience. At the same time, he should show preference for those words that work harder, carrying fuller meanings with greater precision.

THE IMPORTANCE OF WORD SELECTION

A high-level vocabulary will lose an uneducated audience, just as low-level diction may offend an educated group. In other words, talking down to people runs risks no less substantial than talking over their heads. Whatever the level of the readers, they should be addressed in words that are familiar to them. In fact, familiarity is a

From *Supervisory Management,* December 1977.

far more appropriate criterion for selecting words than is mere length. For example, *undomesticated*—long though it may be—is recognizable to many more readers than *feral*, and *ergo* is more likely to be considered pretentious than *therefore*, a longer word. Once more, the accomplished business writer realizes that the "short, short, short" shibboleth does not address the real problem. The shibboleth does not work for paragraphs, it does not work for sentences, and it certainly does not work for words, either. Familiarity is a more reliable guide.

To find out which words his associates and other audiences are acquainted with, Harry Burns listens to the words they use in speaking and observes the vocabulary they are exposed to in their regular reading. Similar projects should be undertaken routinely by business writers as part of their indoctrination in audience-direction.

This method cannot, of course, resolve all doubts; questions will remain. One colleague may be surprised to learn that oscillations are *damped* when they are reduced in amplitude; another may tell you that *cull* is an unusual word. And some words that are indeed unusual have no satisfactory replacement. Should Harry Burns drop these words from his vocabulary? A reasonable answer is for the writer to allow himself to use a certain number of risky words, which are neither so rare as to startle nor so common as to be part of every educated vocabulary. The golden mean is an adequate rule: Neither expunge such words nor overdo their employment. If he is writing for most of the audience, a writer need not pander to every last reader who may happen along.

Regardless of length or familiarity, every word must, of course, carry the precise meaning intended. It is only when two words pass the test of precision that the more familiar of them is selected. In this selection process, precision is not impaired by a trade-off with readability; that trade-off applies only to elaboration and detail. In drawing on one's vocabulary, the precise word is always the correct word. That rule holds for letters and memoranda as well as for procedure manuals and directives.

LEARNING ABOUT SYNONYMS

To satisfy his own objectives as a business writer, Harry finds it necessary to develop a vocabulary adequate to provide precise words as they are needed. (This process requires a continuing effort on Harry's part.) In addition, all business writers must respect the distinctions between synonyms. Those who find themselves repeatedly *determining* things would do well to look into the exact meanings of *discover, ascertain, confirm, verify, corroborate, decide, settle,* and *resolve.* Likewise, for improved expression, it is useful to investigate the differences between *disclose, divulge,* and *reveal* and between *inform, notify, apprise, tell, acquaint, familiarize,* and *communicate.*

No special significance attaches to these examples: Large numbers of synonyms are employed by business writers, and there is much ground to cover. However, the study of synonyms need not become a high-pressure project. For Harry, reflecting at leisure on the distinctions within groups of synonyms has been entertaining as well as instructive. For others as well, this specialized pursuit of common words and their meanings brings greatest enjoyment as a spare-time hobby undertaken at a leisurely pace.

In part, the fine distinctions between synonyms are based on the connotations associated with words having like denotations. Business writers cannot afford to ignore such connotations, because they become part of the message a reader will receive. Frequent use of a word in a certain context can color its meaning for groups of readers. A statistician may have to describe a *bias* in data, but he should recognize that many of his readers will be sensitive to the term *bias* for reasons having more to do with sociological factors than with sampling techniques. Nontechnical use of such a word should be avoided. Similarly, since *integrate* may also arouse emotional responses, it is better, for the present, to *consolidate* functions, *merge* operations, *combine* forms, and *integrate* racial groups.

Time spent in developing an extensive vocabulary and in learning the distinctions between words is well spent. However, a large vocabulary must not be perverted or abused. Its purpose is to provide a business writer with a means for achieving precision. Merely showing off an acquaintanceship with large or unusual words is not a legitimate aim. Moreover, the careless misuse of words becomes more ludicrous as the words grow longer and more pretentious. And reckless use of synonyms merely to avoid repetition of a proper word is a mistake for any writer. When *ambulating the canine* becomes part of everyday speech—heaven forbid!—we can all feel safe in talking that way. Meanwhile, let's *walk the dog,* instead of putting on the dog.

INSIDIOUS PROBLEMS

Some writing problems are avoidable only by paying special attention to them. Figures of speech carry literal meanings that cannot be safely ignored. One may describe a communications problem as a *barrier to be surmounted or cut through.* But if a writer chooses to refer to the problem as a *gap,* then he can no longer *surmount or cut through;* the *gap* will have to be *bridged.* Simple as this rule appears, it is violated repeatedly in business writing out of obvious carelessness. Mixed metaphors—changing horses in midstream—betray similar carelessness. As an example, *grist for the trained eye* leaves considerable doubt as to the author's intent. A business writer may use a series of metaphors to make a point, but he must not create a monster by combining incompatible images. For example, among incongruities, *broad depth* is incomprehensible. A reader is entitled to infer that such recklessness of expression bespeaks carelessness in thinking, insufficient attention to detail, and discourtesy to the audience. As for borderline cases, *far nearer* and *grow smaller* may not disturb many people, but careful readers will wince occasionally when encountering such clumsy expressions.

Foreign phrases often create needless difficulty for readers. To write *vis-à-vis* for *as compared with* is to use a metaphor involving foreign words, a practice not to be recommended. In speech, the French *au fait* ("to the point"), when it is not mistaken for the slang *ofay,* is likely to engender uneasiness, because most listeners will have no handle with which to extract a meaning. However, *de novo* can be understood by people who have not seen it before, and it has a precise meaning not easily expressed in English: *Anew* and *afresh* sound pedantic; *all over again* and *from scratch* are not quite the same. Similarly, *quid pro quo* (literally, "this for that,") is often preferable to *something in exchange.*

Rhyming words and echoes have a habit of stealing unnoticed into prose and disconcerting careful readers. The only known protection is to reread copy for the specific purpose of discovering unwanted rhymes, echoes, or alliteration. There is no excuse, of course, for anything as obvious as *sales volumes attained contained stock market influences. . . .*

No matter how familiar you may think an acronym or abbreviation is, it could trouble some readers. For that reason, the first time an acronym or abbreviation is used, it should be explained, either parenthetically or indirectly, by spelling out the full title. Even so widely known an agency as the FDA should be called the Food and Drug Administration the first time it is named in a piece of business writing.

JARGON AND POMPOSITY

In every field, specialists develop words that are usually understood only among initiates. The underlying motivation for such technical jargon ranges from justifiable to mischievous. There may be an understandable desire to simplify communication by giving a name to something in order to avoid endlessly describing it. Even more defensible is the recognition of a need for a term more precise than those already in existence. Experts do need new words to describe their discoveries and inventions, and imprecise language and endless repetition of descriptive passages can be avoided by a neologism in the form of a freshly coined word or an old word given a new, technical meaning. However, much jargon appears to have no better reason for being than to baffle outsiders and create a spurious air of sophistication among an in-group. Regardless of origin or motivation, *buzz words* are seized upon and spread by so many people that conscientious business writers have to decide whether to use or avoid them.

Those legitimate neologisms that improve communication should be used, but only after being defined to assure that readers understand their meaning. Definitions may be presented either subtly or directly, with equal effect. However, those illegitimate buzz words that are used by supercilious persons to establish a presumption of knowledgeability or superiority should be handled very cautiously. In writing that is meant to endure, recent coinages should be adopted slowly and then only if they show signs of longevity, and they should be dropped quickly when they appear to be going out of style. In casual speech, more leeway can be permitted, provided there is no risk of confounding listeners and that the particular word or phrase has not been overworked.

When a common word is given a new technical meaning, the danger of misunderstanding is greater than when a new word is coined. Sometimes different disciplines latch on to the same word, each imparting its own meaning and contributing thereby to the general confusion. For example, a mathematician's *game strategy* applies to all situations in which participants exercise options that affect the probabilities of success of other participants, but when a psychologist talks of *games*, he is thinking solely of insidious strategems. *Strategies* vs. *strategems*—with a world of difference between them. Furthermore, to computer people *games* are exercises in simulation, based on mathematical models that reflect the essential relations and parameters of the real world. Clearly, a lay reader stumbling over the word *game* needs guidance as to the particular meaning intended.

Much of what is known as *bureaucratese* or *gobbledygook* is not really jargon but rather an overblown manner of writing. Far too many business writers reach for long words, *endeavoring to secure maximum utilization of existing equipment* when they should be *trying to use the machines they have*. There is no excuse for such pomposity. It is, in fact, laughable. Nothing more need to be said about overblown language; the fact that it is widely employed in misguided efforts to display erudition is saddening. There are easier ways to appear ridiculous.

MISUSED WORDS

Business and technical writers have developed a body of misused words that neither qualify as jargon nor serve any useful purpose. They are plainly mistakes that have been thoughtlessly perpetuated and that ought to be corrected in the interests of clarity.

One such abused word is *parameter*, which seems to have been corrupted by its similarity—in sound only—to *perimeter*. A *parameter* is neither a boundary nor a limit nor an option nor an ordinary variable (in the algebraic sense). A *parameter* is a value that remains constant within a given system while varying from one system to another. Thus gravity is virtually constant on earth, constant on the moon, but it has different values in the two places. So gravity is properly called a parameter. In common with all other parameters, it helps to define a system—in the case of gravity, a system of forces on earth, on the moon, or anywhere else.

Another frequently misused word is *reticence*, which seems to be confused with *reluctance* in many minds. Actually *reticence* refers to one kind of reluctance only: an *unwillingness to speak*. Hence it is incorrect to talk of a *reticence to act*.

Similarly, an amendment may *substitute for* original wording, in which case the original wording is *replaced by* the amendment. But the original wording cannot be *substituted with* the proposed amendment, as business authors have written. Furthermore, the amendment is an *alternative*, not an *alternate*. To *alternate* is to go back and forth, and a group that meets on *alternate* Tuesdays will be meeting every other week.

Some technical words and combinations of words are bandied about by business writers in disregard of original meanings. Thus *significant difference* loses some of its precision when used loosely by nonstatisticians, and *discrete* is unfamiliar as a substitute for *separate* or *discontinuous*. A *leading indicator* is not a prominent pointer but rather a harbinger, a measure whose variations foretell what another variable will do. Such an indicator *leads*, while other measures *lag*. To *quantify* is not merely to *count* or to *number*; to *quantify* is to *measure* or to *express a quantity*. The word is useful in describing activities in which a system of measurement is imposed for the purpose of comparing or grading specimens. Thus levels of air pollution may be *quantified* by measuring the density of airborne particles (as in a pollen count) or by testing for toxicity among humans. The temperature-humidity index is another example of *quantification*. Incidentally, *quantize* is entirely out of place in business writing. The term comes from quantum physics, and its meaning in that field is technical.

It is hard to understand how such an outlandish construction as *imbalanced* could appear in reputable publications, yet it does. It is like whistling into the wind to suggest that the participial form of the verb *unbalance* is *unbalanced* and that typists transcribing from pencil copy have a difficult time distinguishing between *un-* and *im-*. Nevertheless, *imbalanced* must be resisted as an impossible derivation from a noun whose parentage is itself doubtful.

Another word that ought to be let alone is *demean*. Since it has two distinct denotations—a neutral one relating to *demeanor* and a pejorative one relating to *mean* (in the sense of *base*)—the word *demean* is ambiguous. By contrast, *bemean* has but one denotation, that it carries unmistakably: to *debase*. Consequently, *bemean* is preferable for its clarity.

MAINTAINING A VIEWPOINT

Recognition of a viewpoint—and adherence to it—can avert serious confusion in a writer's selection of words. For instance, one company's *payment* is another company's *receipt*. In writing about an accounts receivable activity, the receiving company's viewpoint should be maintained consistently. Its mail brings *receipts,* and any mention of *payments* will only confuse readers. However, *remittances* and *remittance slips* may properly be referred to, because the neutrality of these terms is well established in business usage. Similarly, *sales to customers* is an unambiguous, if redundant, phrase. But an expression like *customer purchases* can hardly be clear, except perhaps to the customer himself.

Euphemisms are not misused words, but rather abused substitute words. The employment of a euphemism to soften the harshness of reality, while perhaps noble in its intent, is a futile gesture; for no matter how delicate a surrogate word may be, sooner or later it acquires the meaning of the word it replaced. Thus to *let a person go* is to *fire him; termination* and *severance* are virtually synonymous with *dismissal,* and *separation* is almost there too. Since euphemisms are transparent, the effort to invent new ones is singularly unrewarding.

Dysphemism—the use of an indelicate surrogate word—is much harder to account for than euphemism. Perhaps the leading business dysphemism is the use of *attrition,* which means to *wear down by friction.* That standard definition seems far removed from the thoughts of those who proudly assert that *economies will be effected without layoffs, and staff reductions will be accomplished by attrition,* but some dictionaries now list this as accepted usage. Bordering on dysphemism is the use of *enormity* where *immensity* is meant. The *enormity* of a crime correctly refers to its exceptional wickedness and not its size.

THE PROBLEM WITH NEGATIVES

The following sentence illustrates an indefensible combination of words that is frequently found in business writing: *Poor motivation cannot help but produce absenteeism.* Since either *cannot help producing* or *cannot but produce* would work, there must be an extra word in the original. *Can only produce* avoids the double-negative construction.

Other combinations involving negatives can be troublesome in business writing. In the following examples, if *not less than* is replaced by *at least,* the meaning is retained and the reader's thought process is assisted: *Capacity was not less than 50 percent in excess of demand. In excess of* can also be replaced by *higher than*, to yield: *Capacity was at least 50 percent higher than demand.* Similarly, *not unlike*—an example of litotes—does little for a business writer. The way to achieve an appearance of moderation in business writing is to avoid overstatement. Artificial devices tend to annoy busy readers by their hint of pedantry.

Just this sort of pedantry was apparent in a 1950s plague that at last gives signs of subsiding—although unfortunately some vestiges of it still remain. This was a sort of game in which participants vied with each other to find words on which to tack the suffix *-wise*. Only *temperaturewise* could someone say that the air was hot or cold. Instead of bad weather, there were bad days *weatherwise*. One figure was higher than another *percentagewise*. An activity preceded another *timewise*. Having rediscovered such legitimate words as *lengthwise* and *likewise*, the founders of the game apparently dreamed of the day when every sentence would end in *-wise*. But the game attracts fewer devotees these days. It seems to be on the wane *popularitywise*, which is all to the good *wisdomwise* (or *wisewise?*).

MISSPELLINGS

Some words are so frequently misspelled that they deserve special attention. The most serious spelling errors, of course, are those that lead to confusion between words.

To illustrate, to *forgo* is to *pass up*, and an opportunity *forgone* is one that has not been seized. However, a *foregone* conclusion is one that was settled in advance; and *foregoing comments* refers to *previous comments*. The prefix *fore-*, which appears in *forewarn* and *foretell*, is not to be confused with the prefix *for-*, which is illustrated by *forget* and *forbid*. They come from different sources.

A similar confusion involves the suffixes *-fore* and *-for*. When speaking of a development and the reasons *therefor*—a stilted construction, in any case—the absence of a final *e* distinguishes this adverb from the more familiar connective *therefore*.

Effect and *affect* trouble many people. In business usage, only *effect* is a noun, as in *cause and effect*. The verb *effect* is closely tied to the noun; it means to *bring about a result*. The verb *affect* is less cogent, meaning only to *exert an influence*, which may be either strong or weak. *Temperature may affect a machine's operation, whereas air-conditioning can effect a lowering of ambient temperatures.*

Uncertainties concerning the singular and plural forms of nouns also cause spelling errors. The singular of *criteria* is *criterion;* the singular of *phenomena* is *phenomenon;* the singular of *data* is *datum;* and the singular of *media* is *medium.* Some Latin plurals are well established in English—*memoranda* is perhaps more familiar than *memorandums*—but other Latin plurals are less well entrenched: *Formulae* is readily replaced by *formulas.* When in doubt, Anglicize the plural, usually by adding an *s.*

Making adjectives of nouns and verbs can confuse the unwary writer. For example, *desirable* has no *e* before *-able. Usable* is better without the *e,* but those who want their *e* may have it and write *useable. Knowledgeable* takes an *e* after *dg,* whereas *judgment* is preferred over *judgement* (despite former President Ford's tri-syllabic pronunciation of the word).

Finally, there are those rare words that follow their own unique rules of spelling. *Recision* and *rescission* have similar meanings; either one may describe a withdrawal of a previous pronouncement. But the words come from different roots, and hybrid spellings just won't work.

29

Sentence Control: Solving an Old Problem

Paul Richards

The blunt note at the top of the report told a familiar story.

"The next person who writes a report this wordy can type it himself, read it to himself, and take it with him when he looks for a new job."

The department head was fed up with reports whose meaning was buried in pages of word silt.

When the author came to me for help, the source of his problem was obvious. The sentences in his report averaged 26 words. In this, they weren't too unusual.

As an industrial writing consultant, I find that most business writers who flounder on paper do so by first losing control of their sentences. Reports and memos I see typically turn up sentence averages of 24 to 26 words; many average near 30. And the more profound the authors want to appear, the longer their sentences.

Most business writers don't realize that good professional writing averages roughly 17 to 20 words a sentence. That's true of *Newsweek*, *Time*, and *The Wall Street Journal*, as well as the works of writers like Michener, Steinbeck, and Hemingway.

From *Supervisory Management*, May 1980.

In countering the mistaken belief that wordiness equals wisdom, I've found that students improve quickly by keeping four rather simple guidelines in mind.

1. TEND TOWARD SHORTER SENTENCES

From childhood, most of us are taught to capture at least one complete idea—or thought—in each sentence. But ideas and thoughts have no dimension, and that's where the trouble starts. Writers are tempted to include too many parts of an idea in one sentence. Such sentences often become freight trains, carrying an overload of implications and qualifiers, frequently shunting off on side-tracks or advancing to their destination only very slowly. As a result, they can hardly be read—let alone understood.

To express clearly their ideas, writers should divide them into individual parts. This doesn't mean pulverizing them so finely their whole outline disappears. It means looking for logical dividing lines, then fitting the parts together in progressive, faster-moving sentences.

For example, this 58-word sentence—taken from a company memo to employees about their stock plan—holds every scrap of information the author felt was needed, but even a doctorate student would have a labor to understand it.

All these comments concerning the federal income tax treatment are based on present statutes, and it should be understood that in the future statutory modifications may be made, either in the laws themselves or in their respective interpretations, which will modify that tax treatment or the requirements needed to be in compliance with the applicable statutes.

Divide this blockbuster and look what happens.

These comments about the federal income tax treatment are based on the present law. But the law could change or be interpreted differently in the future. If that happens, your tax treatment or the requirements to satisfy the law will likely change too.

These three simpler sentences—averaging 14 words each—make the idea much easier to grasp. And in 15 fewer words.

Why does dividing and shortening help? Mainly because most

ideas aren't simple and short; they are often quite complex with many dimensions. This is especially true of our own ideas, since we formed and developed them and thus have special thoughts about what they reveal. So when we try to explain them in writing, we're often tempted to convey their every facet at once, to forestall the reader's misunderstanding them.

But our reader begins by knowing little or nothing about our ideas, so we have to *build* carefully his or her understanding. If we try to push the reader from zero to full enlightenment in one sentence, we rarely succeed. The clarity we're striving for often gets lost in a cloud of commas, clauses, and conjunctions.

Here's another example where the author started with a large idea, didn't break it down, and built a runaway sentence. If he'd thought to divide his 53-word monster, it could have been tamed into a much clearer series of shorter sentences.

The subject is employee benefit plans:

> Plan participants may obtain additional copies of the following summary annual report for a reasonable charge, or inspect without charge the latest full annual report or any parts of the report, including a list of any assets held for investment and a list of transactions involving more than 3 percent of plan assets.

Now let's look at the edited version:

> For a small charge, plan members can get copies of this summary report from the benefits office or the administrator. Or they can inspect the full report free at the benefits office. The full report lists assets held for investing, and transactions involving more than 3 percent of plan assets.

Note the edited version uses *fewer* words than the original, yet delivers more information, and does so in a tone that could offend no one's intelligence.

2. WRITE SENTENCES THAT AVERAGE 17 TO 20 WORDS

Wait before you brand this guideline as too mechanical or simplistic. It works, and it passes the most rigorous intellectual test. No information is so complex or abstruse that it can't be clearly conveyed in sentences *averaging* around this range.

For insight on this, analyze the work of good professional writers—especially those popular with a wide audience. You'll find the most successful among them adhere to this technique. Of course, they don't do it by counting words but rather through experience or innate story-telling skill.

If you feel this will lead you into a "See Dick run" sort of simplicity, look at this passage from *Henderson the Rain King* by the Nobel Prize-winning novelist Saul Bellow. It starts off with an 83-word sentence, but the subsequent four sentences bring the overall sentence average down to 21 words.

> We were seated face to face on a pair of low stools within the thatched hut, which gave the effect of a big sewing basket; and everything that had happened to me—the long trek, hearing zebras at night, the sun moving up and down like a musical note, the color of Africa, and the cattle and the mourners, and the yellow cistern water and the frogs, had worked so on my mind and feelings that everything was balanced very delicately inside. Not to say precariously.
>
> "Prince, I said, "what's coming off here?"
>
> "When stranger guest comes we always make acquaintance by wrestle. Invariable."

The next five sentences lower the average further:

> "That seems like quite a rule," I said, very hesitant. "Well, I wonder, can't you waive it once, or wait a while, as I am completely tuckered out?"
>
> "Oh, no," he said. "New arrival got to wrestle. Always."

With that, the ten-sentence average is down to 15 words. The first sentence is a well-written *long* sentence, using simple, concrete words. Then the length pattern of the subsequent sentences, 4—7—10—1—10—18—4—5—1, quickly brings the writing back into the easy reading range.

But that's fiction, you might say. It makes no difference; the rule applies equally to both fiction and nonfiction. Good writing of any kind establishes close idea contact with readers—and that's best done if they can readily understand you.

Consider the wartime speeches of Winston Churchill. They were meant to inform, to persuade, to motivate—exactly the aims of most business writing. Studying them reveals that many of Churchill's most compelling and memorable sentences were *under* 20 words long.

> Never in the field of human conflict was so much owed by so many to so few [17].

> Give us the tools and we will finish the job [10].

> We shall fight on the beaches [6]; we shall fight on the landing grounds [7]; we shall fight in the fields and in the streets [10]; we shall fight in the hills [6]. We shall never surrender [4].

The stationery Churchill reserved for urgent orders contained the terse headline: "Action today." What if this had been written: "It is recommended that implementation of the instructions contained in this document be commenced and, if possible, completed before the conclusion of the current business day." Would that have been more impressive? More urgent? Clearer? Hardly.

Unpracticed writers persist in the notion that length equals depth. But skilled professionals know that readers get exhausted wading through lengthy syntax; they're neither impressed nor motivated, they're just fatigued.

3. VARY YOUR SENTENCE LENGTHS

Keep in mind that the 17-to-20 rule deals with *average* sentence length, not the length of each individual sentence. Your sentences can, and should, vary greatly in length—so long as they fall in the readable range, *on the average.*

Clarity does not rule out well-written long sentences. Ernest Hemingway was considered a powerful "short sentence" writer. Yet two facing pages in *For Whom the Bell Tolls* contain sentences of 153, 74, 67, and 60 words. Despite these, the *average* length of all sentences on those two pages is 21 words.

To achieve that, Hemingway mixed sentences of differing lengths, framing several under ten words and some as short as one or two. You should do the same. This practice automatically gives writing *variety*—a key to catching and keeping reader interest. Make no mistake, it doesn't prop up weak content. But it does infuse strong content with vitality, the essence of good writing.

Unvarying sentence length (as when *all* sentences fall in the 17-

to-20 word band) steals power from even good material by building up an annoying sing-song cadence that calls attention to itself and away from your message.

This report from a business traveler holds valuable information, but it just lies there. (To get the full effect, read it at your normal reading speed.)

> In Phoenix I visited several outlets for our industrial line. These visits were arranged by our local area sales representative. He had explained various areas where each needed merchandising help. At the first, I detailed our new volume discount program. The sales manager was interested but expressed several key doubts. He said his business was composed mostly of small buyers. Their individual purchases were too small to generate much discount. He asked if he could consolidate account purchases into groups. I told him this wasn't currently part of the plan. But I said I'd check with you for an answer.

Simple, clear, and direct, but also choppy, dull, and uninspiring. Imagine it going on for another two or three pages. But vary the sentence lengths, and it comes to life.

> In Phoenix I visited several outlets for our industrial line. Our local area sales rep had arranged the visits and explained what merchandising help each dealer needed. At the first, I detailed our new volume discount program to the sales manager who was interested but had several key doubts. Most important, he said his customers were primarily small buyers whose individual purchases couldn't generate much discount. He asked if he could consolidate account purchases into groups, even though that's not part of the present plan. I said I'd check with you for an answer.

This sentence pattern of 10—17—22—17—19—9 averages 15.3, delivers the message in six fewer words, and, above all, starts speaking with force.

(I obviously engineered the word count in the first memo to make the contrast clear. But the point is equally valid in less flagrant cases.)

4. INCREASE THE VARIETY OF YOUR PUNCTUATION

Of all the declarative writing tools, the most overlooked—and awkwardly used—is punctuation. This probably stems from the baseless belief that punctuation is governed by inflexible rules that only trained grammarians understand. Many writers feel it's safer to use minimum punctuation than risk breaking a rule.

What a waste! Punctuation needn't be complicated or awesome. Writers with even a basic feel for the liveliness of language can easily learn to punctuate with a sure hand. And doing so adds a dimension of vitality to writing that can be gained no other way. Good punctuation imbues an unvarying flow of written words with the vigor and urgency of spoken language. It yields freshness; it gives pace and tone; it makes written ideas more compelling to readers.

Most significant: Good punctuation enhances the clarity of even the longest sentences.

In developing this touch, take heart from knowing that writers like Shakespeare, Milton, and Shelley had no consistent pattern of punctuating. Poet E. E. Cummings even eliminated capital letters. Lincoln changed punctuation between drafts of the Gettysburg Address (even *after* he'd given it), obviously seeking the right *effect*, not the right "rule."

So if you differ from the purist in some usage, who cares? The resulting vigor of your writing will more than offset the small (and largely imagined) risk you take.

A little classifying may help in your use of punctuation. These classes are not absolute or even complete, but they're a good memory guide.

Timing and Pace

These are the main tasks of the period, semicolon, and comma. Think of them in a musical sense.

A period equals a full rest (between sentences): Tomorrow is Saturday. I thought it would never get here.

A semicolon equals a half rest (between independent clauses): Smoking is not a virtue; it's a very expensive vice.

A comma equals a quarter rest (any time you need one): All things considered, we should postpone our decision on the building.

To use these well, learn to appreciate the value of pace and timing in writing. With a little effort, you can quickly develop an adequate sense of where pauses should occur and how long they should be. Then, just use the right marks to get them. If that sounds rather subjective, it's intended to. Writers invented punctuation so they could enliven their writing with the varied movement and flow *they* wanted; and that's still your best guide to using it.

Emphasis

Where word alignment alone can't adequately turn your volume up or down, punctuation can.

Use an exclamation point for loudest volume (but only after a short declarative sentence): This must never happen again!

Emphasize important words *within* a sentence by underlining: He has been bankrupt *four* times.

Draw attention to an important aspect of a larger idea you're expressing by isolating it with dashes: The third objective of this program—and by far the most important—is to reduce attrition.

The colon serves a similar purpose, in two uses.

First, to introduce a list: The subjects of the three operator seminars will be: job safety, product quality, and labor turnover.

Second, as an emphasizing link between an important point and an introductory statement that precedes it: Most important: We must guarantee on-time delivery.

Parentheses turn the volume *down* on a thought that departs from your main message. They tell your reader that this information isn't really essential, but it may be useful: This new model calculator (the fourth we've introduced this year) can perform more functions than any other in its size and price range.

Tone

Two punctuation marks can affect this—the question mark and quotation marks.

Questions can often add a friendly, human tone to your writing. For example, in these sentences, contrast the chill of the first with the warmth of the second: If we're to process the claim you recently submitted, you have to send us more information. Can you help us process your current claim by providing some additional information?

Questions are also useful transition devices. For example: We've set an ambitious production goal for next year. How do we reach it? By hiring qualified people and training them well.

Quotation marks not only set off direct quotes; they can also denote words or phrases used in a special sense: The draft of my manuscript was returned by our attorneys with several "corrections."

Punctuation used well (which includes not using it to the point it becomes conspicuous) can vitalize your writing while keeping your sentences from running out of control.

By keeping these four guidelines in mind as you develop your reports, letters, and memos, you'll reap an important benefit—easier readability. Readable sentences (an endangered species in much business and government writing today) are also apt to be clearer. And clarity yields good communication!

30

Writing:
Don't Let the Mechanics
Obscure the Message

Robert F. DeGise

Many time-saving, cost-reducing, and better-way-to-do-it ideas are never put on paper. Although they may have been verbalized, such productive thoughts too often evaporate in the heat of daily activities. Even when they aren't forgotten, the prospect of putting them in writing has scant appeal for many knowledgeable and experienced managers and supervisors who are the first to admit that writing is not their strong suit.

Another deterrent to getting ideas into writing is reluctance to begin a writing task. Even professional writers are susceptible to this difficulty. For many, putting something in writing clamps a rigid structure on their spoken words. In translating from the spoken to the written form, they lose the ease and directness of face-to-face conversation.

Such reluctance to write is unfortunate, because writing something down is beneficial even when the communication will be pre-

From *Supervisory Management*, April 1976.

sented orally. If, for example, you're going to give oral instructions, writing them down beforehand will bring your thoughts into sharp focus. And it lets you make a visual check on their organization and sequence—vital elements in communicating effectively. You can even put your first draft aside for a day or two and then look at it again with an eye to improving the presentation of the instructions or adding to them.

The guidelines that follow on ways to achieve an informative writing style de-emphasize preoccupation with such mechanics of writing as grammar and punctuation and focus on effective communication. This is not to say that such mechanics are unimportant— but concentration on them while you're putting your thoughts into written words can be counterproductive. Leave such mechanics for the last step—and if you're not good at them, let someone who *is* blue-pencil your draft.

1. *Keep words simple.* Simplifying the words you use will help reduce your thoughts to essentials, keep your readers from being "turned off" by the complexity of your letter, memo, or report, and make it more understandable.

It's laudable to know a lot of words, but it's better to know when not to use them—especially when they might confuse the reader. A good vocabulary represents knowledge; an accumulation of "ten dollar" words to drop into a report to impress your readers does not.

Of course, if your exact meaning lies in a five- or six-syllable word, use it. And you may occasionally want to use a long or uncommon word to hold reader interest. Because our language is rich, you usually have a choice between long, unfamiliar words and shorter, more familiar ones. Here are some examples of long words with their simpler synonyms:

ascertain	find out	procure	get
commence	start	subsequently	later
endeavor	try	terminate	end
facilitate	make easy	utilize	use

Generally, you can increase the exactness of your language by using words with narrow bands of meaning. This minimizes the possibility that a reader might misinterpret the particular meaning you want to convey. But if you are sure your reader will understand your meaning, use the word when there is good reason to do so.

2. *Don't sacrifice communication for rules of composition.* Before you pitch out your grammar books, let me explain.

On the positive side, grammar operates as a kind of language controller that regulates the structure and relationship of words. Instead of exchanging single words and incoherent thoughts, we can send and receive messages through an orderly arrangement of word combinations. But most of us who were sensitized to the rules of grammar and composition taught in our schools never quite recovered from the process. As proof, we keep trying to make our writing conform to rigid rules and custom without regard to style or the ultimate purpose of the communication.

A rigid system of rules tends to interfere with or replace thought—and you can't write well without thinking. If you find this happening as you write, remember the advice previously given: Forget syntax while you're writing and straighten it out later or get someone else to straighten it out.

You may, however, have to give a final verdict when there is a choice between a colloquial expression and one that hews to the rules of grammar. Although the rules remain relatively constant, our language is continually growing and changing. Some words, expressions, and even punctuation considered wrong ten or fifteen years ago are considered correct or at least acceptable now. What makes them right or wrong? Usage. Yours and mine. So when the choice is between an easy, unaffected expression in common usage and a stiff grammatical construction, I would opt for the former unless it is likely to offend your readers.

By and large, readers want to understand your message. They don't have the time to correct your grammar, and they don't want to correct it. Splitting an infinitive in the interest of clearer communication will rarely be condemned except, perhaps, by the most extreme language purists.

Since the precision of language is imparted through the order of words in a sentence, your objective should be this: to choose and arrange your words so that the reader can readily discern their relationship—so he or she can quickly understand you and respond appropriately to your message.

3. *Write concisely.* This means to express your thoughts, opinions, and ideas in the fewest number of words consistent with completeness and smoothness. But don't confuse conciseness with brevity; you may write briefly without being clear or complete.

Clarity is lost if, in a desire to be brief, you leave out important facts or omit words necessary to show the relation between your ideas.

Concise writing focuses on significant and relevant facts and leaves out the insignificant. In short, a concise report wastes no words; it gives your reader the most information in the least time.

4. *Be specific.* Vagueness is one of the most serious flaws in written communication because it destroys accuracy and clarity, leaving the reader to wonder about your meaning or intent. Occasionally, vague writing is intentional—designed to conceal a lack of specific facts or even to withhold certain facts from readers. Deliberate vagueness may conceal the true costs of a project, for example, or the extent of an error. It is not wise to go in for this kind of

Figure 30-1. Vague vs. specific terminology.

Following are some examples of vague terms and expressions with their more specific counterparts.

Vague	*Specific*
engine malfunction	power loss, overheating, bearing failure
hazardous driving conditions	slippery surface, icy pavement, heavy fog
poor housekeeping in factory	spilled oil, dirty rags, paper, cluttered aisles

(Vague)   The company is urging everyone in the shop to use protective equipment.

(Specific) The company is urging everyone in the shop to wear safety glasses and safety shoes.

(Vague)   All engines undergo thorough preparation before shipment to a dealer.

(Specific) All engines are tested, painted, and inspected before shipment to a dealer.

vagueness, however, because when the true facts surface—as they often do—you will be in for a much harder time than if you had given an accurate picture of the situation from the beginning.

Expressing facts in specific terms not only promotes clarity of communication, but also gives it directness and vigor. The examples in Figure 30-1 illustrate the improvement in clarity and impact achieved by making vague terms and statements specific.

Following these guidelines should help you get started on a writing project and communicate better with your readers. But whatever guidelines you follow, if they make you uncomfortable or leave you with expressions that "just don't seem right," go with your judgment. In the final analysis, you have to communicate in your own style, one that does not conflict with your feelings about what seems right—and that style is usually the best one for you and your readers.

31

How to Write Better Letters

James Menzies Black

You know what a cliché is. It is a stereotype, a commonplace conversation piece like, "New York's a wonderful place to visit, but I'd hate to live there," or, "It's not the heat, it's the humidity." It is the prefabricated phrase, the ready-made set of words, packaged for instant use, that saves the speaker the trouble of thinking about how to express an idea. Some people sprinkle their talk with clichés like—to fall back on a cliché—raisins in a rice pudding, and as a result you can anticipate almost everything they are going to say.

Now, it is a strange thing, but many a person whose conversation is lively, imaginative, and stimulating becomes a cliché expert the minute he gets near his pen or typewriter. His prose is studded with a curious and pompous mixture of quasi-legal phrasing, eighteenth- and nineteenth-century mannerisms, and antique Latin ornaments that are as out of place today as a gable on a split-level house.

Evidently too many people regard letter writing, particularly business letter writing, as some kind of formula. They have a supply of stock expressions which they keep in their inventory of words to requisition on appropriate occasions.

MEET MR. BROMIDE

Would you like to interview a cliché expert in the business-letter-writing field and get his opinion on the subject?

Question: Oh, Mr. Bromide! I understand you are something of an authority on stilted letter writing. Could you tell us how it is done?

Mr. Bromide: Your esteemed favor of the tenth instant to hand and we beg to advise you that we will act favorably on your request.

Question: Tell me, Mr. Bromide, when you must reply to a letter, how do you begin?

Mr. Bromide: The speaker usually commences a letter of reply in the following manner: "Replying to yours of March 1, we beg to advise. . . . " However, there are acceptable alternates such as, "We wish to state that your letter of March 1 is before us," or "Your letter of the first instant of March is on our desk."

Question: Then you always refer to yourself in the plural?

Mr. Bromide: Not always. Please find that we sometimes write in the third person, thus becoming "the writer."

Question: Now, Mr. Bromide, if you enclose something in a letter would you say, "Enclosed is. . ." or "Attached is . . ."

Mr. Bromide: My goodness, no! That's much too easy! This writer makes a production of it. We would say, "Attached hereto . . ." or "Enclosed herewith. . . ."

Question: I notice you include many Latin phrases in your letters. Are you a student of Latin?

Mr. Bromide: Never had a lesson in our life. But you are advised hereby that these phrases reveal that we are educated, and they are impressive when the contents of our letters are duly noted. Therefore we utilize such legalistic lingo as "herewith," "whereas," "hereby," whenever we can fit it in. The writer is also delighted when he can insert such actual snatches of Latin as "per," "in re," or "sine die" in a letter. They lend a certain tone, don't you think?

Question: When you get to your closing remarks, how do you proceed?

Mr. Bromide: Then we really go to town. We are as 'umble as Uriah Heep. Phrases flow from our pen like, "Assuring you of our continued interest, we beg to remain, Yours very truly," or, "We thank you in advance for your esteemed favor. Believe me, we are Yours sincerely."

Shall we thank Mr. Bromide and leave him to his letters? Obviously he is satisfied with his methods. His vast store of phrases, like a comedian's jokes, can be adapted to any occasion. Sometimes he may actually be able to get a message in between his notion-counter expressions, although you probably have to dig pretty deep to find it. The business man who comes under Mr. Bromide's influence will be composing letters that sound like the postcard stereotype, "Arrived safely. Having a wonderful time. Wish you were here."

Don't be a stuffed shirt behind a postage stamp. When you are writing to someone, you are talking to him on paper. Why not use phrases or words that come naturally to you? It is a curious thing, but we all show signs of Jekyll and Hyde when we write. Our objective seems to be to eliminate completely our true personality from our prose.

If you have trouble with your letters, ask yourself why. You have an adequate vocabulary. You have at your command the words you need to express yourself when you talk. Why can't you put these down on paper when you write a letter? Why do you freeze up, get tight and restricted? Nobody is asking you to be like Lord Chesterfield, whose letters are considered models of epistolary style and elegance. All you have to do is be yourself—just talk to the other fellow through your fountain pen.

YOU CAN IMPROVE YOUR LETTERS

You probably dictate your letters. Now, if your secretary were the person to whom you were writing letters, how would you phrase them? Talk to her just the way you would if she were the intended reader. With a little practice it soon becomes easy and natural, and you have found the answer to good letter writing. You are a flesh-and-blood personality in your written prose, not some stranger on verbal stilts, uneasy and mentally musclebound. You are at home on paper.

If you want to write a good letter, you can do it, but you must plan what you want to say and determine how you want to say it before you begin. Then, after you have finished, read what you have written and cut away the unnecessary words, trite or stilted expressions, and clichés. Almost immediately your letters will begin to improve and your prose will start to perk up.

Here is a plan for self-improvement.

1. *Define your subject.* The title of a book is its "come-on." It is also an indication of its content. That is why an author tries so hard to select a provocative and interesting one. When you write a business letter, the reader wants to know your purpose immediately. Why not explain it in the opening sentences? That way you catch his interest and lead him on. If you hide your topic behind a thick hedge of preliminary statements, you are likely to lose your audience.

2. *Organize your material.* Don't just start dictating, for you are likely to ride off in all directions and completely confuse the reader. Think out what you want to say and organize your material logically beforehand. It may be best to jot down the main points you expect to cover before you begin. Some people, before they dictate a final draft, write out their letters in longhand, or at least parts of them, to make sure they have selected exactly the right words to convey their thoughts. Whatever you do, don't scattershot your ideas, such as by giving conclusions in the opening paragraphs and then adding a few introductory remarks toward the end.

A typical letter has a typical sequence. It is:

◦ The opening, in which you specify the subject about which you are writing.
◦ Your introductory comments.
◦ Your supporting facts.
◦ Your conclusions and recommendations.

3. *Be polite.* Never put your bad temper in a stamped envelope. When you say something, it can be forgotten or at least forgiven. When you put it in a letter, it becomes a written record, and law courts are full of people who got angry on a typewriter. Don't tell anybody off in a letter, even if he deserves it. Abraham Lincoln had a habit of writing to people with whom he was annoyed, but he didn't mail the letters. He kept them on his desk for a day or so and then rewrote them. Having released the steam of his anger in the first draft, he was able to be moderate and even-tempered.

4. *Make sure your letter is clear.* A well-organized letter says what it wants to say. It contains no double talk. So read your letters ever so carefully before you sign them. Make certain they are not ambiguous or vaguely worded. If you are uncertain about the clarity of a particular paragraph, why not try it out on someone else? If he does not quite understand your thought, you had better rewrite it.

The best writers use simple, expressive words. They avoid polysylla-bles and the obscure, and they do not clutter their prose with tech-nical phrases or abbreviations.

5. *Keep it short.* When you write a business letter, get to the point. Your letters are requests for another person's time. Make sure they don't overstay their welcome.

CLEAR THINKING LEADS TO CLEAR WRITING

A company in New London, Ohio, was attempting to get its workers to return to their jobs. A strike had been in effect for three weeks. A series of letters had been sent to all the employees, urging them to vote to accept the management's offer at the next union meeting. This is the reply the director of personnel received from one of the employees:

> Dear Tom:
>
> I did not want the union or the strike so I voted against the union and also the strike. A few weeks ago we looked up 26 members ready to go to work we went to C-D- to find out what to do, we never could locate him so it blowed over. You have written three letters to me, why don't you call a meeting to find out who is interested and what to do about it. Don't put my name in it, it sounds dangerous. If you call a meeting don't call it at the plant call it at some one house any where in New London.

This is a pathetically laughable confusion of words, unpunctu-ated, inarticulate, and ungrammatical. Yet the writer does convey the general idea: "A back-to-work movement is dangerous, and al-though I and a number of others are willing to go back to our jobs, we don't want any trouble." When you analyze what the employee has said, his message is much clearer than many of the perfectly punctuated, grammatically precise letters that you receive from bus-iness associates. This man, with only a fourth-grade education, was clear in his thoughts. He simply lacked the skill to express them well. There are many managers who have the technical ability to write but have not trained themselves to think in an orderly fashion. Their letters are even more confused, but the confusion is hidden behind a slick façade of good grammar. The letters sound all right; they just don't say anything.

Thinking clearly isn't too difficult for anybody with ordinary intelligence. If you have the ability to reason logically, you can do it under almost any circumstances, but you have to train yourself. Letter writing, or writing of any kind, may be an unfamiliar and unnatural mode of expression to you. But if you have the ability to reason, you can accustom yourself to a different medium of communication. Actually, it can be stimulating and pleasant, for it gives you the opportunity to develop your creative ability. All you have to do is take it easy, put yourself in the place of the person to whom you are writing, and then tell him what you want him to know. You have the words. You use them every day. You know how to spell the words—at least most of them—and when you don't, there is the dictionary. So what's so hard about that? It is simply understanding what has to be written and in what sequence.

WHY NOT TRY FOR A LITTLE COLOR?

You are not a novelist, nor are you aiming at deathless prose. You are a practical man writing a business letter. But if you take time to consider how to make a phrase come alive, it will add something to your letters; it will lift them out of the routine.

The business agent of a union, a flamboyant, picturesque character, had that talent, and his letters were passed around the offices of the companies with which he negotiated contracts. He had little education, and his grammar wasn't all that it could have been, but he made his points in highly colorful language that kept them from slipping through the chinks of memory.

After he had settled a contract with one company, he wrote to its president to say that he hoped both sides had the same interpretation of a certain section of the agreement. He concluded by warning: "If you try to slip something over on me there, I'm going to make more noise than a jackass in a tin barn." Not elegant phrasing, is it? But he left no doubt of his meaning. There was no ambiguity. He punched home his thought in one vivid sentence that was not likely to be forgotten. He was himself; he wrote the way he talked.

When you write a business letter, you are representing yourself and your company, but you reflect your company's personality through your own. Dr. Rudolph Flesch, in *The Art of Readable Writing*, says: "Your language differs from that of anybody else. It's part of your own unique personality. It has traces of the family you grew up in, the place where you came from, the people you associated with, the jobs you have had, the schools you went to, the books you have read, your hobbies, your sports, your philosophy, your religion, your politics, your prejudices, your memories, your ambitions, your dreams, and your affections."

There is nothing so distinctly you as the words you put on paper. Be proud of them, for they are a part of your personality delivered by a postman.

If you want to write letters that speak their piece, you can do no better than follow the advice of the eaglet in *Alice in Wonderland.* "Speak English," he said. "I don't know the meaning of half the long words, and what's more, I don't believe you do either."

The purpose of writing is to communicate. If you succeed, you will have expressed your thought in exactly the way your reader would have liked to say it.

THE TEN "DON'T DO'S" OF GOOD WRITING

1. *Don't "beg."* You are not asking for a handout. Nor are you a king, so don't write "we" unless you are speaking for your company. Don't "state." You are not handing down a Supreme Court decision. Don't tell somebody his letter is "in your hands" or "on your desk" or "before you." He doesn't care where it is as long as you have read it, and he does want you to "read," not "duly note" it. Remember, too, a letter is a letter, not a "communication," and a date is a date, not an "instant."

2. *Don't tighten up.* Stiffness is all right in an upper lip or in a dress shirt, but in a letter it makes your words read like a picket fence. Be relaxed and loose when you write, and don't try to translate your thoughts into strange, unusual words that are completely foreign to the way you ordinarily say things.

3. *Don't send a crossword puzzle to your reader.* He is not interested in solving a cryptogram. To organize your material, you must keep in mind that a letter has a beginning, a middle, and an end, and it's up to you to put the right things in the right place.

4. *Don't be longwinded.* Keep the short story short and say what you have to say once. You are a letter writer, not a revolver, so don't be a repeater.

5. *Don't "write down."* You are not teaching school and your

reader is not inferior or necessarily ignorant. The condescending person is never liked, and the condescending letter is hardly likely to win friends or influence people.

6. *Don't be a bully boy.* Never get tough in a letter. Spoken words vanish into the air, but when you put them down on paper, they stick around longer than a 30-year mortgage, always ready to jump out of somebody's file to refute your claim that you were misquoted.

7. *Don't be rude.* Abrupt, curt letters annoy even though you may not have intended to be discourteous. Always read your letters over before you mail them and try to put yourself in the place of the recipient by asking, "How would I like it if I got a letter like this?"

8. *Don't attempt to be too literary.* You are writing a business letter, not a sonnet. If you are a good craftsman, your letters will show that you have imagination, wit, and intelligence, but there is no need to try for the grand style in prose. The destination of your letter after it gets past the reader is his filing cabinet or wastebasket, not an anthology.

9. *Don't climb on a platform.* You are writing a letter, not preaching a sermon or arguing from a soapbox. You want the reader to meet your mind, not study your ultimatums. Keep away from such phrases as "we insist," "unless we hear from you," "you are put on notice."

10. *Don't write in a hurry.* Good writing is not a matter of rules. There are tricks to the trade, and you learn them by practice. If you have ideas, an interest in your reader, a normal curiosity about language, and the willingness to broaden your background through good reading, you can equip yourself to write, and it is entirely worthwhile. Letters are a means of communicating. If you write them well, you become more valuable to your company and enlarge your chances of promotion.

32

Memos That Get Things Moving

Harold K. Mintz

When you send a memo, you want to inform recipients, to change their attitude, to get them to take action—in short, to get things moving. The key to writing effective memos is organization, provided that your information is accurate and relevant and your style designed for maximum impact.

Memo organization is not a static, repetitive chore; it changes with the subject and with each group of readers. With one subject, the chronological approach may be most suitable; with another, the question-and-answer approach may be best. One group of readers may prefer the general-to-specific organization; another group may lean toward a cause-and-effect organization.

Whatever kind of organization you choose (based on an assessment of the readers' needs), you should:

◇ Tell the readers only what they need to know.
◇ Tell them what it means.
◇ Tell them what action, if any, to take—and when to take it. Later on, we will discuss ways of organizing a memo to achieve these objectives.

From *Supervisory Management*, August 1973.

Memos can move up and down at all levels or sideways across departmental and divisional lines. They can go to one person or hundreds—to superiors, to peers, to subordinates. Occasionally, they may even go to customers, suppliers, and other interested outsiders.

Although memos can run to ten pages or more, short memos—one or two pages—are preferable. In this era of documentation overkill, there is a persuasive argument for brevity. Have your memo typed single-space, with double spaces between paragraphs.

THE IMPORTANCE OF ORGANIZATION

The overall organization of a memo should ensure that it answers basic, relevant questions concerning its subject: What are the facts? What do they mean? What do we do now?

To supply the answers, a memo needs at least some of the following elements: summary, conclusions and recommendations, introduction, main discussion, and closing. Incidentally, these elements make excellent headings to break up the text and alert readers to upcoming topics.

A memo may be well worded and contain all the needed information, but still fail in its objective. Why? Usually the reason is illogical thinking, which results in poor organization characterized by digressions, irrelevancies, and illogical or ineffective sequence of information.

The writer of a good memo keeps his purpose and the reader's needs uppermost in mind; he includes all material bearing upon that purpose and those needs. In addition, he arranges the material in a logical sequence. To meet these requirements, always outline your material before you start writing.

Figure 32-1 shows a poorly organized memo (with real names and dates changed) that was distributed in a "sick" division of a national corporation. At the time, rumors were ricocheting wildly that the division was up for sale; top management was saying nothing. Understandably, morale plummeted. Employees concerned about their jobs were doing little work aside from updating their résumés. This situation was allowed to fester for days before the memo was issued.

Note that the key facts are buried in the fifth paragraph. They should have been headlined and highlighted, as in the reorganized memo (see Figure 32-2).

Figure 32-1. Original memo, with names and dates changed.

To: All Managers   Date: 6-18-80

From: J. L. Dunphy   Telephone: 4321
           Medical Instruments
           Division (MID)

Subject: Published statements concerning possible acquisition
           of MID by Zillion Corporation

On Thursday, June 12, the *Wall Street Financial News Wire*
carried the following news item:

"Zillion Corporation said there is absolutely nothing to rumors
that it is negotiating to buy ACE's Medical Instruments Division."

In response to inquiries generated by this news item, ACE
Corporation has also stated that this rumor has no basis in fact.

Although both Zillion and ACE have both stated that there is
no substance to this rumor, a number of newspapers, including
the *New York Sentinel,* carried the Wall Street news item with
the result that many of our employees, customers, suppliers,
and others with whom we do business will be exposed to this
rumor—either in the form of a denial, as published, or in a
distorted form that omits the denial.

In order to preclude further speculation on this subject, I
would like to make it clear to you that the management of
ACE is definitely not conducting discussions with Zillion and
has absolutely no intention of selling its Medical Instruments
Division to anyone.

It is important that you convey this fact to the members of
your organization, and anyone else you come in contact with,
should you be questioned with regard to this rumor.

                              J. L. Dunphy
                              Vice President and General Manager
                              ACE Medical Instruments Division

---

PRINCIPLES OF ORGANIZATION

Logical organization of a memo will help your readers understand the message. To achieve such organization, you must first know the underlying objective of your memo. Then you can proceed to the first two steps: Select all the information relevant to the objective and organize the information under major headings arranged in logical sequence.

Here are some approaches to organizing information:

Chronological. A historical account of a project may start at the very beginning, or may start with current happenings and "flashback" to earlier periods.

Geographical. A monthly memo reporting national sales figures

Figure 32-2. Same memo reorganized to highlight the two key facts. Memo is also "de-fatted."

Subject: Facts regarding Rumor of MID Acquisition by Zillion.

Fact 1. *Ace has no intention of selling its MID to Zillion Corporation or anyone else.*

Fact 2. ACE is not conducting discussions with Zillion or anyone else.

I urge you to convey these crucial facts to members of your departments and to anybody who asks about the rumor.

This rumor has appeared in many newspapers. For example, on June 12 the *Wall Street Financial News Wire* carried the following news item: "Zillion Corporation said there is absolutely nothing to the rumor that it is negotiating to buy ACE's Medical Instruments Division." A few days later the *N.Y. Sentinel* published the same item.

As a result of all the publicity, many of our employees, customers, suppliers, and other business associates have been exposed to this damaging rumor.

I consider it the highest priority that you clarify Facts 1 and 2 to everybody concerned.

---

may be broken down by regions and states. Other approaches may include: top to bottom, east to west, inside to outside, etc.

Known to unknown or simple to complex. Since you know more about the subject of your memo than your reader does, remember that what is simple to you may be complex to him.

General to specific. Here, you lead off with a general, comprehensive statement and then support it with specific examples. You may also reverse this, going from the specific to the general.

Cause and effect. In this arrangement, you discuss the causes of an event or situation and its effects. If the effects are more dramatic or startling, you may first discuss them and then the causes.

Question and answer. Here, you answer questions to arrive at a desired goal: informing readers, winning their goodwill, or convincing them to do what you want.

The problem, the analysis, the solution. State the problem, analyze it, and give its solution.

Functional. Mechanical or electrical products, for example, may be discussed according to their functions. This principle also applies to the functions of specialists (in marketing, research, product development, etc.).

Most important to least important. Recipients of your memo want to know quickly what is important, why, and what to do about it. That explains why conclusions and recommendations should often be placed at the beginning.

FRONT MATTER—ESSENTIAL HEADINGS

Every memo contains five essential headings at the top: (1) the name of the firm or company, (2) *To*, (3) *From*, (4) *Subject*, and (5) *Date*. These headings may appear in various sequences and positions.

Name of firm: This should be on all business stationery.

To: Use the recipients' first and last names without *Mr.*, *Mrs.*, or *Ms.*, but with a professional title such as *Dr.* or *Colonel*. If the memo is slated for several people, put their names after the *To* and before the *From*. But if the list is long, put only the primary recipient's name after *To*. The other names can go into a distribution list at the end of the memo.

From: Your name and title go here. In an informal memo, you may omit your title.

Subject: State the subject specifically in a dozen words or fewer, if at all possible. Notice that the subject line in Figure 32-1 does not even come close to the employees' basic question: What about us?

Date: All memos require dates.

FRONT MATTER—OPTIONAL HEADINGS

The front matter may also contain optional headings: references, memo number, attachments, addresses, and your telephone number.

References. References may be letters, memos, reports, or any other documents that pertain to the subject. If references are needed, number or letter them and give all the information necessary to retrieve them: titles, names of issuing organization and author, publication date, etc. In the memo text, refer to these documents by their assigned numbers or letters.

Attachments (or enclosures). Occasionally, a memo requires such attachments as photographs, tables, calculations, charts, copies of correspondence or contracts, etc. Handle attachments as you do references; see above. (Attachments are also discussed later on under back matter.)

Addresses of writer and readers. In large organizations (say, over 500 employees), spell out departmental and divisional names when departments and divisions are located in different geographical areas. Sometimes departments are assigned mail stop numbers to help expedite mail delivery. These names and numbers will ensure prompt delivery of your memos.

Writer's telephone number. It pays to include your phone number because telephone contact is a quick way to answer questions about your memos. Add your area code whenever necessary.

ELEMENTS OF MEMO TEXT

Some of the following elements of memo text are optional.

Summary. Every memo longer than two typed pages should open with a summary, preferably in five to ten lines. The summary should be written after the memo is written, in nontechnical, jargon-free language so that recipients at all levels can understand it.

This will help to decide in seconds whether they want to read the entire memo, a part of it, or just the summary.

Although a summary cannot supply all the facts, it gives their overall meaning and highlights the central idea. Items that belong in a summary include the following, if they are applicable: findings, conclusions, and recommendations. If space allows, procedures and any unusual circumstances may be mentioned.

If you anticipate favorable—or, at best, neutral—reactions to the memo, it's best to place the summary at the very beginning. In that prime position, it will get readers' undivided attention and let them know, quickly, the significance of the memo.

But if you expect a hostile reaction, a summary (especially one that states conclusions and recommendations) at the very beginning might turn off many people. Instead, lead off with a statement of the problem or situation, then discuss it objectively (but stressing advantages of your side), and close with conclusions and recommendations. With this approach, you may swing key readers around to your banner by the time they digest your analysis.

Introduction. The primary objective of an introduction is to get the reader "on board" so that he can understand the rest of the memo. You can orient him by stating in the first paragraph the purpose of the memo and the importance and scope of its subject. If you think the reader needs more background or a definition of terms, you can add another paragraph (or more) to the introduction.

This approach applies both to one-shot memos and to those that introduce a series of memos. Of course, if a memo is one of a series that has already started, the first sentence should plunge into the ongoing subject.

Many one-shot memos require no introduction at all. Memos announcing meetings, new lunch periods, promotions, vacation policies, transmittal of a document, etc. should state the necessary facts and stop. One paragraph may wrap it up.

Where both a summary and an introduction are appropriate, an alternate arrangement is to lead off with an "on-board" type of introduction and then move into a summary. You can, of course, omit from the summary any items covered in the introduction.

Other possible items for an introduction are:

A question or an answer to a question.
A thank-you statement.
A statement of good news or the approval of a proposal.

If the recipient's goodwill is important to you, there are two things to avoid in the first paragraph. Don't say *no*; instead, give him valid reasons for the turndown and, if possible, an alternative course of action. Then the *no* may not sting as much. Also avoid saying that he made a mistake. If you can, first give him a deserved compliment. If that is not possible, you may use the passive voice to salve the recipient's ego: "The wrong paint was ordered" rather than "You ordered the wrong paint."

Main discussion. The heart of a memo, its main discussion, may range from a few analytical paragraphs to pages of analysis. Although a memo must stick to one subject, the spectrum of subjects is almost unlimited. Here are a few: a new decision; a policy change; a request for information; a complaint or an answer to a complaint; minutes of a meeting; report of a trip.

Facts and figures characterize a main discussion that serves the readers. Information is what they need in order to make a decision or to successfully fulfill any other responsibility.

Here is where organizing skill enables you to marshall the information under various headings: statement of purpose, approach to the problem, account of work done, theory, equipment, methods, results and their analysis (including negative results), conclusions, recommendations, and plans for future work.

Conclusion (closing). As used here, the word "conclusion" means the end of a memo, not a decision reached on the basis of findings or results.

If your memo warrants a conclusion—and many do not—the conclusion should be brief and should include no new information or opinion. Since it comes last, it will probably fix the reader's impression of the whole memo. Above all, the conclusion should stress in new wording, the key idea and perhaps even the attitude that you want the reader to carry away.

Other possible items for a conclusion are a summary of major points, acknowledgment of assistance given, a look-ahead at work to be done, a critical question directed at the reader, a demand or request for action by the reader, or a request for an answer by a certain date.

BACK MATTER—OPTIONAL ELEMENTS

The complimentary closes and signatures used in letters are omitted from memos. You may or may not, however, sign your memo.

Distribution list. Memos are extremely flexible in distribution; they may go to one person or 1,000. Most memos, however, are aimed at fewer than a dozen people. In selecting recipients of memos on a long-term project, ask yourself two questions: Are these people involved with the project and, if they are not, should they be kept informed? If either answer is *yes*, add their names to the list. If your answer is not clear-cut, and if you're concerned with only a handful of people, ask them if they want the memos. Remember: You may waste time for your boss if you send him copies of all your memos.

Any memo dealing with a sensitive, controversial, or vitally important topic should, for self-protection, be sent to two or more people. Long after a weighty memo has been distributed, an only recipient who originally favored your position may later oppose you for personal or political reasons and may even claim that he didn't receive your memo. Sending it to others will at least partially disarm the opposition.

The principle of having back-up recipients also applies to any idea that you want to protect as your own. If you devise a new process, product, or marketing strategy, announce it in a memo—with one copy to your boss and copies to others concerned.

Arrangement of list. Names on a distribution list usually appear in alphabetical order, since most people readily accept that order. But if you know the recipients' ranks, you may list them by rank where this seems appropriate.

Placement of distribution list. If the list contains a dozen or fewer names, the logical place for it is after the *To,* provided there is enough room. A dozen names should fit on two lines. If the list is longer than two lines, place it at the end of the memo—but don't forget to reference it after the *To* (for example, *distribution list on page 3*).

Attachments. Attachments should provide evidence that supports and clarifies the subject of the memo. How much of the attachments should be included in the memo proper? Brief quotations or key points, or merely summaries of the attachments? Clear-cut answers depend on the circumstances surrounding the memo and on the readers' needs. Often it is impractical to include a multi-page attachment. But including a quotation or photograph or table from an attachment may well multiply the memo's effectiveness.

33

Developing a Meeting Memo

Tom Adams

We all complain about spending too much time in meetings, but the real crime related to meetings is not the loss of time but rather the failure, at the conclusion of the meeting, to clarify for all what was agreed to, what the assignments are, who will do what, and so forth. In other words, it is not the time spent in the meeting that is so costly but rather our failure to capitalize on the fruits of the meeting.

Although a quick review of the decisions reached, assignments given, and the like at the end of the meeting is well worth the time, perhaps a more effective technique is a meeting memo that captures the essential aspects of the meeting. Like most written communications, such a memo has an advantage over oral communications in that it is a permanent record of the conclusions reached.

From many years spent in attending meetings, I have determined what are essential elements in a good meeting memo. There are 13 in all, and each is shown in the accompanying sample. The memo format described will neither eliminate the need to know how

From *Supervisory Management*, July 1980.

to manage a meeting nor provide guidance in how to avoid having meetings, but it will enable you to make the best of it once you are there.

Before reading the descriptions below, take the time to examine the sample memorandum in Figure 33-1.

1. **To.** Here, you note the name of the person(s) to whom the group (meeting attendees) and its actions are ultimately responsible. The identity of this person or persons is usually obvious. If not, force it out. If those present at the meeting are responsible to different people—that is, the group is responsible to co-leaders—then the memo should be addressed to both of them. When the group is self-created, the memo should be addressed to the membership, that is, the attendees themselves.

2. **Via** (optional). The name of the person(s) between the author of the memo and the principal recipient of the memo, can be given. When "via" is used, it usually implies the concurrence of the content of the memo by the middle person. When this is not the intent, avoid its use. Sometimes the middle person wants to have room to "move"; if that's the case, then make him or her a co-receiver of the memo.

3. **From.** The name of the group leader, coordinator, facilitator, or chairperson goes here. It's the place for the name of the official "author" of the memo—not necessarily the person who wrote the memo. (In some organizations, letter- and memo-writing convention require the name of the sender to appear in the closing of the memo.)

4. **Date of memo.** Usually the date the memo is typed. Consider using the same date as the date of the meeting; it can help for later reference.

5. **Subject.** For recurring meetings, like ones devoted to discussion of project status, the work of task forces, and so forth, use a number with the subject title—for example, "Meeting #3—MIS Project Status." Be specific in titling; it can help later on. Instead of "Meeting Notes," use "Follow-up Meeting #2 on Paper Shortage."

6. **Date of meeting.** The date the meeting was held should be noted. You can include the day as well—for instance, January 4, 1980 (Friday).

7. **Attendees.** Here, you list the name and representing organization of each person attending the meeting. Consider including phone numbers and/or office addresses.

Figure 33-1. Sample memorandum.

To: Christine Howard, Chief
           Management Services Branch

Via: Barbara Rigby, Director
           Research Unit

From: Tom Adams, Technical Support Manager
           Research Unit (ext. 4616)

Date: January 7, 1980

Subject: Meeting #8 Statistical
           Reporting Work Group

January 4, 1980 meeting #8 attended by:
     Tom Adams (Research)   Russ Owen (Fiscal)
     Earlene Singer (Research)   Tony Garcia (Fiscal)
     Greg Brown (Research)   Elizabeth Johns (Fiscal)
     P.K. Drew (Consultant)   Alice Wilson (Management Support)

Action items
1. Elizabeth will call Earlene (Research) by next Monday (1-14-80) for Research's input into the design of the management audit team's utilization data questionnaire to be used in the initial audit sessions.
2. Three research staff persons will participate with Fiscal in the audit of the first facility (1-21-80). Earlene will be available to assist Elizabeth in the utilization audit. Greg and P.K. will conduct the special encounter date audit as a follow-up to the utilization audit.

Progress items
1. A revised schedule of the audits has been prepared by Fiscal (see Attachment 1).

Discussion items
1. How the audits could be combined was discussed. The revised schedule of visits (Attachment 1) shows that the planned financial audits have been shifted from two to three weeks and now are scheduled to conclude in early March. Greg (Research) commented that this delay may prohibit Research from participating as fully in the joint audits as had originally been hoped.

February 3, 1980 Meeting #9, to be held in Conference Room 1540 at 1:00 P.M. (Russ and Tony will present Fiscal's Data Quality Assessment.)

Attach.

cc: Statistical Reporting Work Group Members and their Management

8. **Action items.** This is where you list the decisions made and the agreements reached. Tie assignments to people by name. When possible, give target dates. The author can take slight license here to clarify agreements made. Often these are only partially formulated during the meeting itself; it's up to the author to bring clarity to the action items but always in the *spirit of the group*.

One note here: In the normal course of a meeting, action items are continually being generated. At the close of the meeting, even though a meeting memo is to be prepared, it is still a good practice to restate them for the attendees and gain their concurrence.

Action items are placed at the front of the meeting memo because they serve as a good lead-in for the next meeting.

9. **Progress items.** The status of projects and tasks of concern to the membership are recounted. In some situations, this is the main body of the memo. Entries here should be limited to status messages—state what has been accomplished since the last meeting, what is being worked on now, what the next milestones or accomplishments will be, and when they will occur (target date). Resist lengthy discussions; for details, refer the reader to other memos or reports on the subject.

10. **Discussion items.** This is the catchall column for items worth recording but not action items or status messages. Here is a good place to spell out those "For the Record" statements. Attention to detail and careful recording of key ideas and positions will be appreciated by both the attendees and the readers of the memo. The author should try here to be sensitive to the subtle differences and shifts in positions of attendees and try to capture those differences in words that help clarify positions and that can later be used to bring about consensus at subsequent meetings.

11. **Notice of next meeting.** The time, date, and location of the next meeting belongs here.

12. **Agenda of next meeting** (optional). For recurring meetings, the action items recorded in the previous meeting memo are usually the agenda for the next meeting. However, when possible, it is a good practice to state the major items of discussion planned for the next session.

13. **Recipients of copies of the memo.** This is where the "readers" of the memo are listed. People need to know who else is receiving the information contained in the memo. When the list of names to receive copies is long, you should include a statement such as, "Branch Managers and above."

34

Improve Your Report Writing

Marshall Smith

"I'm a supervisor, not a writer!" This reaction is understandable when you're struggling with an unwieldy report that's due in two hours. But the fact remains that a supervisor's reports can go far toward making or breaking him—especially in today's company, where a report may have to travel upward through many organizational levels.

When should you write a report? When you are assigned one, of course—but that is not the whole answer. Try assigning yourself a report on occasion. Self-assigned reports can help you solve problems and get things done.

Suppose, for instance, that you have discussed a project orally with your boss and failed to make your point. If he said *no* to the project because he didn't fully understand it, a carefully constructed report may well change his mind.

Sometimes it's best to skip altogether any preliminary discussion. If, for example, the person you want to communicate with is quick to cross swords in a conversation, or if the written word im-

From *Supervisory Management*, December 1968 and January 1969.

presses him more than the spoken one, simply get a report to him as soon as possible.

In any case, a written report gives you a chance to tell your entire story. You may be stopped if you try to do it orally.

The task of turning out a report is not an easy one. The necessary research, organization, writing and editing involved amount to hard work, even for professional writers. However, any normally intelligent person who applies his efforts in an organized, systematic way can write a good report.

GETTING ORGANIZED

Here are some steps that can help you go about writing a report in the most effective way.

1. *Define the report.* Be as precise as possible; if you don't know what direction you're headed in, you're lost before you start. Ask yourself—and answer—these questions:

What is the ultimate purpose of this report? What should it accomplish? Why should it be written?

How important is this report, and how much effort should I spend on it?

What kind of report is needed? Should it be a justification or recommendation report? If so, what should be recommended? If this is another attempt to justify a previously rejected project, what was the basis for rejection? What did previous reports contain, and why did they fail?

If this is a progress report, what functions, dates and subject matter are to be included? Is the project under fire? Should this progress report therefore serve as a combination progress and justification report? Perhaps it should combine a report on progress with a recommendation to cease, try another approach or expedite.

If it is a descriptive report, exactly what area or areas are to be described, and in what detail?

Who will read the report? Will it stop with my immediate boss or will it go on to his boss or beyond?

What are the requirements, prior knowledge and background of the person who will sign or take action on the report? This is the person I want to influence, the one I must communicate with.

Should this be a formal report, or should the style be casual? Is an outline or discussion draft needed before the final report is submitted?

When must the report be completed? Can it be completed during regular working hours, or should I plan to work extra hours?

2. *Pinpoint information sources and plan research procedures.* You can save a lot of time and effort by mapping out exactly how you're going to gather information for the report. For instance, you might list or outline all sources of information, their relative accessibility and the best time of day and week for consulting each. Sources include, of course, both people and documents.

When you can't borrow a document or have copies of it made, be prepared to take notes. In some cases it might be a good idea to arrange to use a dictating machine.

3. *Collect all pertinent information.* The more important the report, the greater the need for thoroughness in gathering information.

The information you gather can change the very nature of the report. What started out as a clear-cut, one-route trip may soon present several profitable alternate routes. Even a supervisor whose mind is made up on the subject before he starts his research may find new information that changes his thinking entirely.

If the report will require careful, accurate documentation, decide during this step how you're going to handle it. You may decide to use a bibliography, or you may decide to cite information sources in the body of the report. Whatever your choice, making it beforehand can avoid a lot of backtracking later on.

Even when all research appears to have been completed, ask yourself:

Have I overlooked any source?
Do I have all the information I need?
Could I try another approach?
Are my notes complete in all detail?
Have all alternate routes been explored?
Does my information conform to the purpose of the report?
Will this information help to achieve the desired result of the
report?

The answers may indicate that you should continue your research before going to the next step.

4. *Select and arrange in logical sequence the information to be used.* Before outlining or writing the report, study the information you collected and arrange it in logical sequence. Information that seemed inportant at the start may no longer be applicable. Some information may be put aside without further consideration.

Don't, however, discard the information that you won't be using in this report. File and keep all researched information until you are certain it cannot ever be used.

Arrange the remaining information in groups—placing like material with like material.

5. *Outline the report.* An outline is a form of advance planning, and advance planning can prevent wasted effort. In preparing an outline, you are organizing the information into a plan or pattern to follow when you start writing.

Some supervisors prefer to make a mental outline, without committing it to paper. Some supervisors outline by topic and subtopic, some by key words or phrases, some by sentences. As long as an outline serves the supervisor's purpose, it can be as detailed or sketchy as he desires.

An outline becomes more useful for long reports with several sections or in instances when the writing may be interrupted. After an interruption, even the barest outline can remind you of the plan you had in mind.

Another useful feature is that an outline permits you to concentrate on one topic at a time, in or out of sequence. You can work on setting up the section that interests you without worrying whether it's next in line. Then, when you've got it set up, you can fit it into its proper place in the outline.

Never let an outline hem you in. Remember that it is simply a pattern made of movable parts that can be adapted or adjusted to any changes you want to make.

GETTING IT DOWN ON PAPER

Getting started is the hardest part, even for professional writers. Facing that blank sheet of paper is an ordeal, and there are numerous ways to avoid it. You can get a drink of water. You can sharpen a pencil. You can think of something more pressing to be done at the moment.

The report, however, remains unwritten. You must put other thoughts aside, fasten yourself to your chair and start typing or writing.

It is said that you must be in the mood for writing—that inspiration must hit you before you can write well. This may be so.

But in most cases, the act of taking the plunge and applying all your concentration will induce the mood and the inspiration.

The supervisor who says that he can't enjoy writing has probably never stuck with it long enough to get into the right mood. By sticking with it long enough, he would experience the exhilaration that comes when previous effort and present concentration begin to pay off. When he hits this creative spurt he would rather wear the pencil down to a nub than get up to sharpen it. Or, if he uses a typewriter, his fingers can't move fast enough over the keyboard.

Keep Going

When you're in this creative phase, ignore such matters as spelling or finding the precise descriptive word. You can attend to these technicalities later. At the moment, you must focus all your concentration on getting the flow of your thoughts down on paper.

Any interruption or distraction can destroy the mood that is releasing your train of thought. You may have been able to do piecemeal research on the report, and you may later be able to edit it piecemeal, but the writing should be done at one sitting.

If the report is important to you, find a way to shut out all possibility of interruption. Executives can solve the problem by announcing that they are not to be disturbed and that their phone calls are to be held. But most report writers must find other methods.

One answer is to go to the company library or some other quiet place. Another is to write the report at home during working hours, if this can be arranged. Or you may have to schedule the writing for evening or early morning hours. When this is the case, schedule it for the time when you work best. One supervisor does his really important writing between 3:00 A.M. and 6:30 A.M. Before retiring early, he sets his alarm for 2:30 A.M.; he makes a pot of coffee immediately after he gets up. By the time he arranges his notes and gets everything in order on the dining room table, it is about 3:00 A.M., the coffee is ready and he is awake enough to begin the job. This supervisor finds that he can accomplish more good writing in the middle of the night than he could during an entire interruption-filled day at his office.

Choosing the time and place to write is clearly an individual matter. But if the report is reasonably important, choosing the right time and place is well worthwhile.

Where do you start in writing the report? With the first paragraph? It's true that the first paragraph is important. If the report doesn't interest the reader at the outset, he may never finish it.

You don't, however, have to begin at the beginning. Some professional writers always write the body of an article before attempting any kind of beginning or ending. This practice might be considered a violation of the outline you've set up. But those who follow this practice insist that it works. They point out that they often find lead paragraphs buried in the body of their article. After writing the body of the article, they select its most interesting phase, pull out that part, and shape it into the opening paragraph.

One successful writer of mystery novels never knows "who done it" until he has finished all but the last chapter in his first draft. Then he reads over the entire mystery and decides which character is the best candidate for guilt. After that, he writes the ending and, to make everything come out right, goes back through the other chapters and modifies them to fit the ending.

Another mystery writer uses an almost opposite approach. After determining the solution to a hypothetical crime, he writes the last chapter as his first step. Then he develops a cast of characters and works out a series of events leading to the last chapter.

Supervisors can adapt these approaches to report writing. One supervisor may find the going smoother if he begins at the beginning; another may not be able to focus on the report proper until he has worked out the conclusion.

Still another may find it easier to write the body of his report before he can write a hard-hitting introduction and a recommendation at the end that will clinch his case. Actually, he can start anywhere his interest leads him. He always has the outline to check for what must then be filled in or expanded.

Using Illustrations

What about illustrations—graphs, tables, charts, and the like? Properly used, they can be most effective. Some reports, in fact, may consist entirely of such illustrations, with a minimum of prose for explanatory purposes.

For a narrative report, here is a good rule of thumb: Use the illustration when it will add to the reader's comprehension of an important or complicated point. Remember, however, that there is no magic in visual illustration. A confusing tabulation, a hard-to-follow chart or a poorly executed graph will hinder rather than help comprehension.

EDITING WHAT YOU'VE WRITTEN

The next step is to edit what you've written. Getting the report down on paper is an accomplishment, but there is still more work to be done. To faciliate the physical task of editing, it's best to have what you've written retyped with double or triple spacing so that you can write in changes between the lines. Leaving a half-page margin on right or left makes room for more extensive editing.

Editing demands an entirely different mood from that of researching or writing. Cool objectivity is called for; self-criticism is a must. What seemed a compelling phrase in the fire of writing may on cooler inspection be nonsensical or objectionably florid. The fact of being in black and white does not transform the report into holy writ. In fact, the opposite is true; the first draft is only a starting point.

A routine report submitted in a standard manner at periodic intervals probably won't require extensive editing. But for an important report—one intended to represent you in an influential way—you cannot take too many pains.

The editing processes discussed below are presented separately for clarity. Actually, however, many of them can be combined into one.

It Takes Practice

With practice, you can learn to edit with fewer and fewer readings. The overall objective of the following processes is to get your meaning across in the clearest way possible for the greatest impact on your reader.

1. *Edit for logical sequence.* In the heat of writing the report, you may not have presented information in its most logical sequence. Even if you carefully followed a detailed outline, you may now find that certain paragraphs will be more effective in another location on the page. Or a sentence might have greater impact if you change its position within the paragraph.

Physically, there are various ways to rearrange parts of a report for better sequence. You may, for example, cut sections apart and paste or tape them together in a different order. You may use arrows and lines to indicate material to be transposed during the next typing. Or you may number or letter sections to denote the desired sequence. The method used is unimportant as long as it accomplishes its basic purpose; to present the information in logical

sequence from sentence to sentence and paragraph to paragraph—
leading the reader in an uninterrupted fashion to the conclusion.

2. *Edit for completeness.* At this stage, it's a good idea to ask
yourself these questions:

◇ Have I included everything of importance to the reader?
◇ If a statement or fact is likely to be questioned, have I
  furnished adequate documentation?
◇ Will the reader have any unanswered questions?
◇ Is the report complete in every respect?

When you are satisfied that your report is complete in every
detail for the reader, you should move on to exactly the opposite
approach.

3. *Edit for brevity.* The main question here is: Will the reader
need *all* the information that I have given him?

Read the report sentence by sentence, paragraph by paragraph
to determine what can be deleted without harming the report. You
may find that you can cut half of it without loss.

Massive surgery may in fact vastly improve the report's clarity
and conciseness. Sometimes a report may require many readings
and many deletions before it boils down to the point where it can
effectively accomplish its purpose.

During this process, you must be fully aware that you are
writing not for yourself, but for your reader. The overriding purpose
is to present the essential facts, uncluttered by extraneous, distracting information.

When you have cut the report to its bare bones, you are ready
for the next step.

4. *Edit to separate opinions from conclusions.* Have you included any of your opinions that are not justified by facts or supporting information?

Everyone is entitled to his opinion, but seldom in the context
of a report to someone else. If the opinion is fully justified by facts
and supporting information, it is a conclusion, not an opinion.

Opinions that are presented as conclusions can be traced to
unclear thinking. Make sure that there is a logical connection between a conclusion and the information upon which it is based.

Sometimes, of course, you may want to present your opinion as
such. Clearly label all opinions with such phrases as: "In my opinion
. . .", "In my judgment . . . ", "These facts suggest a tentative
conclusion . . ."

5. *Edit for accuracy*. You must check all statements, figures and facts for accuracy. Even one inaccuracy can cast doubt on the entire report.

6. *Edit for precise wording*. Do not, for example, write, "John Doe objected to performing the task" when you actually mean, "John Doe *refused* to perform the task."

If your report is to convey what you mean, you must pay careful attention to finding words that most clearly express your meaning.

Watch out, too, for vague claims; always specify the exact amount or degree of what was achieved. For example:

Cost improvement (how much?)
Time saved (how much?)
Material saved (how much?)
Quicker payout (how much quicker?)
Lower depreciation (how much lower?)
Fuller utilization (what percentage?)
Improved security (in what manner and to what extent?)
Greater efficiency (how so?)

7. *Edit for correct spelling and punctuation*. Everyone has access to a dictionary, so there is no excuse for any misspellings. If you're a poor speller, use the dictionary extensively; a misspelled word will detract from your report.

If you're unsure of punctuation, consult a good secretary or a manual on punctuation.

8. *Edit the title, the introduction, and the conclusion*. Special attention to these parts of your report will pay off.

Because the reader may form his opinion after reading only the title and the introduction, an inexact title and a weak introduction put the report in double jeopardy. Combine these with a weak conclusion, and the report has failed even if the body of the report is excellent.

If you edit in no other manner, rewrite and rewrite the title, the introduction and the conclusion.

When you've finished editing the report, rewrite or retype it for neatness and legibility. If you're submitting it in handwriting, rewrite or reprint it so that every letter is legible. If it is to be retyped, make sure that there are no smudges or strikeovers in it.

If time permits, put the report aside for a while. Forget about it as much as possible. Then re-edit it—again, critically and objectively. If you make major changes, retyping or rewriting will be necessary.

If at all possible, have someone else read the report to see if it makes sense to him. You know your intentions so well that you may have read them into the report instead of writing them into it. Carefully consider any recommendations made or questions asked by the trial reader and, if they're valid, change the report accordingly.

35

Write Clear Reports:
A "Readability" Index

Dan H. Swenson

The ability to get ideas across in writing is about the most useful skill a person can have. Evaluating the effectiveness of what we write is the first step in achieving good communication. To improve people's writing ability, Robert Gunning created his "Fog Index." The index is the most widely used "readability" formula in business, and it's the test we'll use in this discussion. Like other readability formulas, the Fog Index focuses on sentence length and word difficulty to determine the level of writing skill. By identifying readability in terms of grade level, the Gunning test is relatively simple to use and interpret.

OUR PURPOSE

Before we have a look at the Fog Index, the purpose of this test should be explained. A readability test provides feedback on the general reading level of a written document. This feedback can be

From *Supervisory Management*, September 1980.

an indication of the appropriateness (in terms of reading ease and comprehension) of the writing for a particular audience.

Generally, we gain our greatest comprehension from material we can read easily, slightly below the level of our reading ability. Most business reports should not exceed the 11th or 12th grade level of readability. Of course, specialized or technical business reports may exceed this. However, when reports exceed the 14th and 15th grade level, they may be understood only by a few.

The Fog Index, like other formulas, only serves as a guide. "It is a warning system, not a formula for writing," Robert Gunning cautioned. Readability tests are only one check on writing clarity and effectiveness. Since your report must be understood, you will want to consider every means of improving it *before* you send it on. But if a readability test indicates that you are way off the mark in terms of what your intended audience will comprehend, you may have a substantial rewriting job ahead.

By all means, simplify your writing. Where you can, use short words instead of long ones, simplicity instead of complexity. Keep your sentences short. But don't go to the opposite extreme: don't write "primers" for reports. Although you may read that the average sentence length for most business reports is 17 words, don't restrict your writing to 17-word sentences.

THE FOG INDEX

The Gunning Fog Index is used to signal "fog" in writing. Fog clouds meaning for the reader and can be created in many ways. Two major sources of fog are sentence length and word difficulty. When sentences are too long and words too big, fog appears.

In some business writing the fog gets so thick that only a knife can cut it. This is especially true in writing designed to impress rather than to inform. Some "bureaucratic" reports, for example, abound with pseudotechnical words strung together for this purpose. Gerald Cohen's *Dial-A-Buzzword* describes such a vocabulary. He calls it "phrase building," a process of creating vague but impressive buzzwords by connecting almost any three polysyllabic words together. For example, such phrases as "integrated interactive analysis," "overall capabilities criteria," or "modular parameters performance," are nearly incomprehensible unless accompanied by definitions. And such phrases should be avoided *unless* accompanied by definitions.

The Fog Index can detect such "pompous" writing. This is its value.

APPLICATION

The Fog Index is calculated by the following steps:

1. Select one or more samples. Count out 100 consecutive words at random. If you are testing a lengthy report, two or more samples may be taken. Count each word, even "a's" and "i's". Do not count figures that are not spelled out. Count hyphenated words as one word.

2. Find the average number of words per sentence. This is done by dividing the total words in the sample by the number of sentences.

3. Find the percent of difficult words in the sample. Count the number of difficult words and divide by the total number of words.
   ◦ *Include* each word of three syllables or more as a difficult word.
   ◦ *Exclude* words of three syllables or more that are capitalized (except words that are capitalized because they start sentences).
   ◦ *Exclude* words of three syllables or more that are formed by two simple words, such as "chairperson" or "businessman."
   ◦ *Exclude* verb forms of three syllables in which the third syllable is *es* or *ed*, such as "processes" or "converted."

4. Add the average number of words per sentence and the percent of difficult words. Then, multiply this sum by .4 in order to determine the readability level (in terms of grade level).

Here's an example. Follow these four steps:

Step 1: Just count out 100 consecutive words.
Step 2: Assume there are *eight* sentences in the sample.

$$\frac{100 \text{ words}}{8 \text{ sentences}} = 12.5 \text{ words per sentence}$$

Step 3: (Assume 15 difficult words in the sample.)

$$\frac{15 \text{ difficult words}}{100 \text{ words}} = .15 \text{ difficult words}$$

Multiply .15 by 100 for the next step. Thus, .15 × 100 = 15.
   Step 4:

$$
\begin{array}{r}
12.5 \text{ words per sentence} \\
+ \ \underline{15} \quad \text{difficult words per 100} \\
27.5 \\
\times \ \underline{0.4} \\
11 \quad \text{grade level of readability}
\end{array}
$$

   If this calculation had yielded 11.7, for example, it would be read as 11th year (grade level) and 7th month.

   Here is an application of how the Fog Index works. Take this example:

> A presidentially appointed interagency Task Force on Workplace Safety and Health, birthed by President Carter's campaign promise to relieve businesses of excessive OSHA-type regulations, will soon release recommendations on incentives supplementing OSHA regulations, duplications and gaps in federal agency jurisdiction, and ways to improve the safety and health efforts of all federal agencies. The task force also examined the possibility of more closely stabilizing worker compensation insurance premiums with injury rates, establishing an injury tax so that more of the burden of injuries would be on the employer, eliminating the tax deductibility of excessive workplace injury costs, and giving credits for reducing injury costs.

   First, you try it. After you have completed your test, compare your results with these.

   Step 1: The sample contains *104* words.

   Step 2: The sample contains *two* sentences. So, the average number of words per sentence is determined by dividing 104 by 2:

$$
\frac{104}{2} = 52 \text{ words per sentence}
$$

   Step 3: The sample contains 32 difficult words. "Appointed," "Interagency," and "president" were excluded as difficult words in accordance with the rules previously stated. So, the percent of difficult words is determined by dividing 32 by 104:

$$
\frac{32}{104} = .3077 \times 100 = 30.77
$$

Step 4:

$$\begin{array}{r} 52 \quad \text{words per sentence} \\ \underline{30.77} \text{ difficult words} \\ 82.77 \\ \times \quad \underline{.4} \\ 33.1 \quad \text{grade level of readability} \end{array}$$

The Fog Index in this sample is 33.1—33rd grade-level plus one month! And the sample is from an actual business document, a newsletter prepared by a company for its employees!

Here is another writing sample:

In order to maintain stability in the workforce and help ease the situation connected with the dislocation of employees due to some major changes in our operations, the following procedures should be followed:

No full-time employee is to be hired in the company without first checking to see whether there is a qualified person elsewhere in the company available for the job. Ralph Johnson will act as a clearinghouse for all new hires or layoffs. He will attempt to match jobs and people, considering their qualifications. He will also instigate the necessary procedures in order to accomplish this objective. Supervisors will be asked to evaluate qualifications of all persons involved in these moves.

Step 1: The sample contains *113* words.

Step 2: The sample contains *six* sentences.

$$\frac{113}{6} = 18.83 \text{ words per sentence}$$

Step 3: The sample contains 23 difficult words. The verb "connected" was excluded.

$$\frac{23}{113} .2035 \times 100 = 20.35 \text{ difficult words.}$$

Step 4:

$$\begin{array}{r} 18.83 \text{ words per sentence} \\ + \quad \underline{20.35} \text{ difficult words} \\ 39.18 \\ \times \quad \underline{0.4} \\ 15.67 \text{ or } 15.7 \text{ grade level in readability} \end{array}$$

This would be fine if all employees could read at the senior-college level. But they can't.

How would you rewrite the memo in order to cut the fog? Rewrite it, then compare your work with the following:

We have made some *operational* changes to upgrade our firm. These changes may result in some job changes and new *opportunities*. To help in this process, these steps will be taken:

1. Our employees will be informed and given first priority in consideration for new job opportunities within our firm.
2. Mr. Ralph Johnson will handle all new hires and lay-offs.
3. Further, Mr. Johnson will attempt to match new jobs with our present employees where he can. He will set up the procedures to do this.
4. Supervisors will be asked to assess the qualifications of those involved in these moves.

Step 1: The sample contains 98 words.
Step 2: The sample contains *eight* sentences.

$$\frac{98}{8} = 12.25 \text{ words per sentence}$$

Step 3: The sample contains 10 difficult words.

$$\frac{10}{98} = .102 \times 100 = 10.2 \text{ difficult words}$$

Step 4:

$$
\begin{array}{r}
12.25 \text{ words per sentence} \\
+ \; 10.20 \text{ difficult words} \\
\hline
22.45 \\
\times \; 0.4 \\
\hline
8.98 \text{ grade level in readability}
\end{array}
$$

Now this is more like it. The readability level of the memo is the 9th grade. The memo was rewritten to gain economy and clarity in expression. Unnecessary words, particularly difficult words, were eliminated. More sentences were used. Some sentences were numbered.

CUTTING THE FOG

Here are some suggestions for cutting fog:

1. Eliminate unnecessary words—long and short.

2. Write concise but thoughtful sentences. Don't make a sentence do the work of a paragraph. Write naturally. Use long and short sentences. Don't just write in long sentences.

3. Enumerate your sentences and paragraphs. This will help you organize your thoughts into logical units for the reader's consumption.

4. Prefer the simple words to the complex ones.

5. Don't use words to impress and confound.

6. Don't use words of which you are uncertain.

7. If your expression or meaning gets tangled in a sentence or paragraph, don't leave it for the reader to untangle.

8. Omit the needless repetition of words.

9. Don't start sentences with "There" and "It" if they don't refer to something specific. Too often they become "nonsensical subjects," being not only vague, but also requiring more words in the attempt to communicate. For example, in "There is a possibility that the report is in error," to what does "there" refer? Identify the subject by saying: "The report may be in error." This does a clearer job with fewer words. In, "It is my opinion that the report may be in error," to what does "it" refer? "It" sets up a need for a long, passive expression. Say instead: "I think the report may be wrong."

10. Minimize the use of "thingified" words. Thingified words are verbs that have been changed to nouns. When this change is made, the word often becomes polysyllabic. Thingified words can be recognized easily because they end in *-ent, -ing-,* and *-ion.* Like nonsensical subjects, thingified words often require more words to say less. An example: "The discussion went on for hours." Say instead: "They talked for hours." Or: "We can provide the management." Say instead: "We can manage." Or: "Delivering is our business." Say instead: "We deliver."

And you'll deliver.

36

Job Descriptions— Critical Documents, Versatile Tools

Richard I. Henderson

Have you looked at your job description lately? Or those of your subordinates? If you haven't, you may be in for a surprise. However accurate they were when originally written, chances are that they don't accurately reflect the jobs as they stand now. Why? Because departments and units, and the jobs within them, are like living organisms—they expand; they contract; they move up, down, and sideways; sometimes they merge. It's a good idea to jot down changes in jobs as they occur, in preparation for the day when job descriptions are updated.

But although job descriptions are not etched in stone, once and for all time, they are quite important—to you and to your organization. And the continuing emphasis on complying with such federal legislation as the Equal Pay Act and the Equal Employment Opportunity Act makes them more important than ever before. They are,

From *Supervisory Management*, November 1975.

for example, critical documents in any dispute over qualifications required for specific jobs, equal pay for equal work, and the like.

Before examining the structure and development of job descriptions, let's take a look at their many uses in an organization. Their main areas of use are in (1) personnel administration, (2) compensation administration, (3) legal compliance, and (4) collective bargaining. (Smaller organizations may not have any job descriptions; larger organizations may have them only for higher management. And the organizations that have job descriptions for all employees may not avail themselves of all their possible uses.)

PERSONNEL ADMINISTRATION

Well-written, up-to-date job descriptions give organizations a key tool in planning human resource requirements and in using human resources properly. A brief look at some major functions within personnel administration underscores this point.

Manpower planning. Used in conjunction with organization charts, manning charts, and functional statements, job descriptions identify the work to be performed in particular jobs and show the interrelationships of these jobs with others in the organization. A systematic review of them can reveal manpower gaps or superfluous positions.

Recruiting and screening. The person who recruits and screens candidates for a vacant job is seldom the one responsible for its performance. An accurate job description is vital in giving recruiting and screening personnel a clear picture of what the job is all about.

Hiring and placement. The responsibility for final selection and placement is normally shared by a personnel specialist and the immediate supervisor. In cases where the personnel specialist has total responsibility, however, he must rely heavily on the specifications concerning knowledge, responsibility, and physical working requirements in the job description. If these are not clear, he or she will be hard put to find a candidate whose qualifications match those required by the job.

Current pressures from government and society mandate the appropriate application of various testing procedures used in screening, hiring, and placement. That is, any tests given must be strictly in line with job requirements—a constraint that leads us, once again, to the importance of an accurate, up-to-date description of job duties and responsibilities.

Orientation. Letting a prospective employee or new hire review and analyze the job description helps him get a more complete picture of what will be expected of him, compare that picture with his current image of himself, and judge how the picture presented meshes with his expectations and aspirations.

Training and development. Really current job descriptions enable those responsible for training and development to tailor their programs in ways that will prepare employees for the demands of the job today and tomorrow. Well-written job descriptions identify the specific education, experience, and skills required for adequate performance.

Career ladders. Accurate job descriptions are the links used in developing upward-mobility programs—programs that may be a part of a company's affirmative action efforts. Personnel specialists scrutinize them for relationships among jobs and focus on those indicating that the education, experience, and skills gained in one job can lead to the next step or job in a career-ladder program. The process also identifies areas in which a candidate is deficient—a state that he or she must remedy through some form of education or training before an upward move is possible.

COMPENSATION ADMINISTRATION

Any compensation system requires the evaluation and classification of jobs in terms that relate each to the others. This, of course, is what good job descriptions do. Consider, for example, these compensation-related matters:

Job evaluation. Nothing is so basic to the design of equitable compensation structure as the development of job descriptions that permit differentiation among jobs according to their respective knowledge and responsibility requirements.

Grading and classification. The development of appropriate grade levels, classifications, or families of jobs begins with the proper description of each job. From such descriptions, common job elements are identified. With the description of sufficient common—and uncommon—elements, it is possible to group jobs into families, grades, or classes.

Compensation surveys. Such surveys are meaningless without some basis for comparing results. Here, again, job descriptions give work pictures that enable organizations with widely varying outputs to compare pay practices for the jobs they have in common.

Pay structure. "A fair day's pay for a fair day's work" is more a relative consideration than an absolute one. What's *fair*? How much *work*? How much *pay*? The pay structure must deal equitably with these questions in identifying and assessing contributions and rewarding accordingly. One of the first steps in developing an equitable pay structure arises in the accurate and valid description of jobs.

Standards of performance. A job description that accurately identifies both job content and accountabilities (results of satisfactory performance) provides a basis for developing performance standards. These standards are, of course, critical matters during a supervisor's appraisal of subordinates' performance and any consequent recommendations for pay raises, promotions, and the like.

LEGAL COMPLIANCE

Changes in government legislation—as well as changing emphasis in enforcement patterns—have highlighted the importance of the job description. Here are some of the major legislative acts bearing upon employers' treatment of and dealings with employees.

Fair Labor Standards Act (FLSA). Although this is certainly not a new influence in the world of work, revisions in some of the Department of Labor regulations have forced organizations to take another look at the impact of the FLSA. Jobs included within the exempt and nonexempt categories have had some redefinition. When job descriptions are used to support exempt status, they must accurately identify the work *actually* being performed; the work activities and requirements specified in the job descriptions must meet with FLSA exemption criteria.

Equal Pay Act. The job description is a primary defense when an organization is accused of paying a lower wage rate to an employee of the opposite sex for performing—under similar conditions—work requiring equal skill, effort, and responsibility. The job description should clearly identify the degree of skill, effort, and responsibility required as well as the conditions under which the job is to be performed.

Title VII of The Civil Rights Act (Equal Employment Opportu-

nity Act of 1964). This act makes it an unlawful employment practice for an employer to discriminate against any individual with
respect to hiring; compensation; or terms, conditions, and privileges
of employment because of race, color, religion, sex, or national origin. This act in no way prohibits an organization from hiring or promoting on the basis of qualifications and merit. It does, however,
place the burden of proof concerning qualifications or merit on the
organization. Again, the job description is a valuable management
tool—for defining the requirements of a job and setting the base
standards for job performance. Accurate identification of employment standards as well as the identification and elimination of artificial employment barriers will help any organization meet EEOC
mandates. (Artificial employment barriers arise when job duties are
essentially unrelated to the primary content of the job or when the
job calls for the employee to perform duties significantly above the
normal level of duties required on that job.)

Occupational Safety and Health Act (OSHA). Most job descriptions contain a section that describes job conditions. This is especially true of jobs with elements that endanger the health of the job
holder or elements that are considered dirty, distasteful, or otherwise unsatisfactory by most people. These safety and health considerations should be specified in the job description. (Naturally, too,
the company must have in effect measures to protect employees
against dangerous conditions and comply with OSHA standards.)

COLLECTIVE BARGAINING

A key labor principle is equal pay for equal work. Many union demands focus on the inequity of varying pay rates for similar work or
on an imbalance in wage structure among comparable organizations.
The job description provides a stepping-stone for standardization in
pay rates for similar kinds of work. If a union urges uniform rates
indiscriminately and unjustifiably, the organization must defend itself by (1) recognizing and identifying jobs that are truly similar and
(2) protecting pay levels that discriminate among jobs because they
require different levels of knowledge and responsibilities and provide different contributions.

Figure 36-1 shows a job description of an exempt position.
Later on, we'll go into greater detail concerning elements of the job
description. In the meantime, here's a brief look at each.

Figure 36-1. Job description of an exempt position.

Supervisor of Data Processing Operations
Job Title

Exempt	012.168
Status	*Job Code*
July 3, 1975	Olympia, Inc.—Main Office
Date	*Plant/Division*
Arthur Allen	Data Processing—Information Systems
Written by	*Department/Section*
Juanita Montgomery	12 740
Approved by	*Grade/Level Points*
Manager of Information Systems	14,800-17,760-20,720
Title of Immediate Supervisor	*Pay Range*

SUMMARY

Directs the operation of all data processing, data control, and data preparation requirements. Performs other assignments as required.

JOB DUTIES

1. Follows broadly based directives.
   .1 Operates independently.
   .2 Informs Manager of Information Systems of activities through weekly, monthly, and/or quarterly schedules.
2. Selects, trains, and develops subordinate personnel.
   .1 Develops spirit of cooperation and understanding among work-group members.
   .2 Ensures that work-group members receive specialized training as necessary in the proper functioning or execution of machines, equipment, systems, procedures, processes, and methods.
   .3 Directs training involving teaching, demonstrating, and advising users on productive work methods and effective communication in data processing.
3. Reads and analyzes wide variety of instructional and training information.
   .1 Applies latest concepts and ideas to changing organizational requirements.
   .2 Assists in developing and/or updating manuals, procedures, specifications, and other matters relating to organizational requirements and needs.
   .3 Assists in the preparation of specifications and related evaluations of supporting software and hardware.
4. Plans, directs, and controls a wide variety of operational assignments performed by five to seven subordinates; works closely with other managers, specialists, and technicians within Information Systems as well as with managers in other departments and with vendors.
   .1 Receives, interprets, develops, and distributes directives ranging from the very simple to the highly complex and technological in nature.
   .2 Establishes and implements annual budget for department.
5. Interacts with people representing a wide variety of units and organizations.
   .1 Communicates both personally and impersonally, through oral and written directives and memoranda, with all involved parties.
   .2 Attends meetings of professional organizations in the field of data processing.

ACCOUNTABILITIES

Successful completion of scheduled activities. Increased use of facility services through expansion of user understanding and satisfaction with delivered product.

Figure 36-1. *(continued)*

JOB SPECIFICATION

Factor	Subfactor	Degree	Substantiating Data	Points
Knowledge	Education	5+	Requires knowledge of theory and concepts related to hardware and software applications. A minimum of a four-year business administration program preferred, with technical school certificate or CDP certificate required.	98
Knowledge	Experience	6+	Must have at least five years of experience and training in data-processing operations, data preparation, and programming.	130
Knowledge	Skill	7−	Requires great skill in interpersonal contact as well as technological skill in methods, systems, and equipment used in data-processing operations.	95
Problem Solving	Interpretation	5+	Analyzes and evaluates broad amount of theoretical and technical knowledge on the efficient use of data-processing resources and their effective interface with human resources.	78
Problem Solving	Compliance	4	Develops from both specific and abstract sources directives and procedures that are understandable by the operating personnel responsible for output.	42
Problem Solving	Communication	6	Requires broad communication abilities. Must be able to communicate technical or sophisticated concepts in simple terminology/basic language. Must maintain liaison with other departments and hardware vendors.	123
Decision Making	Interpersonal	5−	Frequently exchanges routine and nonroutine information as well as "state of the art" knowledge; instructs, coaches, trains, and counsels subordinates and nonsubordinates performing similar assignments in their work areas; closely coordinates activities involving other managers.	73
Decision Making	Managerial	4	Receives general supervision with broad guidelines; directs small group of subordinates performing technical functions in operation of data-processing system within a multi-programming environment.	53
Decision Making	Assets	4	Has some opportunity for influencing planning and control of rather narrow field involving capital assets valued at less than $500.000. Assists in establishing, implementing, and controlling budget for the operation and training of personnel and the purchase of material at less than $150.000.	48

Total Points: 740

THE MAKEUP OF A JOB DESCRIPTION

Although there is no universal description form, a complete job description should contain the following sections: job identification, job summary, job duties (including descriptions of any dangerous, dirty, or uncomfortable assignments), accountabilities, and job specification. (If there is no job specification section, there must be an employment standards section—to follow the job duties section.) A format commonly followed in job descriptions is to place the job identification, job summary, job duties, and accountabilities sections on one side of the page, with the job specification section on the other.

Job identification. This section contains such information as job title, status (exempt or nonexempt), job code (if any), date written or revised, location of job by plant/division, department/section, title of immediate superior, grade/level and points (if used in the evaluation process), pay range, signature of the person writing the description, and signature of the person approving it.

Job summary. This section is a brief, narrative picture of the job that highlights its general characteristics. In a few carefully selected and presented words, it indicates clearly and specifically what the job holder must do on his or her job. It provides sufficient information to identify the major functions and activities of the job and differentiate them from those of other jobs. This section is especially valuable for a quick overview of the job.

Job duties. Duty statements describe activities that must be accomplished in the performance of the job and for which specific accountabilities can be set. Normally, measures of performance can be applied to these duty statements, and they can be used as a basis for setting the primary goals of the job.

This section represents a summary, usually in outline form. It is not meant to be all-inclusive, but rather to describe duties related to major performance requirements. Normally, one sentence may describe each major duty or responsibility. In developing this section, the writer must not fall into the trap of doing a task analysis or breakdown. This area contains major *duties* and *responsibilities,* not the *tasks* necessary for their performance.

Accountabilities. This section briefly describes the major end results achieved when job duties are performed satisfactorily. It serves as a guide in setting performance goals and standards; it is useful as a reference in preparing performance appraisals.

Job specification. This important section describes the human qualities necessary to perform the job. It gives a rundown on compensable factors selected by the organization to determine the worth and value of the job. (Compensable factors are those that identify qualities common to many jobs. Although various compensable factors have been used by various organizations, some of the more common factors are knowledge, skill, responsibility, working conditions, effort, physical requirements, problem solving, know-how, decision making. Later, we will take up the matter of compensable factors in greater detail.) It describes the degree of quality required for the particular job under consideration. This factor analysis of the job provides the basic data for evaluating it and comparing it with other jobs.

Properly developed, the job specification serves as employment standards for the job. The organization that does not use an evaluation system based on compensable factors must develop an employment standards section that accurately describes the necessary knowledge and the physical and emotional requirements demanded of the incumbent. The job specification or employment standards section is extremely important—not only because it prescribes the standards for selection and promotion, but also because it regulates the pay of the job. The rise of affirmative action programs mandates that the qualifications specified be bona fide occupational qualifications and that there be a demonstrated relationship between qualifications and job.

DIFFERENTIATING BETWEEN JOB AND POSITION DESCRIPTION

In discussing job descriptions, it's necessary to note that some companies distinguish between *job descriptions* and *position descriptions*. Before seeing how, let's look at the way the U.S. Department of Labor defines *position* and *job*:

Position: a collection of tasks constituting the total work assignments of a single worker. There are as many positions as there are workers in the organization.

Job: a group of positions that are identical with respect to their major or significant tasks and are sufficiently alike to justify their being covered by a single analysis. There may be one or more persons employed in the same job.

Organizations that differentiate between job descriptions and position descriptions usually do so on the following basis:

Position description	*Job description*
Exempt	Nonexempt
Upper and middle management	All others
Upper and middle management and professionals	All others

In making such differentiations, organizations usually assume that it is more difficult to describe positions precisely. Thus, they require a more general narrative form for describing positions than for describing jobs.

Many specialists in this area, however, feel that such a separation is unnecessary. If you take the viewpoint that all members of an organization are responsible to some extent for planning their own work activities, solving problems, and making decisions connected with their jobs, there is no need to differentiate between job and position descriptions. The same format and procedures apply to the most senior job in the organization and to the lowest as well.

GETTING IT ON PAPER

Now for the actual writing of a job description. The objective is to write one that is brief but accurate and useful for a variety of management functions. Success in writing it depends on information available to the writer. A combination of the job-analysis data and the writer's own knowledge can produce a job description that will be a valuable job-information tool.

Even in companies where information is gathered by a job analyst, the person who writes the first draft may be the incumbent. By the time the final version appears, several people may have gotten in on the act, including the incumbent's superior, his or her superior, and perhaps the analyst's superior in the personnel department.

The kind and number of participants in this writing stage are affected in part by the person in charge of the job-description program. If the company has never before had job descriptions, the program is often initiated by a fairly high-level executive. But if the program is designed for the rewriting of existing descriptions, a lower-level executive—usually in the personnel department—is placed in charge.

Earlier, we showed a sample position description for a managerial job. Now let's look at a sample description for a nonsupervisory position—shown in Figure 36-2. (To compare this lower-level job description with a managerial position description, see Figure 36-1.)

In discussing the writing of a job description, we'll do so by taking up, section by section, the description format we've followed throughout, using Figure 36-2 for reference.

Remember that the format discussed is designed to fit into two pages, preferably the front and back side of a single sheet of paper. The front side contains the identification, summary, duties, and accountabilities sections, with the specification section on the reverse side. Whatever format is used, all organizational job descriptions should follow it. Those writing descriptions should receive similar instructions and follow identical guidelines so that, in total, the job descriptions will provide a common basis for comparison in determining equitable compensation structure.

Job Identification

Note in Figure 36-2 that the job identification section contains lines for entering job title, status, code, date, writer, approver, title of immediate supervisor, plant/division, department/section, grade/level, and pay range. For organizational purposes, the identification section is the first cut at defining the job and establishing a ranking order with other jobs. It outlines department, division, or functional groupings and serves as a guide for career ladder or upward-mobility programs.

Job title. The most important element in the identification section is the job title. A job title that correctly and precisely identifies the job is valuable (1) to the jobholder, (2) for purposes of job relationships, and (3) for comparison purposes with comparable jobs in other organizations.

The job title indicates to anyone reviewing the job description its field of activity, its relationship to that field, and its professional standing. (Incidentally, any job title should afford the jobholder some prestige and personal satisfaction.) The title should be as specific as possible—"Payroll clerk," for example, rather than "clerk." Every effort should be made to eliminate any reference to sexual identification in the title.

The job title is especially important in comparing a job with jobs in other organizations. This comparison process is critical in the development and utilization of wage and salary surveys and for recruiting purposes. To achieve a basis for comparison, job titles

Figure 36-2. Job description of a non-exempt position.

Computer Operator	
Job Title	
Non-Exempt	213.382
Status	*Job Code*
July 1, 1975	Olympia, Inc.—Main Office
Date	*Plant/Division*
Arthur Allen	Data Processing—Information Systems
Written by	*Department/Section*
Juanita Montgomery	7 406
Approved by	*Grade/Level Points*
Senior Computer Operator	$7,800—$9,360—$11,232
Title of Immediate Supervisor	*Pay Range*

SUMMARY

Operates digital computer and peripheral equipment under general supervision. Performs other assignments as required.

JOB DUTIES

1. Follows specific technical and scheduling directives.
    .1 Follows technical directives and assigned schedules under spot-check supervision.
    .2 Processes data according to defined procedures and schedules.
2. Operates digital computer and associated peripheral equipment.
    .1 Monitors equipment; maximizes operating time; minimizes program errors.
    .2 Analyzes error messages; identifies possible causes.
    .3 Notifies proper authorities of machine malfunctions and program errors.
    .4 Corrects errors within specified areas of authority and responsibility.
    .5 Stores outputs and completed inputs in proper location.
    .6 Performs preventive maintenance as specified.
3. Reviews and analyzes data inputs.
    .1 Recommends changes in scheduling and application to maximize efficient use of equipment.
    .2 Assists in testing new applications.
4. Maintains logs and records.
    .1 Details individual running time of each program.
    .2 Records all equipment malfunctions and program errors.
5. Receives, stores, and maintains D.P.C. inventory.
    .1 Unloads delivery truck.
    .2 Maintains stockroom in orderly manner.
    .3 Maintains stock records.
    .4 Notifies appropriate authorities of inventory requirements.

EMPLOYMENT STANDARDS

1. Knowledge and ability:
    .1 Must know basic principles of operating a digital computer and associated peripheral equipment.
    .2 Must be able to read and understand technical computer operation manuals.
    .3 Must be able to follow prescribed standards and procedures.
    .4 Must be able to follow computer scheduling instructions.

Figure 36-2. *(continued)*

2. Physical requirements:
   .1 Must be able to lift and store 60-lb. boxes.
   .2 Must be able to load and off-load 20-lb. disk packages.
   .3 Must be able to stand for ten hours a day.
3. Emotional demands:
   .1 Must be able to withstand relatively high pitch and levels of noise.

ACCOUNTABILITIES

Timely completion of assigned schedules.
Prompt recognition of machine malfunctions.

JOB SPECIFICATION

Factor	Subfactor	Degree	Substantiating Data	Points
Knowledge	Education	4	Requires completion of vocational-technical program or equivalent on-the-job training.	64
Knowledge	Experience	4	Equivalent on-the-job training may be up to one year.	64
Knowledge	Skill	5	Requires ability to operate medium-size computer and peripheral equipment.	63
Problem-Solving	Interpretation	4−	Analyzes error messages and takes corrective action in accord with procedures manuals and operating practices.	38
Problem-Solving	Compliance	4−	Requires ability to read and understand technical computer operations manual.	37
Problem-Solving	Communication	4	Must maintain records of operation and communicate results.	53
Decision-Making	Interpersonal	2+	Notifies authorities of machine malfunctions and program errors.	28
Decision-Making	Managerial	3−	Follows technical direction and assigned schedules under spot check supervision. Has no supervisory responsibilities.	35
Decision-Making	Assets	2+	Has some opportunity for influencing the planning and control of work assignments.	24

Total Points: 406

must be kept current and jobs with similar duties and similar requirements must have the same or a similar title. The *Dictionary of Occupational Titles*, (to be discussed shortly in the job-code section) gives valuable aid in settling on titles for this purpose.

Job status. This section permits quick and easy identification of the *exempt* or *non-exempt* status of the job in relation to its compliance with Fair Labor Standards Act requirements.

Job code. The job code permits easy and rapid referencing of all organizational jobs. The code may consist of letters or numbers in any combination—though each code must, of course, have enough characters to cover all jobs in the organization. It could be a four-character alpha-numeric code (B 735, for example) or a six-character numeric code (213.382, the code in Figure 36-2) as used by the U.S. Department of Labor, Manpower Administration in its *Dictionary of Occupational Titles* (DOT), or any other suitable combination.

The DOT can serve as an outstanding guide for developing job descriptions. It not only contains job titles and an excellent method for coding jobs, but also describes work performed, worker requirements, clues for relating applicants and requirements, and training and methods of entry for specific types of work. The two volumes of the DOT provide a fundamental guide for job-comparison purposes among all organizations.

A brief review of the manner in which the DOT utilizes its six-character code will aid any organization that develops its own code or that uses the DOT code. Let's look at 213.382, the DOT code for a computer operator (see Figure 36-2). The first three digits—213—signify occupational group arrangement:

2   —Clerical and sales occupations.
21 —Computing and account recording.
213—Automatic data-processing equipment operator.

The second three digits—.382—represent worker trait arrangement (respectively, to data, people, and things).

.3   —Computing (data).
.38 —No specific relationship (to people).
.382—Operating-controlling (things).

The other elements in the job-identification section are more or less self-explanatory. The date is the one on which the final version was written. It should be noted that some organizations dispense with *plant/division, department/section, grade/level, points,* and *pay range* because they consider them unnecessary or because rapid changes or variations would require frequent revisions of the job descriptions. In some companies, jobs are not graded and the point system is not used. Where no pay range has been set, the specific pay for the job is entered.

Job Summary

As you can see from the job summary in Figure 36-2, brevity, clarity, and specificity are called for. In writing this section, get to the heart of what the jobholder does on his job, describing the general purpose of the job and listing only its major functions or activities. Including the sentence, "Performs other assignments as required," provides a measure of flexibility necessary in every job.

To achieve the twin goals of brevity and clarity, try this approach:

◇ Start a phrase or sentence with an action verb. (See the list of action verbs at the end of the chapter.)
◇ Explain the requirements of the job—that is, amplify the verb by telling *what* is done.
◇ If necessary for further amplification, explain the purpose of the job, using an example to describe the *why* or *how* of the job.

Job Duties

This section gives a summary, usually in outline form, of typical duties and responsibilities of the job. These duties and responsibilities normally fall into such major areas as operational activities, interpersonal activities, technical activities, and financial activities. Depending on the job, a duties statement may include involvement in all four of these activities or fewer. This section is not meant to be all-inclusive, but rather to describe duties related to major performance requirements. Normally, one sentence or one to three phrases in outline form may describe each major duty or responsibility and will assist the incumbent and his manager in identifying significant areas for goal-setting. Improved performance in any of these areas is a contribution that should have direct impact on the attainment of work-group and organizational goals and objectives. Some of the major duty or responsibility categories are:

1. Quantity and quality of supervision received.
2. Quantity and quality of supervision given.
3. Interaction in teaching, counseling, coaching, training, or development of others.
4. Ability and requirements for analyzing and evaluating action-oriented instructional information.

5. Requirements for following instructions or orders.
6. Amount and quality of directions, instructions, and suggestions transmitted.
7. Degree of accountability for human and other resources in planning, operations, and/or control of the job.

Here, too, as in the summary section, action verbs are useful. Consistency in selecting and using words is important because many words have a variety of meanings. Establish a meaning for a word and stick to it; avoid ambiguous words. Also take care to avoid a common pitfall for the unwary description writer: overdescription of the job. Too often, descriptions of every job in a department appear to describe the combined activities of all the job duties.

Employment Standards

When a job description does not include a specification section, or if the specification section does not adequately identify employment standards, then an employment standards section should be included here. (Note that the description in Exhibit 6 has both an employment standards section and a job specification section.) Employment standards relate to (1) education standards, which may include an actual description of the language and mathematical skills required as well as reasoning skills needed to comply with job-performance standards; (2) experience standards; (3) skills and ability standards; (4) physical standards, which may include actual lifting or pressure exerted (by pounds) in the performance of the job; (5) emotional standards, which describe unusual psychological pressures exerted on the incumbent in the performance of the job, and (6) certification or licensure requirements. Not all of these standards, of course, are applicable in every job.

Special care should be taken, here and in the job specification section, to comply with mandates of the Equal Employment Opportunity Act. These place the burden of proof concerning standards and qualifications on the organization. Practically, this means that employment standards must be accurately identified so that any artificial employment barriers are eliminated. Artificial employment barriers arise when employment standards and their related job duties are essentially unrelated to the primary content of the job or when the standards call for the employee to have skills to perform duties significantly above the normal level of duties actually required on the job. Such artificial barriers result in the screening out of candidates who are in fact qualified to perform the job. Clearly, accurate identification of standards is vital in protecting a company from charges of discrimination toward one or more groups.

Whenever possible, use quantitative words. For example: "Must make 20 customer contacts daily," not "Must make *many* customer contacts daily." And avoid drawing conclusions: "Must perform work requiring the lifting of 94-lb. bags of concrete," not "Must perform strenuous work." It is unnecessary to use stilted, twenty-dollar words; commonly used, simple English words and terms are preferable.

Accountabilities

This section briefly describes the major end results achieved in the satisfactory performance of the job duties. It acts as a guide for the goal-setting process that integrates job requirements with incumbent contributions.

Job Specification

This section contains the significant factors necessary to perform the job. This factor analysis of the job provides the basic data for evaluating the job and comparing it with others. Obviously, it is the section that controls the pay level for the job. The makeup of this section will depend directly upon the compensable factors used by the organization and the degree to which they are significant in the job at hand.

The next article will describe in detail compensable factors and subfactors that best describe a job and the process of assigning degrees and point scores to subfactors in order to reflect the significance of each to the job. The job specification section in Figure 36-2 lists the factors used to evaluate the job and gives sufficient substantiating data to select a particular level or degree of each factor. As we shall see, it is possible to develop from these an evaluation process that assigns a degree and point score for each factor.

ACTION VERBS

The following verbs are useful in identifying and defining job functions. Although many of the definitions may seem self-evident, we are defining each in the interest of consistency on the part of the person writing job descriptions.

Administer. Manage or direct the execution of affairs.

Adopt. Take up and practice as one's own.

Advise. Recommend a course of action; offer an informed opinion based on specialized knowledge.

Analyze. Separate into elements and critically examine.

Anticipate. Foresee and deal with in advance.

Appraise. Give an expert judgment of worth or merit.

Approve. Accept as satisfactory; exercise final authority with regard to commitment of resources.

Arrange. Make preparation for an event; put in proper order.

Assemble. Collect or gather together in predetermined order from various sources.

Assign. Specify or designate tasks or duties to be performed by others.

Assume. Undertake; take for granted.

Assure. Give confidence; make certain of.

Authorize. Approve; empower through vested authority.

Calculate. Make a mathematical computation.

Circulate. Pass from person to person or place to place.

Clear. Gain approval of others.

Collaborate. Work jointly with; cooperate with others.

Collect. Gather.

Compile. Put together information; collect from other documents.

Concur. Agree with a position, statement, action, or opinion.

Conduct. Carry on; direct the execution of.

Confer. Consult with others to compare views.

Consolidate. Bring together.

Consult. Seek the advice of others.

Control. Measure, interpret, and evaluate actions for conformance with plans or desired results.

Coordinate. Regulate, adjust, or combine the actions of others to attain harmony.

Correlate. Establish a reciprocal relationship.

Correspond. Communicate with.

Delegate. Commission another to perform tasks or duties that may carry specific degrees of accountability.

Design. Conceive, create, and execute according to plan.

Determine. Resolve; fix conclusively or authoritatively.

Develop. Disclose, discover, perfect, or unfold a plan or idea.

Devise. Come up with something new—perhaps by combining or applying known ideas or principles.

Direct. Guide work operations through the establishment of objectives, policies, rules, practices, methods, and standards.

Discuss. Exchange views for the purpose of arriving at a conclusion.

Dispose. Get rid of.

Disseminate. Spread or disperse information.

Distribute. Deliver to proper destinations.

Draft. Prepare papers or documents in preliminary form.

Endorse. Support or recommend.

Establish. Bring into existence.

Estimate. Forecast future requirements.

Evaluate. Determine or fix the value of.

Execute. Put into effect or carry out.

Exercise. Exert.

Expedite. Accelerate the process or progress of.

Formulate. Develop or devise.

Furnish. Provide with what is needed; supply.

Implement. Carry out; execute a plan or program.

Improve. Make something better.

Initiate. Start or introduce.

Inspect. Critically examine for suitability.

Interpret. Explain something to others.

Investigate. Study through close examination and systematic inquiry.

Issue. Put forth or to distribute officially.

Maintain. Keep in an existing state.

Monitor. Watch, observe, or check for a specific purpose.

Negotiate. Confer with others with an eye to reaching agreement.

Notify. Make known to.

Operate. Perform an activity or series of activities.

Participate. Take part in.

Perform. Fulfill or carry out some action.

Place. Locate and choose positions for.

Plan. Devise or project the realization of a course of action.

Practice. Perform work repeatedly in order to gain proficiency.

Prepare. Make ready for a particular purpose.

Proceed. Begin to carry out an action.

Process. Subject something to special treatment; handle in accordance with prescribed procedure.

Promote. Advance to a higher level or position.

Propose. Declare a plan or intention.

Provide. Supply what is needed; furnish.

Recommend. Advise or counsel a course of action; offer or suggest for adoption.

Represent. Act in the place of or for.

Report. Give an account of; furnish information or data.

Research. Inquire into a specific matter from several sources.

Review. Examine or re-examine.

Revise. Rework in order to correct or improve.

Schedule. Plan a timetable.

Secure. Gain possession of; make safe.

Select. Choose the best suited.

Sign. Formally approve a document by affixing a signature.

Specify. State precisely in detail or name explicitly.

Stimulate. Excite to activity; urge.

Submit. Yield or present for the discretion or judgment of others.

Supervise. Personally oversee, direct, inspect, or guide the work of others with responsibility for meeting standards of performance.

Train. Teach or guide others in order to bring up to a predetermined standard.

Transcribe. Transfer data from one form of record to another or from one method of preparation to another—without changing the nature of the data.

Verify. Confirm or establish authenticity; substantiate.

Postscript: The Basics of Effective Communication

Though it is an integral part of every management job, communication will always remain a distinctly personal art; no two persons communicate alike any more than they are quite alike in other respects. This factor of individual differences obviously makes it undesirable—even if it were possible—to attempt to reduce good communication to any kind of formula or definitive "rules of conduct."

Nevertheless, there are certain basic principles of communication which apply to all situations and all persons. These are so self-evident as to be "common sense"; yet their consistent application in daily interpersonal communication is by no means common. Whether or not we consciously think about them, our success or failure in expressing meaning and intent depends upon how well we observe these ten basic principles of good communication.

1. *Seek to clarify your ideas before communicating.* The more systematically we analyze the problem or idea to be communicated, the clearer it becomes. This is the first step toward effective communication. Because communication is virtually a continuous process, we commonly express our thoughts or feelings without having clarified what we are trying to say or accomplish. "I don't advise

you," says Clarence Randall, "to start talking until you have begun thinking. It's no good opening the tap if there is nothing in the tank." Management communication commonly fails because of inadequate planning. Good planning must consider the goals and attitudes of those who will receive the communication and those who will be affected by it.

2. *Examine the true purpose of each communication.* Before you communicate, ask yourself what you *really* want to accomplish with your message—whether it is to obtain information, initiate action, or change another person's attitude. Identify your most important goal and then adapt your language, tone, and total approach to serve that specific objective. Don't try to accomplish too much with each communication. In general, the fewer the objectives, the sharper the focus of the communication—and the greater its chances of success.

3. *Consider the total physical and human setting whenever you communicate.* Meaning and intent are conveyed by more than words alone. Many other factors influence the over-all impact of a communication, and the manager must be sensitive to the setting in which he communicates. Consider, for example, your sense of *timing*—that is, the circumstances under which you make an announcement or render a decision; the *physical setting*—whether you communicate in private, for example, or otherwise; the *social climate* that pervades work relationships within the company or a department and sets the tone of its communication; *custom and past practice*—the degree to which your communication conforms to, or departs from, the expectations of your audience. Be constantly aware of the total setting in which you communicate. Like all living things, communication must be capable of adapting to its environment.

4. *Consult with others, where appropriate, in planning communication.* Frequently it is desirable or necessary to seek the participation of others in planning a communication or developing the facts on which to base it. Such consultation often helps to lend additional insight and objectivity to your message. Moreover, those who have helped plan your communication will give it their active support.

5. *Be mindful, while you communicate, of the overtones as well as the basic content of your message.* Your tone of voice, your expression, your apparent receptiveness to the responses of others—all have tremendous impact on those you wish to reach. Frequently overlooked, these subtleties of communication often affect a lis-

tener's reaction to a message even more than its basic content. Similarly, our choice of language—particularly our awareness of the fine shades of meaning and emotion in the words we use—predetermines in large part the reactions of our listeners.

6. *Take the opportunity, when it arises, to convey something of help or value to the receiver.* Consideration of the other person's interests and needs—the habit of trying to look at things from his point of view—will frequently point up opportunities to convey something of immediate benefit or long-range value to him. People on the job are most responsive to the manager who takes their interests into account.

7. *Follow up your communication.* Our best efforts at communication may be wasted, and we may never know whether we have succeeded in expressing our true meaning and intent, if we do not follow up to see how well we have put our message across. This we can do by asking questions, by encouraging the receiver to express his reactions, by follow-up contacts, and by subsequent review of performance. Make certain that every important communication has a "feedback," so that complete understanding and appropriate action result.

8. *Communicate for tomorrow as well as today.* While a communication may be aimed primarily at meeting the demands of an immediate situation, it must be planned with the past in mind if it is to maintain consistency in the receiver's view; but most important of all, it must be consistent with long-range interests and goals. For example, it is not easy to communicate frankly on such matters as poor performance or the shortcomings of a loyal subordinate; but postponing a disagreeable communication makes it more difficult in the long run and is actually unfair to your subordinates and your company.

9. *Be sure your actions support your communication.* In the final analysis the most persuasive kind of communication is not what you *say* but what you *do*. When a man's actions or attitudes contradict his words, we tend to discount what he has said and perhaps to view it as an attempt to mislead us. For every manager this means that good supervisory practices—such as clear assignment of responsibility, adequate delegation of authority, fair rewards for effort, and consistency in policy enforcement—serve to communicate more than all the gifts of oratory.

10. *Last, but by no means least: Seek not only to be understood but to understand*—be a good listener. When we start talking, we

often cease to listen in that larger sense of being attuned to the other person's unspoken reactions and attitudes. Even more serious is the fact that we are all guilty at times of inattentiveness when others are attempting to communicate to us. Listening is one of the most important, most difficult—and most neglected—skills in communication. The complex art of listening demands that we concentrate not only on the explicit meanings another person is expressing but on the implicit meanings, unspoken words, and undertones that may be far more significant. It demands, in other words, that we learn to listen with the inner ear if we are to know the inner man.

The Contributors

TOM ADAMS is Data Processing Manager/Analyst, Department of Social Services, Sacramento, California.

JOEL ANASTASI is a Co-Principal of Schachat/Anastasi Associates, Inc., a consulting firm in New York City.

JAMES MENZIES BLACK is Executive Vice President of the National Metal Trades Association in New York City.

JOHN B. COLBY is Supervising Editor, Exxon Production Research, Houston, Texas.

KEN COOPER is President of his own consulting firm, KCA Associates, in St. Louis, Missouri.

ROBERT F. DEGISE is Publications Editor, Sales Development Department, Engine Division, Caterpillar Tractor Co., Peoria, Illinois.

WILLIAM A. DELANEY is President of Analysis and Computer Systems, Inc., in Bedford, Massachusetts.

RUSSELL W. DRIVER is Assistant Professor of Management at the University of Oklahoma, Norman, Oklahoma.

RICHARD J. DUNSING is Associate Professor of Organizational Development and Director of the Institute for Business and Communication Development at the University of Richmond, Richmond, Virginia.

DAVID EMERY, when his article was first published, was Conference Director of the Executive Communications Course for the American Management Association, Inc.

JULIET M. HALFORD, when her article was first published, was Editor of Personnel magazine.

LOIS B. HART is President of her own management consulting firm, Leadership Dynamics, in Lyons, Colorado.

BRIAN L. HAWKINS is Associate Professor at the College of Business, University of Texas at San Antonio.

RICHARD I. HENDERSON is Associate Professor in the Department of Management, Georgia State University, Atlanta, Georgia.

PHILIP LESLY is President of the Philip Lesly Company, Public Relations and Public Affairs Counsel, in Chicago, Illinois.

EDWARD L. LEVINE is Associate Professor of Psychology at the University of South Florida, Tampa, Florida.

LARRY G. McDOUGLE is Director of Campus Programs, School of Technical Careers, Baccalaureate Studies Division, Southern Illinois University at Carbondale.

V. DALLAS MERRELL is a management consultant who specializes in organization study, problem solving, and management development and lives in Silver Spring, Maryland.

HAROLD K. MINTZ is a Communications Specialist at Honeywell Information Systems, Inc., in Minneapolis, Minnesota.

PETER B. OLNEY, JR., is President of Olney Associates, a consulting firm in Boston, Massachusetts.

LARRY E. PENLEY is Associate Professor, College of Business, The University of Texas at San Antonio.

PHILIP L. QUAGLIERI is Assistant Professor, School of Administration, University of New Brunswick, Fredericton, Canada.

JOSEPH A. RICE is Associate Professor, Systems and Operations, University of Houston, Houston, Texas.

PAUL RICHARDS is a business and industrial writing consultant in Peoria Heights, Illinois.

WAYNE SANDERS is President of Sanders Associates, a management consulting firm in Columbus, Missouri.

ROBERT SCHACHAT is a Co-Principal of Schachat/Anastasi Associates, Inc., a consulting firm in New York City.

ALAN SIEGEL is President of Siegel & Gale, a language simplification and design firm in New York City.

MARSHALL SMITH is Employee Relations Supervisor, the Zia Company in El Paso, Texas.

DAN H. SWENSON is Assistant Professor of Business and Administration Services, Western Michigan University, Kalamazoo, Michigan.

PAUL R. TIMM is Assistant Professor, Department of Business Education and Business Administration, School of Management, Brigham Young University, Provo, Utah.

JEAN W. VINING is Associate Professor of Office Administration, University of New Orleans, New Orleans, Louisiana.

NORMAN WASSERMAN is Vice President of Ruder & Finn, Inc., a Public Relations firm in New York City.

ALAN J. WEISS is General Manager of Kepner-Tregoe, Inc., in Princeton, New Jersey.

ALLEN WEISS is a consultant in business writing in Upper Montclair, New Jersey.

HARRY E. WILLIAMS is a management consultant and registered professional engineer who lives in Seal Beach, California.

MARION M. WOOD is Assistant Professor, Graduate School of Business Administration, University of Southern California in Los Angeles.

AUGUSTA C. YRIE is Associate Professor of Office Administration, University of New Orleans, New Orleans, Louisiana.

Index